PRAISE FOR *DOW*

"This book is an EPIC adventure tale that needs to be added to your collection. This book encourages you to overcome your fears, take calculated risks, and accept hospitality from complete strangers and it will even inspire you to plan your next trek so that you too will not give up on life and accept aging as most people do . . .This is one of my all-time favorite books that I have ever read . . . and now I'll begin reading it a second time. If you are looking for a feel-good experience that will leave you eager to achieve more in your life, start here, read this book, and get ready for your spirit to be forever changed!"

—Patrick Snow,
international best-selling author of
Creating Your Own Destiny

"*Downhills Don't Come Free* is a wonderful book! The whole concept of 'finding your stretch'—that challenging place where you feel most alive—imbues the book with an energy and vitality that jump from the page. It is, in the end, an ode to persistence, endurance, and follow-through, and a celebration of living life fully and ecstatically. This book is not just for those who want to take a similar adventure, but for anyone looking for their 'stretch,' be that physical, mental, or emotional."

—Dale Griffiths Stamos,
Emmy-nominated writer, poet,
teacher, and director

"A highly recommended read"

—Elliotte Friedman
journalist for Sportsnet amd panelist
on CBC's *Hockey Night in Canada*

DOWNHILLS
DON'T COME
FREE

DOWNHILLS
DON'T COME
FREE

ONE MAN'S BIKE RIDE
FROM ALASKA TO MEXICO

WISE Ink
CREATIVE ★ PUBLISHING

JERRY HOLL

ISBN 13: 978-1-63489-942-0
eISBN: 978-1-63489-941-3

Library of Congress Catalog Number: 2017937449
Printed in the United States of America
First Printing: 2017

21 20 19 18   5 4 3 2

Cover design Nupoor Gordon
Interior design by Dan Pitts

Maps by Neal Calvin Peterson

Wise Ink Creative Publishing
837 Glenwood Ave.
Minneapolis, MN 55405
www.wiseinkpub.com

To order, visit www.itascabooks.com or call 1-800-901-3480. Reseller discounts available.

To my parents, Justin and Jerry (Geraldine),
who instilled in me a love of adventure.

And, to my wife, Suzanne, and kids; David, Julia, and Justin, who
let me run with it.

MAP KEY

The maps at the beginning of each chapter are a clever combination of satellite imagery and graphic illustrations of the terrain encountered on my daily route.

The white line traces the path itself along the map, whereas the shaded areas at the bottom show exactly how steep that mountain actually was.

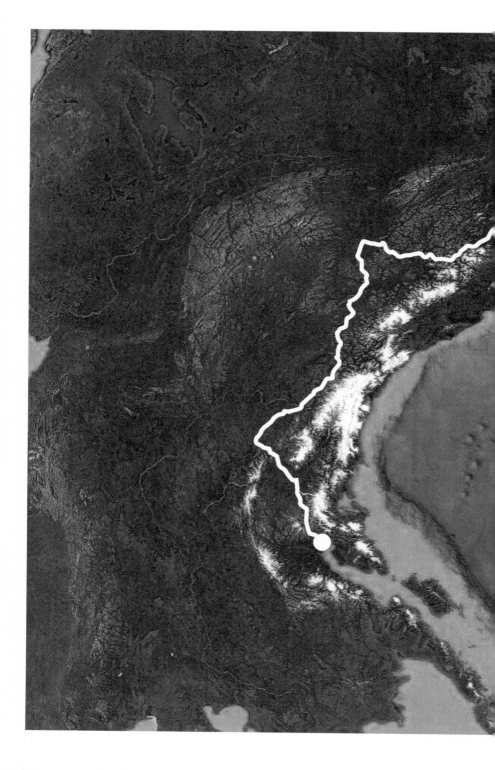

INTRODUCTION

ALASKA TO MEXICO — 3,634 MILES — 51 DAYS
ONE MAN. ONE BIKE. ONE TENT.
June 20, 2012 – August 9, 2012

Whoa, was that movement? On June 27, with my legs churning against a shrieking headwind, I was cycling southeasterly on the Alaska Highway, totally immersed in the vast and pristine Kluane wilderness area of the Yukon. I was starkly alone and lost in my thoughts, grinding my way toward Destruction Bay, a tiny enclave on Kluane Lake—appropriately named due to the vicious winds that had blown down military structures there during the Alaska Highway construction in 1942–43. My face buffeted against the gale as I gazed forward, squinting and straining for focus. *Uh-oh! Shit—my worst fear!* A large female grizzly was foraging on the side of the road. Her big head slowly swiveled toward me; our eyes met as she placed me in her crosshairs. I froze dead in my tracks about a hundred feet from her—*Already too close!* She was a big, dirty-blonde female grizzly in her prime, with a broad face and the telltale hump at her shoulders. Grass clumps fell out of her mouth as she chomped her lunch—but then she froze too as she considered me. *Oh God—a stare down.* My heart spiked with an adrenaline surge. *Don't stare, kemosabe: play it cool—nothing quick.*

Despite her beauty, she was ominous and foreboding. *Goddamn! My problem just tripled—there are her two cubs! She has to be in lockdown protective mode.* The searing reality of being completely alone and exposed in her house trumped my bravado.

"Did you hear about the mauling last week?" flashed through my mind. That was the blunt inquiry the REI saleswoman had made of me a week ago while I was buying bear spray in Anchorage. *Jesus, lady!* I'd thought. *Do you get off trying to scare people?* But it was her oblique warning to me to stay on my toes—nothing's tame where I'm headed. Of course, I'd brushed it off at that moment.

In the prior few days, I'd seen bear scat along the roadside and even mused to myself, *What an inside-out fate that would be.* But suddenly, that possibility became very . . . real.

I'd been making pretty good time and was happy with my progress. *But now, Christ! She's between me and Destruction*—Destruction Bay that is. *I loved that name, until now! Now, all I want is out of here! Distance and separation,* beyond *her,* so I can proceed onward.

I faced one of life's most fundamental questions—*What in hell's name do I do now?* I watched her, warily, for a minute. She averted her eyes, pretending I wasn't there, but she knew damn well I was.

Hmmm. She doesn't appear to be very concerned, but then again, what do I know about grizzlies? What to do, what to do—retreat to safety, or pedal past? I'm so screwed! I thrashed through my limited options. *She could have already had my ass if she wanted! And if I proceed, I won't have to cut between her and her cubs. Maybe I'm okay.*

Already vulnerable to her whims, I steeled myself and simply hoped for the best. As though the intelligence of my feet made the decision—*Click-clack*—I clipped back into my pedals, the sharp snapping sound cutting the air. *What is it about the siren call to move forward?* My gut clenched. In grave trepidation and straining for speed, my ass subconsciously tucked under like a submissive dog's tail, I thrust forward.

With the thin mist of bear spray as my only defense, I made the second-dumbest decision of my entire journey.

PART 1

FINDING MY STRETCH: DECISIONS AND PREPARATIONS

TUESDAY, JUNE 19, 2012
Delta Airlines Flight from Minneapolis to Anchorage

·

Are you bringing a gun?

What in the world would compel you to do this?

Are you insane?

You're going alone?

My husband and I have talked about this—we think you're way too confident.

My buddies and I think you're nuts. You have bigger stones than any of us!

At fifty-seven, I resigned from my corporate job, and in a broader sense from my past, to take on the challenge of a bike ride from Anchorage, Alaska, to the Mexican border despite zero distance experience whatsoever on a bicycle. In the days before I boarded my flight, everyone had something to say about my plan, and few of them were what you'd call supportive—they all boiled down to some form of "How stupid! You're going to fail."

I brushed them off in blind confidence. *Don't let them talk you down, Comanche. This is your time, your journey—not theirs.* But at the same time, I couldn't completely distance myself from doubt. *I don't know what I don't know. How do I deal with that? How will I react?* There's no real answer, so I tried to just push them aside as the characteristics of a blind adventure. Good thing I wasn't clairvoyant, or I'd likely have talked myself out of it. I didn't know it yet, but this trip was going to be my stretch: a big undertaking—beyond the limits of what I knew I could comfortably accomplish—and well beyond a big bike ride.

Contrary to my detractors, my wife, Sue, was extremely supportive, even enthusiastic. *Too enthusiastic?* But she occasionally reminded me that I tend to be an ignorer of problems. *Not a great trait, but sometimes it works to your advantage.* In my mind, any potential problems were still days away: anticipate, to be sure, but worry only when it's time to worry about them. I redirected my attention to the few prerequisites needed to just get me to Anchorage and on the road.

Fasten your seat belts took on an entirely new meaning for me. In the hold of the jet that streaked nonstop from Minneapolis to Anchorage was my brand-new bicycle, a Surly Long Haul Trucker. I liked the name because it described what I was about to do. I couldn't feel more ready. But my bold confidence was about to go out the window.

The weather was crystal clear, and I was fortunate to have a window seat in the jetliner. For the last three hours of the flight, I looked down at nothing but heavily glaciated mountain wilderness. I did the math. *Three hours at upwards of 500 miles per hour covers more than 1,500 miles of rugged terrain in this segment alone! And from 40,000 feet, I can see about 250 miles to the horizon—and there's no sign of civilization!*

I stared out the window, transfixed by the razor-sharp mountain peaks, plunging ice fields, white ribbons of merging glaciers with their toppling seracs glinting reflected sunlight, and endless valleys in the wrinkles of the earth. The visual pierced me like a spear. *Oh my God! I have to ride through this? And this is only a portion of the trip? WTF! Am I in way over my skis? Can I do this? What in hell am I thinking?* What was previously just bar-talk bluster now became real. For the first time, I got a visceral visual of the magnitude of this journey and what I'd really signed up for. It was all so raw, so real—so vulnerable. *Mommy!*

Still, as daunting as it looked, I found my predicament kind of funny and felt strangely invigorated by it all. *Well? Get on with it. The blind adventure of this trip is exactly what I want.*

***

I was lucky and I knew it. I had come to a point where my kids were essentially raised, and I had the good fortune and wherewithal to fund this type of endeavor. I was luckier yet in that I felt vigorously healthy. I thought about two good friends, both about my age, who'd had recent health scares. Each had felt sluggish and eventually been diagnosed with occluded coronary arteries. In each case, docs had uncovered 95 percent blockage in the left anterior descending artery, commonly called the widow-maker. They'd both caught it just in time, and the docs jacked multiple stents into their respective hearts to restore blood flow. In contrast, I was fortunate—I felt great! *Why bother to go to a doctor for a pre-trip checkup? My body is just plain telling me I'm ready.* But my friends' close calls served as a great reminder: *Get out there and live while I can. Get moving!*

For the past several years, I'd caught myself looking out my office window and dreaming when I should have been working. I dreamed of being outside in the natural world—and of big, hairy, audacious adventures—in faraway places. *God I've had some great experiences!* But in the same thought I also lamented, *Christ, there's so much more that I haven't done—and the second hand is relentlessly sweeping!*

And sure, each position I've had takes a certain talent, but over time every position would devolve into an all-too-sclerotic daily pattern, an ordinariness. . . . *Shit! I'm anesthetized—the unchanging daily routine is a form of business process anesthetic—I'm becoming the functional walking dead!* I was slowly dying in place. *Sure, I'm breathing fine. But am I alive?* I so feared this living death. I longed for new growth and excitement. Then I asked myself a simple question.

When am I at my best?

I had an epiphany as I thought it through. *In a strange way, it's not when I'm the most comfortable. It's when I'm a little on edge and uncertain, and when my hair is on fire. It's when I think I have most of the pieces to solve a problem, but I'm not quite sure—the problem is still fuzzy, and I don't really know if I can put it all together—but at the same time, I'm enthusiastic about the possibilities and opportunity. That's when I feel most alive. Why not spend my remaining time there? My God! Listen to me! The jury is in: I need new stimulation—I need something bigger!*

I'd read numerous stories of people who'd dared to do the unusual and pursue their dreams. *I'm a complete sucker for real-life adventure stories.* I felt an unmistakable jealousy every time I heard or read about someone who had the guts to quit talking about their dreams or ideas and actually take them on. *What did Henry Ford say, "You can't build a reputation on what you're going to do"?*

I'd always place myself in adventurers' shoes—pondering what I would do in their sticky situations. *Do I have the guts? Do I have the stuff to survive their story? There's only one way to know: Pick your journey and go. Just go.*

I, like many others, had tackled a variety of shorter outdoor activities and adventures that provided immediate thrills and quick adrenaline fixes throughout the years—mountain climbing, downhill skiing, scuba diving, backpacking, grueling cross-country ski races, backcountry canoeing, skydiving, running with the bulls, and more. Some of these were high-intensity weekend warrior–type activities, such as the American Birkebeiner and the NorthShore Inline Marathon. But those types of events, while grueling, demanded only a short burst of output and focus—I could see the end in a few short hours. Over time I got bored with their relative sameness each year. I didn't realize it at the time, but these quick hits prepared me well to take on this larger journey.

And I needed something more, something strikingly different, something sustained, something that would be a monumental stretch for me. *I want it to be in a remote location, gruelingly physical, and breathtakingly beautiful, and I want to do it completely on my own. I don't want any guides or seasoned experts. I want to be nimble and not have to rely on anyone else for support—mental or physical. I don't want anyone pulling me along or, in mountain climbing terms, to be short-roped. My new adventure will be intensely personal and at my own pace—I don't want to slow anyone down, or conversely, to be slowed down.*

I wanted it to be something that would require constant perseverance, even—especially—when I might not want to continue. I wanted, in other words, an experience that would force me to grow—something life-changing.

At the same time, it had to be somewhat realistic. Like most people, I didn't have unlimited resources, and I wouldn't break my own bank doing it. In short, it had to be a stretch but not a break: It couldn't be delusional; I had to have an honest chance at it.

Sue had been encouraging me to venture on for several years. She would ask, "What are you waiting for? You've spent your entire adult life making sure everyone else is covered. You've been deeply involved with the kids, we've paid for our house, and I've been fortunate to do what was most important to me—be able to primarily raise the kids." She maintained that if I hadn't married her and had kids, I probably would have explored most corners of the earth by this point. Now that the kids were through college, she said, "Go. It's your turn."

"It's your turn." What a gift!

And so, in May 2012, I resigned. *It's time—time to leave yesterday's ways and look to tomorrow's dreams and possibilities.* However, I had one small problem: I had no idea or real vision of what *tomorrow* looked like. I just knew it would be vastly new and different from what I'd done in the past.

***

I quickly considered what I would do. It didn't take long for me to decide that I'd start with a solo bicycle ride from Seattle to San Diego. Then I mentioned my plan to a sage. "Jerry," he emphasized with piercing eyes and furrowed forehead, "If you're going to go—go big." Despite all the reservations that others had expressed, somehow he sensed that I had more in me than even I knew. That one-liner was the best piece of advice I've ever received. *My God, I was thinking way too small!*

I decided on the spot to ride from Alaska to Mexico. *Geez! I thought Seattle to San Diego was a stretch; now this is a stretch on top of my stretch!* My decision was that spontaneous and simple. Now, I never was much of a cyclist. I didn't belong to biking groups, and I'd never biked beyond a casual twenty or so miles in a day—certainly not on a bike loaded with gear. Nor had I trained for this type of trip. *It's not specifically biking shape, but I'm in decent enough shape overall,* I figured. *I'll have plenty of time to ride myself into it along the way. No big deal.*

Due to my inexperience, I didn't know what to plan for. *Oh, screw the minute details—I just have to get the few big things right and use good judgment to figure out the rest as I go—it's more efficient. Plus, I can't possibly contemplate every eventuality. There are probably a thousand minor details I'll miss, but they shouldn't be showstoppers—and if it's not a showstopper, don't sweat it. Why try to fine-tune rough estimates?*

Besides, I'm not going to the goddamn moon—I'm just getting on a bicycle! So with that my plan was, well, no plan: it was mostly an attitude. *C'mon—I can camp, I can pedal, and I know how to work out, so what's the big deal? I'll just string a few of those days together. I'll just buy a bike, fly to Anchorage, and start pedaling. I'll see what I run into and learn what I need to along the way. Let the journey itself teach me.*

There is never a perfect time to jump—so jump now while I can. If I try to be OSHA compliant, I'll never go!

***

I only gave myself a couple of weeks to get equipped. In a few quick shopping sprees at the bike shop I made sure that I had gear decent enough that I wouldn't have to fight it in the wild.

I bought the Surly Long Haul Trucker solely because, about a year before, I'd crossed paths with a persnickety cyclist in a Minnesota regional park who happened to be biking to Seattle from Grand Rapids, Michigan—and that was the bike he chose for his long-distance travel. So I bought that same bike without ever riding or testing it.

I also knew I'd want bike tools and spare parts. "What do I need?" I asked my bike shop guru. "Grab a bag and throw the junk together that you'd bring."

"Follow me," he replied. In a bike version of the old show *Supermarket Sweep*, he grabbed a cart and, with me lagging well behind, quickly strode the aisles, playing the parts rack like a piano— tossing in a foldable spare tire, a bike multi-tool, chain oil, spare tubes, a tire changing tool, tube-repair stuff, and who knows what else. He jammed them all into a compact tool bag. *Perfect. I can just pack this bag as is.* I didn't know how to use any of it anyway. Since I hate mechanical maintenance, I also didn't take the time to learn. *How hard can it be?*

I also needed a small tent, an ultrapackable sleeping bag, cooking gear, and clothing. According to my camp-store gizmo guy, the MSR Hubba Hubba was hands-down the tent to carry on a trek like this. With one set of connected poles, it assembled quickly and had the added bonus of a pole construction that created vertical end walls, thus providing more room than you usually find in a two-person tent. Also, as it was self-supporting after assembly, I could pick it up and carry it around until I found just the right place to staple it to the ground each night. *A breeze.*

I bought a Mountain Hardwear down sleeping bag, good to about thirty degrees F, that packed smaller than an NFL football via a compression sack. I already owned a high-quality inflatable camping air mattress—its ability to come between me and sticks, rocks, roots, and trenches, plus the thermal layer it provided between me and the cold ground, promised a solid night's sleep. I needed about five minutes to blow it up each night. *Not exactly what I'll look forward to after I blow a lung pedaling all day, but, there's a price to comfort.*

Specialized clothing also helps, so I bought two sets of bike shorts, two quick-dry bike shirts, a set of warm leggings, and a set of arm sleeves. *Just legs and sleeves? As weird as Michael Jackson's one glove!* I added one lightweight, water-resistant windbreaker and one wind vest to the quick-dry T-shirts, polypro zip-top, Gore-Tex shell, long-sleeved wind-stopper jacket, and wind-stopper vest I already owned. *Discarded? One three-piece suit!*

I'd never worn biking shorts and even made fun of them once or twice. But on this trip I figured I needed every advantage I could get, so I bought the best biking shorts available. I asked the cycling guy, "What do people wear under the bike shorts?" He sort of smirked. Then he saw that I was serious.

"Nothing," he told me.

"What?" I laughed. He didn't. "They go commando?" I asked, just to be sure I was hearing him right.

"Yep."

Alrighty, then. Yippi-yi-yo, cowboy! That was news to me. But then I realized I'd found the title for the blog I was planning to write throughout the trip: www.goingcommandoblog.wordpress.com

As an aside—my daughter, Julia, insisted that I write a blog each night. "Dad, we need to know where you are and how you're doing!"

God, I have no interest in writing a meandering blog. "Julia, where I'm going, there aren't any cell towers," I lamely protested. "Even if I write, I won't have a connection to send it. But yeah, okay, whatever." *Just accommodate her for now and get past this discussion—sheesh!* Julia read the false commitment, so she made me swear to it. "Okay, okay already—you have my word," I relented. I didn't fool her for a second.

The bike shorts I selected had a soft chamois bottom side that would minimize chafing, but my cycling guy also convinced me to buy some anti-chafing butter as well. When I checked out, I sheepishly placed it on the counter and commented to the cashier, "I hope the butter doesn't make my butt slide off the seat." My comment fell flat as she shot me a *what-a-perv* sideways look. *Okay, then.*

My efforts to pack light took a hit with regard to electronics. My iPad, iPod mini, iPhone, and Kindle all came along—that's a lot of electronics. But I wouldn't be able to charge every night, and each device served a different purpose. I didn't want to use the iPad for my e-books or music because I needed to save the battery for my blog. The Kindle had about a month's worth of charge, and I downloaded five books, hopefully more than enough for the whole trek. The iPod was so small, its weight didn't matter, and it would be a convenient way to listen to music while I lay in my tent. And even though I wouldn't have cell service in Alaska beyond Anchorage, and none at all in Canada, I brought my iPhone for Wi-Fi hot spots and to serve as my camera. I packed two chargers for the Apple devices and planned to plug in at every opportunity.

Lastly, my kids had insisted I carry an emergency beacon communicator. *I don't want one—it's a negotiated settlement. But, it will make them happy. And who knows? I might need it.* I hoped I wouldn't.

Finally, I broadly eyeballed my route and made travel arrangements. I just needed to make sure my bike and gear didn't exceed size and weight limits for shipment on my plane.

I felt I was up to the physical challenge of this trip, including some discomfort, but there was no way to know how I'd be affected by the repetitive motion cycling demands—or by a trip this distance. Then there were the wild cards. *What if I get appendicitis, have a heart attack, or crash in the middle of nowhere?* There wouldn't be any ready help or nearby medical facilities. *Hiccups will happen; they're bound to in a journey of this scope. I just don't know in what form, or how I'll handle them.* But I felt physically strong and ready, so I ignored *(I mean accepted)* those prospects. *Why burn excess energy worrying about these possibilities? I can't change them—they go with the territory.*

The physical or psychological effort of the journey—the big issues—didn't cause me upfront anxiety. My anxiety was mostly centered on the small, mechanical-type issues, starting with packing and shipping my gear to Alaska, and how the hell I'd put it back together when I arrived in Anchorage. *I just don't want mechanical problems. I hate fixing things. It's not that it's complicated. I just don't like it.* So I adopted my mechanical strategy: *Hope for the best.*

I left the last-minute tasks like assembling my bike shipping box for the day before I was to leave. *Thank God for dads!* I hate puzzles, and my dad, who *is* mechanical, helped me assemble the special bike box and tape it all together. I disassembled a few parts so the bike would fit in the box and then crammed everything in. I topped it off by jamming other gear into the box until it reached the airline weight limit.

I still had to figure out how to pack my five bike bags as airline luggage—while still meeting airline weight restrictions. *I'm down to the wire.* I stood there and eyed all my gear, imagining packing it all into the bike bags and then onto the bike once I was in Anchorage. I never did a dry run—packing the bags or riding a loaded bike. *Not the best approach. But what the hell! I'll figure it out in Anchorage.*

TUESDAY, JUNE 19, 2012—AFTERNOON AND EVENING
Anchorage, Alaska

I landed around noon local time and was relieved to find my bike waiting at the baggage claim, along with the two large duffle bags into which I'd squeezed my bike panniers.

I struggled to get it all to the curb, caught a van-sized taxi into Anchorage, and checked into a fleabag hotel. Then I found a UPS store from which to ship the bike box and bags to my brother Steve's house in San Diego, so it would all be waiting for me at the other end of my journey—a distant eventuality I couldn't even imagine at the moment.

Back at the hotel, I thankfully remembered how to reassemble the pieces of my bike. *That only took me an hour—not bad, considering. Elation! It tests out—I'm ready to roll!*

I still needed a few supplies, so I grabbed a couple of empty bags, clipped them to the bike, and took off. *First things first!* I pedaled to the Anchorage REI to buy a canister of bear spray.

"Hey, did you hear about the big mauling last week?" the saleswoman asked.

I'd felt that possibility was still too distant, so, instead of quaking in my shoes, I laughed. "Was that constructive?" I responded, getting a laugh out of her, too. She showed me two sizes of bear spray, small and large.

"I'll take the jumbo. I need all the help I can get."

"It exhausts all its contents in just nine seconds," the saleswoman said. "But you have to wait until the bear gets close enough so you don't exhaust it too early."

"Got it!" I replied with false courage, at a loss for more meaningful words at the moment. *Just cash me out and get me out of here, lady.*

I couldn't quite absorb that I was actually talking about this subject; it was so distant from my concerns of just a couple of weeks ago that it hadn't yet sunk in. But, with some other unlucky soul having been shredded by a bear just a week ago, now I couldn't ignore it.

My mind rifled through potential scenarios. *I better remember to be upwind or I'll nail myself. I'd better make sure the bear is close enough when I blast him. Will I have the presence of mind to wait that long? Could I hit him on a dead sprint with an over-the-shoulder shot?*

Bear spray was my sole protection. I didn't bring a gun because Alaska would be the only state where I could carry one—Canada, Washington State, Oregon, and California don't allow handguns. *And I ain't no Annie Oakley anyway; who thinks I could even hit the bastard? If a bear charges, I'm probably screwed. But those things happen to other people, not me.* Total denial. I insanely relied on plain dumb luck.

Back at the hotel, I packed and hooked the panniers onto my bike for the first time ever and then finagled all my gear into them, meanwhile trying to properly distribute the weight. *Finally! Good enough.*

I headed out to dinner at 5:00 p.m. A friend had turned me onto the F Street Station Bar and Grill. *My Last Supper.*

While I ate (and threw back a few beers), I got into a conversation with a few guys next to me at the corner of the bar. One man, Anthony, managed cargo operations for a fleet of petroleum services tugboats. I couldn't help but notice he was missing three fingers. "What happened?" I had to ask.

"Well," he replied, "back in the 1970s, I was high on a crane when something went terribly wrong. I reacted before I could even think and grabbed the cable to save myself. My fingers were dragged into a pulley and *schwitt!* My fingers were lopped off." Then he added—dragging out the words in deep afterthought—"That . . . was a bad day." The moment hung awkwardly in the air.

"I'm sorry, Anthony," I finally said softly. I regretted asking. *Get me outta here!*

"Don't worry about it," he replied. "Really, I'm none the worse for it."

The mood immediately turned lighter and livelier as Anthony and his buddies became intrigued with what I was about to do. Like disciples, they crowded in, and several more buddies joined them, offering all sorts of advice on the terrain, weather, what to watch out for, and towns I'd hit on the way. Information spewed direct from their streams of consciousness, and they became animated and loud, interrupting each other and laughing as they all tried to get their two cents in. I soaked it all up. *My kind of guys.*

I noticed that the bartender, Tiffany, stayed close and listened in on our conversation, but she didn't join the fray. No sense butting in on a bunch of half-lit guys, she probably thought. And she was an expert—an expert on BSers. To her, I was just another tall-tale BSer—another barfly Pecos Bill—*Yeah, sure, he's ridden tornados, what an ass,* she likely mused. She's seen us all.

Later, as I settled into my hotel room, I realized this would be my last night in a bed for a while. I stretched out to take advantage and set my alarm. I should have been tired, but wide-eyed, I traced cracks in the ceiling. It was deathly quiet as the song "Come Over," by Kenny Chesney, endlessly cycled in my mind.

Tomorrow, it begins. Where will this take me?

PART 2

WILD:
ALASKA, YUKON, AND
BRITISH COLUMBIA

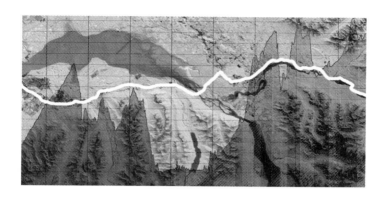

DAY 1
WEDNESDAY, JUNE 20, 2012—ANCHORAGE, AK
Miles to date: 0

My body clock still operating on Central time, I was up at dawn and on the road. The summer solstice sunrise at this latitude was 4:07 a.m. With an odd combination of excitement and unfamiliarity, I pedaled Sixth Avenue westward, out of downtown Anchorage and into the unknown.

I was immediately deflated. *Goddamn! I should have done a trial run on a loaded bike—I'm so wobbly and unbalanced! I had no idea my bike would be so unwieldy with all this weight!* It was the first time I'd ever pedaled a fully loaded bike. I never weighed my bike, but on a deadlift it was heavy—probably around 100 pounds fully loaded. *Along with my 195 pounds of body weight, it's a ton of beef to haul! Will I get used to it? Hope so—nothing I can do about it now. I ain't turning back!*

I'd barely studied my route before I left on the journey, but I knew that I had to travel northeast—away from Mexico—for about 350 miles before I could turn south toward it. *Away first? C'mon, really?*

The sky was battleship gray, overcast, with temperatures in the mid-forties. *At least it's not raining, which is common here. I'd hate to start wet.* I headed up the Mat-Su Valley, where the Matanuska and Susitna Valleys merge. The valleys were shaped by the trifecta of the Alaska Range, the Talkeetna Mountains, and the Chugach Mountains, so I was surrounded by spectacular peaks. In the valleys were the towns of Palmer, Wasilla, Big Lake, Houston, Willow, and Talkeetna—essentially outer suburbs of Anchorage. *I have to take advantage for final needs: these are the last major populated areas I'll see until I make Whitehorse in the Yukon Territory, some seven hundred miles away.*

While there was a bike path from Anchorage to Palmer, about forty miles away, when someone tried to describe all the turns and cut-offs I'd need to make, it quickly became information overload. *That's too hard, and I'm too lazy to figure it all out. I'll just climb on the freeway.*

Within the first thirty minutes of my trip I was pulled over by Alaska's finest, the Alaska Highway Patrol—nice start. *Whoop-whoop!* the rising blast of his siren shrieked. Through his loudspeaker he blared, "Pull over!" He pulled ahead, and I rode up to his window. The bored smirk on his face suggested, *Dude, c'mon, I've got better things to do than chase bicycles off the freeway.* "Bikes aren't allowed on the freeway," he deadpanned. "Where are ya headed?"

"Mexico." I grinned.

The ridiculous thought disarmed him. He smiled as he said, "There's a bike path to Palmer. Get off the freeway at the next exit about a mile up, cross over the freeway, and you'll intersect the bike path. Take a right and it goes all the way into Palmer."

The cop appreciated the spirit of this journey, so he didn't throw me off with a ticket. With my wobblin' load and stylin' garb, I was hardly a threat to society. At least I was already past the Anchorage bike path gyrations; I rode the far-more-straightforward path most of the way to Palmer.

Just before I hit town, I cut onto the Glenn Highway (Hwy. 1), and like flipping a light switch, traffic immediately changed. Even though the Glenn is called a highway, beyond Palmer it was only a single lane in each direction, and the road was empty.

Shortly out of town, the highway rose high along a ridge, well above a pristine lake with cabins strung along one entire shore. But instead of a boat in front of each cabin there was a floatplane—symptomatic of the vastness of this land. I should have paused for a picture of the floatplanes, but I kept pedaling. *Damn, I missed it!*

Beyond the lake I could see nothing but a sea of dark aquamarine-green pines like big ocean swells on the rolling countryside extending to the distant horizon, interrupted by dirty gray mountains thrusting upward, well above the tree line. *Though I'm pedaling my ass off, the horizon doesn't change.*

Alone on the Glenn, I turned up the Matanuska Valley. It didn't take long to see my first bald eagle floating high above, so wild and majestic, symbolic of the soaring freedom we both shared. But our similarities ended there: its movement was effortless, mine wasn't.

With the spring melt in full swing off the high, snow-covered peaks, the rivers were running hard. I loved both the sight and sound of these torrents. I stopped in the middle of every bridge, giving me unobstructed vistas to a horizon of pines and peaks. The roar of the rivers was like the low spooling of a jet engine. The bridges shook and vibrated as I watched the heaving turbulence. *This raging water is trying to tear each bridge from its footings—what a battle! So wild, so untamed.* I was hypnotized by the swirling eddies and fell into the thousand-yard stare. *Follow my finger, you're getting sleepy. . . . Snap out, you've got miles to go!* Alone, looking into the vast distance in all directions, I just took it all in—simply breathtaking. *How can I ever possibly describe this to others?*

I had my first taste of what I thought were hills. I struggled to the crests and then flew on the downhills with the momentum of a barreling cement truck. I let it go on every downhill—I'd earned it—no holding back. I whooped out loud as I flew. Little did I know these were teasers: the real hills were yet to come.

I was learning new basics. *Man! How quickly I can go from hot to cold! How can I be sweating, yet freezing?* I worked into a sopping sweat on the uphills, then shivered as the wind pierced my clothing on the glide down.

It didn't make sense to stop and change clothing for each hill—it was *all* hills, and I'd just be soaked again in a matter of minutes. *Why ruin two sets of clothes in one outing?* I added a layer during a period of light, intermittent showers, and while it kept the direct rain off me, my layers couldn't breathe fast enough to keep up with my effort. *I need to learn how to dress—and undress. I don't have this stuff down. Or, more so, maybe I just have to endure the varying conditions and get used to being wet all day.*

I stopped at wayside pullouts and tiny convenience stores to have a snack and drink. I wanted to stay fueled and hydrated in advance of when I might have an energy problem, since this was all new to me, and I didn't know if or when I might collapse. *Try to stay ahead of the curve.*

At these stops, everybody wanted to talk about where I was going, where I'd been thus far, and why in the world I was doing it. One particular conversation in a convenience store was indicative of all. My eyes caught the female attendant looking through the window as she watched me lean my bike against the outside wall. I strode into the store. "What have we here, darlin'?" she said with a broad smile.

I love her easy familiarity; she broke the ice. "I'm 'Running Down a Dream,' you know, Tom Petty, baby," I replied in playful sassiness bordering on cocky. We both laughed.

"Where are you headed?"

"Mexico."

"Whoa, good for you! That's a long way from here."

"Don't remind me—I might break down and cry," I teased.

"Well, I'm proud of you for taking it on."

"You're a little premature—I can't take credit for what I haven't done."

"Well, how much *have* you done?"

"I'm almost embarrassed to answer. I just started this morning from Anchorage; I'm only about fifty miles in. I've gone nowhere yet!"

It got quiet as I bought a couple donuts and a pint of milk. As I cashed out, she asked, "Do you have any fears?"

"Yeah, I'm mechanically disadvantaged, so I just hope this pig stays together." I waved at my bike outside.

"Well, you be careful out here, this is big country, honey. Good luck, and be safe."

"Thanks, I'll need it."

I came upon some road construction workers next. They gave me inquisitive looks. "Mexico or bust!" I shouted as I passed. They laughed out loud and cheered me on. I also encountered a couple of young hammerheads in a pickup truck with an impressive, yet juvenile array of spotlights attached to the roof. *Ha-ha, they also have an external loudspeaker? Stuff like that is just not a marker for intelligence.* They validated my thoughts because as they passed me, they yelled through the loudspeaker, "Go bike somewhere else!" *What? With all that roof-mounted gear, that's the cleverest you guys can be?* I laughed as I waved. *Aw, hell, they don't get many chances to use their dumb-ass speaker, and like a dog instinctively barks at a doorbell, they just couldn't resist. No harm—I would have probably squawked something moronic too—just kids having fun.*

I continued to Pinnacle Mountain RV & Cafe, an oasis along the Matanuska River. It's a single-pump gas stop with a small campground and RV park—but there was nobody in the park. It also had a small cafe—a big plus!

My bike computer indicated that in the four hours and forty-seven minutes I'd pedaled from Anchorage to Pinnacle Mountain, I averaged 14.4 miles per hour. With that benchmark to go by, I estimated the time it would take to the next *natural stop*—which, to me, was where there would be food. It was too distant to go any further today.

I barely had my head in the door when the upbeat attendant said, "Go set your tent in the woods and get settled. Then c'mon back—and if you're hungry, we also have good food."

"Music to my ears!" I replied. "I'll be back shortly."

"You guys have everything here," I blurted upon my return, pointing to the various snacks, staples, and hardware, and finally to a washer-dryer just off the eating area.

"Yeah, we try to have necessary essentials for neighbors and travelers. By the way, I'm Jill." We exchanged introductions.

"I understand the travelers, but where are the neighbors? I don't see any homes."

"There's a small community of cabins scattered throughout the area."

"I presume you're the gathering spot?" I half questioned.

"Yeah, we see everybody, don't we, Marvin?" Just then, an older man emerged from a back room.

Marvin continued. "Yep, everyone shows up. Up here, everyone needs each other—and a place to go and socialize—and this is the spot. We all look out for each other. We have to. We're a pretty tight community."

They treated me as another neighbor in need and went out of their way to make sure I was comfortable.

"Hey, if you want a shower, we have one around the corner in the back room," Marvin offered.

"That would be fabulous. Is the washer-dryer public?"

"Yep, It's a coin-op."

Although this was only my first day, my biking clothes had a full day's road grime.

I don't know the next time I'll be able to wash. I'd better take advantage of it while I can.

I finally sat down and ordered a mountain of food. As Marvin delivered the platter like an infield grounder, he asked, "How long do you think this journey will take you?"

"I have no idea. I don't know the total distance or what my sustainable pace can be. Bigger yet, since I've never done anything like this, I don't know if my body, mind, or bike will break down. So, I don't know what to expect or what I'll run into—with all that, my wild-ass guess is four or five months."

"Do you have planned stops and know where you'll stay each night?"

"No, I'm adrift with the wind. I'll just see how far I can get each day and then plop down."

"Flying blind," he stated with incredulity.

"Yep, pretty much—a blind adventure."

After a few shovelfuls of chow, I said to Marvin, "Man, I had some climbs and downhills today. I hit thirty-four miles per hour on one downhill—bombing on a loaded bike feels like seventy-five!"

"You ain't seen nuttin' yet. Wait 'til tomorrow. The grade on the Caribou Creek climb is over seven degrees," he replied.

One of the locals chimed in, "You're about thirty miles from the Matanuska Glacier, which is the source of the milky Matanuska River just outside the door. You'll head uphill for about thirty miles and see the glacier, and from there, you'll eventually hit the Caribou Creek climb. That should be interesting!"

"Well, I'm looking forward to seeing the glacier up close, and as far as the climb, I have no idea what to expect on that steep of a climb on a loaded bike. We'll just have to see."

Jill joined back in, "After the next fifty miles or so, it's essentially downhill to Glennallen, and then pretty flat to the little town of Tok." *These are good people, kind and helpful—they live as they say.*

Later, in my tent, I wrote a quick blog entry and then just lay back. *First day completed. Not bad. I actually feel pretty good tonight, but I wonder if I'll feel as good in the morning.* I'd never ridden anywhere near that distance in one day, let alone on a hundred-pound bike. I lay on my side, propped on one arm, and in the dark with my headlamp, I studied my map. *Despite tomorrow's uphill, I'll try to hump it to the Eureka Lodge area.*

Later yet, with my head on my makeshift pillow, a lumpy stuff sack crammed with loose clothes, I listened to the puffs of wind in the towering pines. "One Day I'll Fly Away," sang Randy Crawford. *Love the title—I wonder what tomorrow will bring.*

PINNACLE MOUNTAIN, AK
Miles today: 74

DAY 2
THURSDAY, JUNE 21, 2012—PINNACLE MOUNTAIN, AK
Miles to date: 74

As I ate breakfast, Marvin reiterated, "Eat hearty, Jerry, you'll have a tough day."

"Okay!" I smiled. "Feed me the works! I'll need the fuel."

He was right, but I had no concept of how strenuous it would be. The pass started gentle. *What are they talking about? This isn't so bad.* Well, they knew exactly what was coming: the slope incrementally became steeper by the mile. *It's like heading up a ski jump from the bottom, but it's a* forty-mile *ski jump!*

By about the third mile, I was soaked with sweat and my thighs bulged as I pressed the pedals. I climbed the entire day into the Chugach Mountains. When I looked ahead, the road was a continual ribbon of black leading up, up, up, and then more up, as far into the distance as I could see, broken only by bends in the road. Each time

I rounded a bend it was more of the same, a rising stretch of road to the next bend. Although I never rode listening to my iPod, two songs rifled through my head as I thrashed through my gears: Led Zeppelin's "Stairway to Heaven" and a song I don't even like, AC/DC's "Highway to Hell."

How the hell do I get these tunes out of my mind? On a continuous loop, they made me insane. *Snip that synapse!* I tried to distract myself into other new songs, but they morphed back; "Stairway" and "Highway" destroyed the new songs. They were a constant reminder of the ever-steeper terrain—I haven't listened to them since.

The road hugged the edge of the mountain, so my elevation gain from the valley floor was always in sight. I could look straight across the river valley to the parallel range on the other side and see how high I was. Every so often, I hit a screaming downhill. Like the reprieve of blue sky after a storm, I lusted for the runaway downhills—letting it fly was impossible to resist. On one downhill, I topped off at forty-four miles per hour. *Light the afterburners: what speed can I hit? This is wild, a total dive-bomb—grab your ass and hang on, Luigi! I hope this bike is sturdy because if I blow a tire or if something snaps, I'll be totally toasted and scattered all over Mat-Su County.* Then I did it all over again on the very next downhill.

However, flying didn't come free. After every downhill I not only had to climb back to my previous level but then even higher. In that manner, I seesawed my way uphill the entire day.

Kill me! When I hit the 7-percent-or-more grade of the Caribou Creek climb, it shredded me. *Please pass the EPO, Lance!* I realized how unprincipled I was in times of need. *If I had a gun here, I just might use it—on me, not on a bear.*

Crap! I'm not getting anywhere! My speed was a whopping four miles per hour on certain uphill stretches of the Caribou, and I topped out at six or seven miles per hour on the easier sections. *I have to learn to take a deep breath and be patient—not my strong suit.*

I didn't have much choice—I could hardly change the terrain. I just had to tuck my chin, grind it out, and cope. But strain and pain are great teachers. *Your body can always take more than your mind,*

I tried to convince myself. But I learned a valuable lesson on the Caribou: *Don't even try to make any kind of good time on the climbs. It's a waste of precious energy for little incremental gain. Pick your moments more wisely as to when to make time and distance. Yeah, you hate slow. But accept slow on climbs like the Caribou and save yourself for the flats and downhills, where you'll more than make time.* Just as entertainers have to find their own unique voice and style, I had to find my own personal rhythm and effort suitable for the terrain. And so I learned by feel how to put my mind in a trance, set a machinelike cadence, and find my optimal efficiencies. My legs pumped like rhythmic pistons, learning to not waste motion or burn excess energy.

Since this was the first bike I ever had with clips, I was also learning literally on the go. On the steepest sections I needed enough initial momentum to clip in and still be able to keep going. After one rest break, when I started up again on one of the Caribou's steeps, I clipped in one foot and thrust forward for a start, but I couldn't get enough initial momentum. So, with one foot clipped in and the other slapping at its pedal, struggling to snap in, I lost my inertia, my bike lost its stability, and like a clown bike in the circus, I tipped over. As if fate itself was laughing at my plight, the scene played out in slow motion as I strained to get my free foot down, but the bike tipped away from it—I was helpless to catch my fall.

So, with one foot still locked to its pedal, I lay sideways in the road in a tangle. *How embarrassing!* Naturally, I looked around. *Did anybody see this train wreck?* But, of course, I was completely alone in the middle of Mat-Su nowhere. Like the Joker, ridiculous painted face and all, I laughed out loud. *Did anyone just hear me? Were my friends right? Am I drifting toward insanity out here solo in the wilderness?* The tip-over was pretty pathetic, but at the same time, it was pretty funny, too!

So, aided by my self-inflicted pratfall, it only took me a few stops to remember to gear down before I stopped on a hill. *Then, when I restart again, I'll avoid excess strain in the pedals and that harrowing, drunken-sailor weave. Also, every schoolkid knows to pedal across the grade rather than straight uphill to lessen the apparent slope—elementary, for sure! But crazy, I have to relearn what I've forgotten—the hard way.*

I spotted bear prints in the gravel on the shoulder of the road. *How fresh? I don't know, but fresh enough, since there isn't any erosion around the edges.* I also saw bear scat. I knew bears were everywhere, but this was the first sign—or my first sighting, so to speak. *I really am in their house, not mine. Whoa, this is wild!*

The wildlife also felt different here. For one thing, the ravens were freakishly big. With the rush of the wind or raging water below the only sounds as I pedaled, suddenly the rambunctious squawk of a raven would pierce the quiet. *My God, that's such an otherworldly sound, and it carries far beyond what I imagined—despite the dense, lush woods!* I also passed my first beaver, just puddling about out on a mountain lake. He slapped his tail on the water, a sound like a sharp crack of a whip cutting the air—*wham-wham—kerplunk!* He dove as I struggled by. *Pretty cool, he damn near splashed me!*

Due to the remoteness, my encounters with people were sparse—but everyone I met appreciated my effort and wanted to help in some little way. During one rest, a guy called out from afar and then ran to me. "You too strong!" he shouted as he arrived in a heavy foreign accent that I couldn't immediately place. "I saw you climb," he said with a rising intonation, searching for his English, "and I want you to have this." He thrust a Snickers bar into my hand.

"Thank you so much! You're too kind," I replied. "Where are you from, France?"

"Switzerland, but on the French–Swiss border, on holiday." He had the look of a mountaineer, and with a broad grin of appreciation of my effort, he'd just had to contribute somehow.

At another stop, an old man from Michigan said, "I saw you working up that long hill! I'm so envious, I couldn't even make a small portion of it." *His tone is more sad than envious—a statement of youth long past and elder regret.* "I wish I tried something like this when I could have—when I was younger and stronger," he added.

I offered him a bit of complimentary encouragement: "You're still out traveling, and you have a lot more than you think you have.

Enjoy yourself on your trip!" He gave a feeble salute and struggled back into his car.

On the Caribou climb, a car stuffed full of young women passed me, and they all leaned out their windows, pumping their fists and shouting encouragement: "Alright!" "Good job!" "Keep going!" I gave them my best thrusting fist pump.

Each outpouring of encouragement and goodwill kept me going for miles. *Funny. Those were nice little boosts—take note for others.*

With so few distractions, little things stood out. For instance, I must have been the only person in Alaska not carrying a gun. Every highway sign was peppered with bullet holes. *Boy is this indicative of a knot-headed free spirit here on the frontier's fringes. It's senseless.* But I laughed at every sign.

Each of these bullet-ridden signs showed the distances to the next major towns, often three or four hundred miles away, and I'd mentally calculate when I'd hit each town—several days out, or longer. The simple mental math kept my mind engaged. But even more interesting, time was now measured in days and weeks rather than the minutes and hours I used to keep track of.

I finally arrived and set my campsite at Grandview, a small outpost lodge surrounded by white, snow-packed peaks cutting into a royal blue sky. The lodge had a few RV and tent sites. But best of all, it also had a shower. As basic as it may seem, after being drenched with sweat all day, a shower and clean clothes were my new luxury. However, at this stop I forgot to take my pack-towel to the shower. *Shake like a dog, drip dry, and shut up, chief—it's a shower and won't always be available. With such a simple pleasure, I have to find a way to get clean every night, one way or another.*

The non-riding portion of my day was a series of chores: pack/unpack, set camp/break camp, cook/clean up, launder/repack. *I'm too inefficient! Although I have nothing but time, I'm much—much—busier than I expected, and too much of it is wasted time because I don't have an efficient routine. I need to streamline all these brainless activities.* So I started figuring out a system of what efficiently packed where, for proper bike balance and elimination of my wheel shimmy, and also so I could find or pack my gear quickly. *This is the penalty of no dry run. Big deal! I'll get better every day—it won't be long.*

My tent was about a hundred feet from an RV where four people sat at a picnic table next to a campfire. The owner wandered over to my camp to see what my story was. *I'm attracting a lot of attention—people want to talk.* He was a retired Air Force colonel from South Carolina. He said, "Have you eaten? We have a lot of food, I made ribs. C'mon over and join us."

"I'd love to, but I have so little to contribute to the party," I said, embarrassed.

He just smiled and pointed at my bike in a knowing way. "C'mon over."

I've never been comfortable as a freeloader, but I swallowed my pride and joined them for a welcome plate of ribs, potatoes, cornbread, salad, and corn on the cob. They knew how to eat! Afterward, we talked for over an hour. I'm no cook, so I was doubly lucky they were around. "Thank you for your generosity," I finally said. "I still feel guilty." He waved me off. "I'll tell you what," I continued, "the next time you invite me to a potluck, I'll bring the paper towels and the packaged cookies."

He laughed and simply said, "Goodnight and good luck."

Goodnight was relative, as it was the summer solstice, the longest day of the year, and at this latitude it stayed light until 11:30 p.m. I watched the natural kaleidoscope of evening sunlight play off of Mount Thor and Mount Marcus Baker, two 13,000-footers whose ice fields fed the Matanuska Glacier. As evening fell, the glaciers reflected alpenglow and the colors changed from bright white through a spectrum of iridescent yellows, oranges, and hot pinks. Meanwhile, the shadows of neighboring crags and peaks crawled across the ice fields as the angle of the sun changed. The scenery was in full motion, constantly changing until finally, the motion of the heavens itself flipped off the lights.

I lay awake in the dark. *Does it get better than this?* Trips like this reduce you to the simple—*There's nothing like scrubbing clean, sleeping outside in cold mountain air, a crisp breeze wafting through your tent, burying yourself deep into your sleeping bag, and listening to the whispers of the wind interrupting your inner thoughts.*

The day was a killer to be sure—*I'm pretty sure the Caribou Creek climb will give me night sweats for years to come.* Of the day's meager forty miles, thirty-five were uphill—but I survived. And, although this was only the second day, I realized, *I'm pulling it off—I can do this.*

GRANDVIEW, AK
Miles today: 40

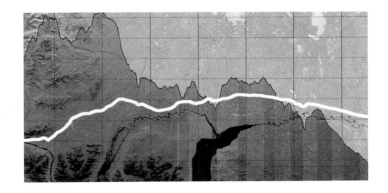

DAY 3
FRIDAY, JUNE 22, 2012—GRANDVIEW, AK
Miles to date: 114

I awoke early with a goofy, euphoric feeling of well-being. Living outside in the gorgeous, wide-open wilderness was so healthy for my disposition. Even though the Caribou Creek climb had wrung me out and made me a little loopy, it did so in a good way. *I have a runner's high—on steroids.*

Like a hood ornament, my chin sliced through a stiff headwind. In need of a break, I paused at a roadside pullout and was treated with breathless wonder to a bird's-eye view of the countryside spread before me. The neon light of early morning electrified the landscape in Technicolor. Brilliant but rockfall-dirty ice fields clung to the purple-gray mountain peaks. Avalanche trails plummeted down the mountains. White-foamed waterfalls of seasonal glacial melt streamed off cliffs. A cotton-like quilt of clouds layered the depths of the valleys. It's easy to let your mind drift in these special places—*this pristine area hasn't changed in eons except for the single sign of mankind, the road itself*—of which I could see traces in the distance—opposing silver crescents of the Glenn shimmering in the sunlight, or just the string-like cut through the millions of trees.

I jolted back to reality from this panoramic viewpoint and had a five-mile downhill cruise for the ages. I let myself go, and gravity sucked me into a freewheeling plummet through a moving postcard and eventually deep into the fog and murkiness below. *This descent is so symbolic of the ever-changing conditions and uncertainties in my life—constant cycles from vast brilliant clarity and warmth to being enshrouded in cold, dark, foreboding clouds and fog. But what the hell, I'll eventually pedal out of the fog—I always have.*

Late morning, about eleven o'clock, I came upon a single Piper Cub parked on a grass strip in front of the remote Red Eagle Lodge. *The Red Eagle International Airport?* It was such a vivid contrast from just a few weeks earlier, when I strode through a packed concourse at LaGuardia or Logan, flashing privilege from my platinum air-miles card as I jostled all the other cattle for position. *Now that I'm not flying, the airline will downgrade me from platinum to plywood status in just a few short months—which suits me just fine! Here, at this short grass strip, status doesn't matter—only survival. Airport security would be no more than wiping the dirt off your feet before boarding, and checking bags would be throwing them behind the pilot.*

The Red Eagle Lodge is a highlight of the Copper Valley area—a lonely stretch with dozens of miles between cabins, outposts, or other signs of civilization. I hadn't eaten breakfast, so I was starving. I pulled off the road to the comfort of a picnic table in front of the lodge. The quiet was remarkable. I was about to munch a granola bar when the silence was suddenly shattered.

"Hello!" a man exuberantly called as he stepped out from an outbuilding and walked toward me.

"Busted! I feel like a trespasser!" I shouted.

"Naw, no problem—everyone is welcome here."

"Well, I hope you don't mind that I just jumped your picnic table." Our conversation paused as he closed the gap.

"I'm Richard." He wore a big grin as he approached.

"I'm Jerry." I extended my hand.

"Well, Jerry, you look like you've taken on quite an adventure. Where are you headed?"

"Mexico!" I said, smiling. "But we'll see how that goes, I've just started." By way of explanation, I added, "I'm starving—I need to pump calories!"

"Well, come on in!" he bellowed. "We've got food."

Richard and his wife, Judy, owned the Red Eagle Lodge. I joined them in the main cabin, which doubled as their house. They set up a buffet of coffee, juices, cereals, fruit, yogurt, toast, and muffins. "Five dollars to eat all you want," he told me.

"I don't think you want to make me that offer," I replied. "You could get totally screwed—you don't know how hungry I am!" *I couldn't be happier.*

He broke out laughing and waved me off. "It's nothing."

Judy offered to make me other food, but what they had was perfect. While I sawed through my unexpected but welcome meal, I visited with Judy, Richard, and their young summer helper from Colorado. It became apparent to me that they were starved for company. *This seems like times long past, when a wayward traveler would bring news of the world as they passed.*

Richard and Judy, however, were well informed on the current news of the world, not to mention smart, articulate, and highly opinionated. Political correctness clearly had no place in conversation in this remote outpost. *Whoa, unvarnished!* Much of what they said, whether I believed it or not, had me belly laughing. *But, despite their leanings, they'd drop everything and rush to aid anyone in need.*

I lingered too long. As much as I enjoyed my hosts, I had to get back on my bike and get moving again, especially because the weather was so good. *The pull to keep moving is constant.* Still, on the way out, I took the time to let Richard show me his Piper Cub. *Between the dings in its wings and a dashboard control panel that's so worn that it's more like an out-of-control panel, it's hard for me to believe this plane is flightworthy!* Richard laughed at the expression on my face. "This plane is my baby," he boasted. "Not only I can coax it to fly, it can get me anywhere." I wasn't so sure of that.

Richard had been all over the contiguous United States and to the most remote edges of Alaska—even to Siberia—in his small plane. In addition to flying, he had taught high school, but had since retired. But what struck me most was his pioneering, self-reliant spirit. *Underneath it all, he and Judy are fabulous people who want me to succeed.*

Reenergized by the breakfast, I clipped in for the next leg of my day. The terrain was rolling hills through wilderness where I only occasionally saw a lone cabin or small encampment. I let my mind wander as I ground out the miles. *Every possible thought and topic rattles through my brain. Where do the hours go?*

By late afternoon I was dragging. Luckily, I found a roadhouse and ordered a late lunch. It's a good thing the food came fast because I was nodding off in my booth. The burger, fries, and paint-can-sized chocolate malt gave me the energy boost I needed to power through the rest of the day.

What the hell is that? About thirty miles out of Glennallen, I began to see what appeared to be an imperceptibly faint but massive structure in the vast distance. At first, I pegged it as an optical illusion because the structure was just about the same color as the sky. *Is that a distant cloud formation, or am I getting mind-fucked? Is that an enormous mountain? Can a mountain reach that high?*

As I rode closer, I realized I was looking at an immense and completely glaciated mountain, just a micro-shade off the color of the sky. I later learned that it was Mount Sanford, a volcano in the Wrangell Volcanic Field. Bathed in the late-afternoon light, it was pure white and so perfect in form it seemed almost too symmetrical, like what I—or a first-grader—might paint in watercolor. As I reached Glennallen, it dominated the horizon, thrusting straight up out of the surrounding countryside to 16,237 feet, overwhelming all surrounding geological features. I later learned that Mount Sanford is a shield volcano, its south face rising over 8,000 feet in one mile, one of the steepest gradients in all of North America.

I stopped for the night in Glennallen, at the crossroads of the Glenn and Richardson Highways. After three days of riding in the outback, this town of 483 people felt like a major metropolitan area. The towns between it and Anchorage were little more than a gas station, convenience store, tiny cafe, and maybe an RV park each.

I checked into the Northern Nights Campground, where the camp receptionist looked me up and down in my cycling clothes and saw my bike leaned against a post outside. "One of my friends owns a roadside restaurant about a hundred miles south and west of here," she said with a grin. *So what?* I didn't understand. "She called me yesterday to report a funny story about a cyclist who'd just left her restaurant. She said everyone in the restaurant had plates stacked full of food, and then this skinny biker comes in and orders nothing but an orange. An orange!" she exclaimed. "Everyone stopped eating to watch. Here this cyclist is the one who needs food the most, and that's all he got. When he left, everyone in the restaurant just cracked up!

"My friend exclaimed, 'It just didn't fit!' and she was laughing so hard as she told the story, I could hardly understand her!"

"Uh, that biker was me." I grinned.

"I suspected that," she said, still giggling.

"Who knows why, but I had an unbelievable craving for an orange. Go figure." What the restaurant owner couldn't have known was that I'd had a huge breakfast about twenty miles earlier, so I wasn't starving, just craving. But I didn't tell this to the camp receptionist. It would have diminished her sense of fun. *Why be a wet rag?*

As I was leaving to set up my tent, she said, "By the way, it's Pie Night in the campground. We'll have a variety of pies laid out in the central courtyard. Come back at seven thirty and get a free slice."

"I don't know, I don't know if your pie can hold a candle to that orange! But, I'll give it a whirl—I'll be back for sure."

I'm positive she immediately called her friend back with this latest edition of the story and a whole new round of laughter. *Small news travels far up here.* Funnier yet, that orange wasn't even on the menu, but they'd accommodated me nonetheless—and only charged me a dollar. *They can laugh at my expense all they want—God, these are good people!*

I pitched my tent as quickly as I could, as weather can change pretty fast in the far north. But rain wasn't to be my problem: for the first time I was killed by mosquitos! Those little suckers just swarmed. I didn't carry any bug repellent because I've always thought its smell and residue were worse than the bugs themselves, so I endured the swarm of skeeters while I pitched my tent. I quickly threw my gear inside, zipped the flap, and then mushed every last mosquito that'd slipped inside. My tent was covered with little splotches of blood— my own blood, exploded from smashed mosquitos. *It's a blood bank gone amuck—what a mess in here!*

I didn't cook if I didn't have to. Well, more accurately, I don't cook—period! Luckily, Glennallen was big enough to have dining options: there were a couple of truck stop/general stores for me to choose from. Out of sheer laziness, I chose the one straight across the street from my campsite. I had a roast beef sandwich, chips, two oversized cans of iced tea, a turkey sandwich, homemade potato salad, a banana, and a cookie. I finally cleaned up with a small tub of ice cream. My version of an eight-course meal, fine dining straight off the shelves of a general store. I hit most of the major food groups: sugar, salt, and fat. And of course I hit the pie plate back at the campground.

After five and a half hours in the saddle, I felt more wiped out than on the previous days. *I'll continue toward Tok tomorrow, about 140 miles away,* I figured, *still heading northeast and away from Mexico. I'll make Tok in two days and then maybe take a rest day.* Although I was tired, all in all, I was shocked at how good I felt.

I awoke deep in the night. *God, I'm hungry. No—starving! Too bad. I'll have to hold out 'til breakfast.* I tossed, famished.

NORTHERN NIGHTS IN GLENNALLEN, AK
Miles today: 81

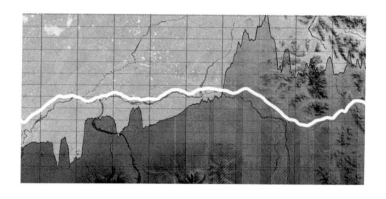

DAY 4
SATURDAY, JUNE 23, 2012—GLENNALLEN, AK
Miles to date: 195

I've been fortunate thus far: outside of a few isolated sprinkles, the weather has been nice. The Wrangell–St. Elias National Park was so drop-dead gorgeous that it would have been a shame to miss. This large, mountainous region is often socked in while travelers pass through, so they don't see a thing, but I was lucky. Out of what would be my passenger-side window, I had stunning views of Mounts Sanford and Drum. *This is a "don't miss" national park, and I'm coming back!*

I stopped at a small lake with a couple of tranquil swans painting a portrait of serenity—*Almost too perfect, like one of those cheesy yoga posters with a feel-good platitude.* But just as I was about to shoot a photograph, an eagle buzzed the swans, nearly winging their heads. I heard the swoosh of air under the eagle's wings, but damn, I missed the shot. In the eagle's wake, the swans honked and squawked, bobbing their necks, totally pissed. *Fucking beautiful! Nature's true drumbeat and drama, not a sanitized artist's view.*

Later, I climbed to an elevation where I had a top-down view of another bald eagle scanning the river below. I watched from above as I pedaled along, his white head swinging side to side, looking for movement as he did wingovers and doubled back into the wind— whereupon he'd slow and then, just before a stall, swing back around, working himself downriver. *Nature's grace.*

Two different cars and a group of motorcyclists each stopped or slowed to ensure all was well. "Everything okay, man?" one guy shouted through his window as he rolled past.

"Yep, all is well! Thanks for checking, though!" I hollered back. Each passing was similar; everybody said *something.* My exposure compelled them to check in. *Everyone has your back up here, even if you're just a visitor passing through.*

In the late morning, I blew past a cyclist who seemed to be crawling in comparison. I felt guilty flying by another rider in the wilderness, so I doubled back and rode tandem with him for a bit. As a pleasantry I asked, "How's it going?"

"F . . . i . . . n . . . e," he said in slow motion.

"What's your name?"

"T . . . o . . . n . . . y." *Uh-oh. I'm going to have to carry this conversation.*

"Where are you from?"

"V . . . a . . . n . . . c . . . o . . . u . . . v . . . e . . . r." *Am I in a time warp? This is going to take all day.*

"What's your destination today?"

"T . . . o . . . k." *That's the longest three-letter word I've ever heard.*

"No way," I said, "that's still about seventy-five miles away!"

"Y . . . e . . . a . . . h," he replied with an innocently crooked smile.

I've asked five questions and received exactly five one-word answers— hate to have him on a talk show! My best guess was that Tony was in his mid-thirties and didn't work. We pedaled a few more painfully slow strokes in silence.

"Where do you normally stay at night?" I was looking for more connections to make a conversation.

"Mostly in motels and lodges."

"That gets pretty expensive day in and day out, doesn't it?"

"I have a credit card." He gave me the same crooked smile, as though he didn't have to worry about the payments.

"You're wearing jeans, Tony?" I inquired, searching for an answer.

"Yeah." He smiled as though it was explanation enough.

"When it rains, they never dry out!" I exclaimed. "Plus, they bind and chafe. Why don't you wear bike clothes? These professional biking dudes have figured out a thing or two about biking comfort over the years."

"I can't afford them with all the money I have tied up in my bike," he replied.

O . . . K . . . , motels and lodges each night, and won't buy spandex. None of it makes sense. But it also didn't take a psychotherapist to realize Tony wasn't altogether *there.*

I tried to figure out just who this person was. *That's it! Tony is a cross between Mr. Magoo and Forrest Gump: nearsighted, naïve, and clueless—and seemingly oblivious.* I remembered one episode in particular when Mr. Magoo ended up high on a skyscraper, meandering along an I-beam being lifted by a crane. When he blindly stepped off the end of a rising I-beam into what should have been thin air, he caught a descending I-beam perfectly, without breaking stride—and, being Mr. Magoo, was completely oblivious to what had just happened. And like Forrest Gump, riding long distances was just what he did. When he finished one trek, he'd simply change direction and start in another—no place in particular to go, and nowhere in particular that he had to be. Riding and riding—and riding.

"I really enjoy it," he stated. Tony was perfectly happy being out there, alone and in his own world. He pedaled painfully slow, and I estimated that he spent twelve hours in the saddle each day to reach his destination—way too much time on his razor-blade seat, especially for the distance attained. But I had to give Tony credit for his persistence: he eventually got places. He had a perpetual smile, and I didn't hear a single complaint. He was clearly no worse for what would have had me in rear-end agony. In a way, I admired Tony—he was completely content and free of worry. *So simple as he just accepts himself, his condition, and the greater world for what it is.*

After a little while, I could no longer ride at that pace. "Tony, my engine is revving, it's time for me to throttle up."

"O . . . k . . . ," he said too slowly, "I'll see you later." He gave me a feeble wave-off, barely getting his hand off the handlebar. In a few short moments I lost sight of him. But later in the day, over two hours after I'd stopped and set my camp for the night, who should come chugging along but Tony, wearing a big smile. *I never thought I'd see him again.* He stopped to eat and told me that he would ride on to the town of Tok yet that night, still forty-five miles away. Even though it stayed light until late evening at this time of year, I concluded that Tony's ride would end well after dark. *Tony and I are the modern-day version of the tortoise and the hare!*

Earlier that day, at about three in the afternoon, I'd stopped at a funky wayside general store in the middle of who-knows-where to fuel up. Four guys there were in the process of closing up early, talking fishin' and huntin' all the while. I settled in a ratty, moldy-cushioned easy chair on their storefront porch to snack, but I kept going back in for yet another item. "Hustle up," they finally said, firmly but kindly. "We're outta here—we're goin' fishin'."

As I watched, one of the guys grabbed a cannon-sized pistol and slipped it into a holster strapped to his chest. "Aren't you guys packin'?" he hollered to his friends, who were piling into the truck.

"Well, are you?" one of them called back.

"Hell, yeah!" he said. "You never know." Whereupon the rest of the crew scrambled out of the truck, retreated to a shed, and came out with rifles that looked more like bazookas. *So much for my little can of bear spray! You never know!* rung in my ears.

However, the day's calamity involved not a bear but a water bottle. As I was riding, I reached down to grab it, but as I pulled it from its holder, the bottle slipped out of my hand and fell to the road, where my back wheel immediately flattened it. An explosion of water instantaneously disappeared behind me. I slowed and circled back to find that I'd broken off the tip and crushed the cap. The precious water streamed in its own little rivulet down the road. I was in the middle of nowhere. *Dash one water bottle—I may need that water. Well, shit happens.*

Of all the problems I'd tried to imagine in advance, this was nowhere near that radar screen. I needed to replace that third water bottle as soon as I could, but it would have to wait for Whitehorse, several hundred miles away.

The second half of the day was a distinctly different tale than the first. The wind spooled higher yet, and I bucked a thrashing headwind for the last forty-five miles. *From now on, I'll add the unknown variable of blistering stonewall headwinds into my calculations.* Seven grueling hours was a long time in the saddle—definitely longer than I wanted. *But as consolation, there's a certain dignity to the struggle.* Late in the day I came upon five guys, each with their Harleys, parked in a hidden pullout. I had to look twice to see them tucked away, deep in the bushes, mostly out of sight.

"Hey, want a beer?" one guy shouted as I rode past. They were firing down brews in the bushes.

"I'd love one!" I hollered back. "But I still have to make time." That got me a beer-induced cheer and a hearty thumbs-up. More truthfully, it was overcast and dark, I was damp to the bone, rain threatened at any moment—and I was freezing. Stopping for a cold beer would have made me even colder yet, and I wanted to get downstream to a campsite and set up before the clouds burst. They were a raw group of knuckleheads; I'm sure I could have had a ball with them and unlocked some colorful wisdom. *I should have joined that group—imagine their stories! The living version of George Strait's "Cowboys Like Us." Next time I'm stopping no matter what. I hate missed opportunities!*

I'd seen several motorcyclists on distance trips over the last few days, and I envied their ability to just effortlessly cruise. But then I had a funny thought: *When I'm cruising on my own motorcycle trips, I envy the cyclists because they're wringing themselves out. What would a shrink make of that? Then again, who cares what a shrink thinks; they're more twisted than their patients! Ho ho—I too easily entertain myself!*

I could have elected to ride fewer miles today but felt I was up for a longer reach. In this far northern wilderness, I aimed to pick *natural* stopping points. Natural stops to me were where I could get food and find a campsite, and yet were far enough downstream to make a full day. I was constantly making judgments on whether to proceed or stop based upon weather, headwinds, terrain, time of day, speed, distance attained, my physical and mental condition—and available food. *There is no right answer. Just pedal and do what you can.*

At the beginning of each day I tried to figure where my optimal natural stop would be—but nobody planned the highway with cyclists in mind. They were more like natural railway stops, so they were often forty to fifty miles or more apart. Some clusters of natural stop points were too short for a day, but continuing on to the next could be a stretch. Or, conversely, I could be making better time than I expected—*For God's sake, keep moving.* So I was flying blind on how far I could get and never knew exactly where I'd end up. *In any case, just take what the day gives you!*

As each mile passed, every one of my senses fired continually: the warmth of the sun on my skin, the shrieking wind through my ears, the frigid cold in the shadows, the rain pelting and stinging my face, the smell of millions of pines in an undisturbed wilderness—inhaling the cleanest air on Earth. The sounds were their own symphony: wild rushing rivers, piercing raven squawks, swoosh of an eagle's wings, slap of a beaver's tail, rumbling thunder echoing off the far shores or wind in the treetops. And, the taste of pure mountain water. All this while I was saturated with a speedball of adrenaline and endorphins. I was punished on the climbs but exalted at the crests, followed by swooping skydive downhills. I was living outside 24/7 with few, if any, places to retreat to for safety or comfort. And the people—both the kind and the strange—only occasionally entered the scene.

I reflected on the last four days. *Traveling here by bicycle is like IMAX all day long, but so much better—it's sensory overload!* I was immersed in rolling *Planet Earth* scenes, frame by frame, drowning in beauty that was live, raw, and real—not sterilized by far-too-safe video screens. *I had to more than see all of this—I had to feel it.* These amazing experiences were mine and mine alone, not limited, polluted, or filtered by a filmmaker or editor's view of the world. *My own eyes and imagination can't be replaced. Funny, just like the book is "always better than the movie" because your own imagination is engaged—you paint your own scenes.*

As each day finally ended, and in the protection of my tent, I was overwhelmed by a feeling of well-being—only to do it all over again the very next day. *How can I describe this to others?* I wished my family and friends could see and feel these moments. *It's hard to imagine how time can be better spent.*

Up front, I couldn't anticipate exactly how I'd be affected by this journey, so I gravitated to the shallow and the trite—*I just want to see if I can do it, and the stories will be a hoot!* But the wonder of it all was heightening my observations and sparking my imagination. *This is clearly new and pure growth.* I wasn't quite sure how I would use this experience in the future, or where it would take me, but I equated it to pure research—personal R&D. After all, when the first research laser came online, scientists and engineers weren't quite sure of its applications either—that came later. *So although it's fuzzy now, I have a funny feeling, a sixth sense, that this journey is paving the way to tomorrow's dreams.*

It's exactly what I'm looking for.

MENTASTA LAKE, AK
Miles today: 96

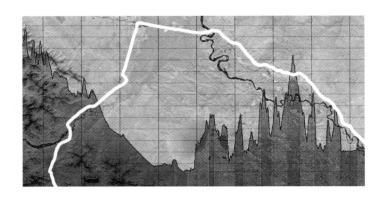

DAY 5
SUNDAY, JUNE 24, 2012—MENTASTA LAKE, AK
Miles to date: 291

I was awakened by a moose at about four o'clock this morning, bellowing and screaming his brains out. *Funny what a guy will do for a girl.* A moose's nose is about four feet long, so it forms a pronounced megaphone, and the sound was so loud that I thought the moose was right on top of my tent. *That son of a bitch just blew me out of my sleeping bag.* Moose can be both erratic and dangerous, and statistically, they cause more human trauma than bears, so I grabbed my bear spray and looked out of the tent.

I didn't see anything. *Truth be told, I can't see shit without my contacts anyway.* But without a visual to confirm what I heard, I decided to roll over and try to get a couple more hours of sleep. *Try* was the operative word: that moose was so lovesick, he never quit his hollering. When I was fully awake, I realized it was the first moose call I'd ever heard in the wild and was still stunned by how loud it was, and how amazing to hear. *Another clear reminder that I'm in their world out here.*

Tok, another major town as these towns go, was only about forty-five miles away from my camp. Since I'd ridden ninety-six and eighty-one miles in the previous two days, respectively, I thought I would make Tok and then dial it back, perhaps even take a rest day. With that shorter distance in mind, I got off to a late start at about 9:15 a.m.

It didn't take me long to realize one more reason that my last forty-five miles had been such a struggle: my front tire was flaccid. A bit concerned, I pumped it full and listened for leaks, but I couldn't find any and decided to just go with it. At each stop, I pinched my tire to check it. *Hmmm, seems okay, so when am I losing my air?* Of course, the answer was "all day long," but it was undetectable with each subsequent pinch test, and I was too lazy to go through the simple effort of reinflating it. *I'll just keep an eye on it—hopefully it goes away.*

I pedaled out of my campsite and immediately rounded a blind corner, where, whoa! Thirty feet ahead stood a moose grazing on the side of the road, probably the dude who'd kept me up half the night. *Moose can be mean. Which way is he going to go?* Face-to-face in a Mexican standoff, neither of us budged. I fished for my camera, but as if he knew what I was doing, he slinked into the thick bush and I never got the shot. Still, he never heard me coming, so I had my first moose sighting of the trip.

I found gentle hills early and then a flattish run into Tok, with a slight tailwind for a change. *I'm flying—but that's relative on a loaded bike.* Despite a few photo stops, I hit Tok in good time, about two and a half hours of saddle time, at 12:15 p.m. real-time.

I took measure of Tok. Despite being a so-called major town, there was nothing special to keep me there. Up here, the black dot on a map that denotes a major town may just be a gas stop and general store. Tok isn't quite that small—there were a few motels and restaurants—but it's not much more than just a crossroads of the Glenn Highway with the Alaska Highway (Hwy. 2).

I stopped for lunch in Tok, and while I was eating a grilled roast beef sandwich and sucking on a malt, in walked a guy in full cycling garb.

He found me and immediately said, "Is that your bike out there?"

"Yeah," I replied, surprised by another cyclist.

"I was pedaling by, saw the bike, and had to stop."

"Where are you headed?" I asked.

"I'm headed south to Whitehorse, over to Watson Lake, and then down the Cassiar Highway to Kitwanga, and then I'll head east on the Yellowhead Highway to Prince George, and eventually to Jasper, Alberta," he outlined. "How about you?"

"I'm going the same direction to Whitehorse, Watson Lake, and Kitwanga, but then I'm headed west on the Yellowhead to Prince Rupert—I'll make my way south on the Inside Passage from there to the northern tip of Vancouver Island, ride the island, and then cross to the US and ride Highway 1/101 to Mexico." I continued, "Where are you coming from?"

"I started in Prudhoe Bay, came south to Fairbanks, and then headed southwest to Denali Park and swung around to here. I've been on the road for a couple weeks."

"Sounds fabulous! How's the stretch from Prudhoe Bay?"

"That treated crushed-gravel road was a mess. The fine grit mixed with the road chemicals has destroyed my bearings and gears. Luckily, the mechanic's shop a couple blocks away had some tools and I've been working on my bike."

"Do you know what you're doing on your bike?" I asked, hoping for further kinship with someone as mechanically inept as me.

"Yeah, I can tear it all down and reassemble it—it's not that hard. I've got it back in rideable shape, but I'll have to replace all my parts when I get home. It's pretty easy." *You don't know who you're taking to*, I said under my breath, *I don't know jack-shit.*

"Where's home?" I inquired.

"Minnesota," he said.

"Oh yeah? Where?"

"Edina."

"You're a cake-eater!" I blurted, laughing. I couldn't help myself. (It's a colloquial nickname for Edina-ites due to their historic aspirations and demographics—well known to most Minnesotans.) He saw the humor, as he hardly fit the mold. I continued, "I'm from Tonka Bay!" (We only lived about ten or fifteen miles from each other in Minnesota.) "How funny. What a small world! I'm Jerry."

"I'm Joel."

As fellow long-distance solo bikers, we had a near-instantaneous mind meld. But unlike me, Joel had substantial long-distance biking experience, so he not only knew what he was doing, but also had everything down to a system and science. Joel joined me for a quick lunch but only ordered a small salad. *What? Don't you want to pound down a steak?* He saw my quizzical look. "I'm a vegetarian," he said. "I'd like to get moving again today, but I'm stuck here in Tok because I have to wait for the post office to open tomorrow [Monday] to retrieve a pre-shipped stock of special beans—I'm low on supply." *All the calories we're tearing through, and he's living on beans?* He turned my preconceived notions on their ear. *Who am I to critique? He is a picture of fitness.*

Joel also planned to divert to a couple of different areas on side trips before Whitehorse. Our destinations would diverge at Kitwanga—still well over a thousand miles from here. *I'm still trying to absorb the magnitude of these distances on a bike.*

The weather was excellent, so despite my thoughts of a rest day, I decided to make hay in the good weather. "I'm going to giddy-up, Joel. I feel strong, and the weather is nice. Good luck on your beans!"

It was the last I thought I'd see of him, so I bade him good luck and farewell, and targeted Naabia Niign Campground, about fifty miles downstream from Tok. It looked to be another natural stopping point because it promised to have both food and campsites.

The 350 miles from Anchorage to Tok had taken me northeast, away from Mexico. Now I turned southeast onto the Alaska Highway. *South finally! It feels good to be pointed toward Mexico, albeit obliquely.*

At sixty-three degrees north, Tok was my northernmost point—just three and a half degrees south of the Arctic Circle. "Downhill from here!"—or at least that was what *everybody* kept saying. *Stupid joke, it's getting old!*

Late in the day, I rolled off the road at a pullout and rode up to a woman, also solo on her bike, talking with a man in a truck. Like Joel, Sarah was cycling to Jasper before doglegging back to Seattle. Her dad was following in his pickup on this portion of her ride so she wasn't alone. He carried all their camping equipment and supplies and would pull ahead about twenty miles to wait while she rode to him, over and over again.

The three of us chatted for a bit, and by crazy coincidence, she was also from Minneapolis. She had been a reporter for the *Star Tribune*, a major paper in the Twin Cities, but the siren of the road called and she'd resigned to ride this summer. *What's with us Minneapolis folk riding bikes thousands of miles?*

It was getting late, so I took off and left Sarah and her dad at the pullout. A few minutes later, I waved as Sarah's dad drove past on his way toward their camp spot for the night. Their camp would be set by the time Sarah caught up with him.

About thirty minutes later, I was straining hard in the pedals on an uphill—in way too high of a gear. I downshifted but had far too much power in the pedals and tension on the chain. *PING!* My chain snapped. I looked down and watched, almost in slow motion as my chain spooled off the sprocket with a low metallic growling sound and a soft thud as it hit the pavement in a pile. I pedaled air, reminiscent of the Wicked Witch of the West pedaling in the sky in the in *The Wizard of Oz.* My bike quickly decelerated—one moment I was full of motion and life, and the next, I glided to a stop, followed by silence of the wilderness—complete with a haunting rush of wind, like a death scene in an old Western movie.

I walked back and stared at my broken chain lying in the road like a coiled snake. *How deflating! I've never broken a chain. What the hell do I do now?* I picked up the chain and stood there, clueless—

looking at it, looking at the bike, looking back at it. *I'm so screwed.* I might as well have been a third grader staring at a physics test.

My mind twisted. *What do I do now? I'll pitch my tent in the bush, curl up, suck my thumb, and figure it out in the morning.* I started making preparations to squat right there. I'd known upfront that I'd have setbacks; I just couldn't contemplate what they'd be. *Stay calm, take a deep breath, lie down, and let the feeling pass. This isn't life or death—it's just a pain in the ass.*

I stood there deflated for a while, but then I looked down the road and, through a mirage, I saw someone in the far distance. *Are they pedaling toward me? Is this for real or a bad joke? Is my mind playing tricks on me?* But, as they got closer—*It's Sarah!* When she pulled up, I was standing next to my bike with a greasy, broken bike chain draped across my hands, looking absolutely forlorn.

Sarah sized up the situation in an instant. "Do you have an extra chain link?" she asked me.

"I don't know," I replied. "The bike shop guy threw a few items into a parts kit that he thought I might need. Let me look." I pulled out the kit and dug in. I hadn't even opened it yet.

The cycling guy was brilliant: there in the kit was an extra snap link. I held it up. "I have no idea what to do with this," I told her.

"There's a way to snap this link and reattach your chain. I did it once on a long ride across the States," she said. "Do you have a maintenance manual?"

"No," I sheepishly replied.

She said, "I have one; I'll dig it out of my pack." She unbundled her pack and found it. On our hands and knees, bent over my bike like doctors huddled in surgery, we studied the chain section of her manual. Then we restrung the broken chain—*Click*—the snap link popped into place! Success! I was back in business. I stood elated with my hands black with grease—hers were just as bad.

Although I'm alone, I guess I'm not completely self-reliant. I couldn't have even begun to fix this without Sarah. So much for solo independence! Most impressively, she didn't criticize—calm as could be, she just straightforwardly worked the problem. She also had three spare links and also carried an entire spare chain in her kit; since I only had the one snap link, she handed me a spare and said, "You'd better take this."

"Sarah, you're a godsend! I was screwed without you. You're going to heaven."

"It's no big deal." She laughed. "It's just what you do, and anybody would have helped."

I pedaled with Sarah until she cut off into a camp area where her dad had their campsite all set. "Do you want to swing in and camp near us?" Sarah asked.

"Thanks for your offer, Sarah, but the Naabia Niign Campground should be about ten miles ahead; I still have energy, so I think I'll knock off the extra miles. But what a stroke of luck that you came along! Thank you so much." I wagged my head at my good fortune. "What are the odds that someone would appear out of nowhere, riding the same brand bike, having a manual, and actually knowing what they were doing? Mind blowing. You're a saint."

So I moved on. The truth was, I didn't want to show how inept and unprepared I was. All I had to share at the moment was a couple of granola snacks in my bag—no real food. *I have absolutely nothing to offer them. Hopefully I can get some real food at Naabia Niign, and I don't want to impose on her any more than I already have.*

I arrived at the campground late in the day. It's located in Northway, Alaska, in the Naabia Niign area—the heart of Athabasca Indigenous country. I checked in and bought a couple Lunchables for my dinner—it's about all they had. *Thank God they have something!* I quickly set my tent, washed, and changed into clean clothes. I was the only person in this camp, deep in the woods and down a long hill from the tiny store, and there was total silence. Practicing bear discipline, rather than dining by my tent I traipsed a hundred yards to the Chisana River's edge with bear spray strapped to my hip like a six-gun, carrying my portable chair, my iPad, and my off-the-shelf dinner: the two packages of Lunchables—real food, at least to me.

While I was finishing my dinner, a big piece of ham fell out of my cracker sandwich and smeared all over my pants. *Ham-flavored clothing—have at it, Yogi! God!* I gave that portion of my pants a Wet

Wipes wash and hoped there were no bears in the area. By then, it was late, past 9:00 p.m., and dusk faded to dark as I sat next to the river and I wrote my daily blog. I realized that I was so caught up in the writing that I'd forget to look up. *I need to do that occasionally—to make sure I'm still alone.*

I'd bucked headwinds again today, but it wasn't bad. The terrain was flattish early in the day, and then I began a series of long climbs—not steep, just long. Near the end of the day there were a few nose-over downhills where I could just coast in the cool fresh air, surrounded by vistas of faraway mountain ranges and occasional glimpses of the distant strips of the road I'd eventually hit.

What a struggle for me to adequately describe this country. Everything in Alaska is immense; the mountains are taller, the valleys broader, the rivers swifter than in the contiguous US. Riding this is an out-of-body experience.

Despite the grueling effort thus far, I felt surprisingly great. For the first five days I'd ridden 74, 40 (all climbing that day), 81, 96, and 96 miles respectively. *I didn't know how I'd do physically. But jeez, I still don't feel like I need a rest day yet!*

The headwinds of the day abated. I lay in the pitch black under the even darker canopy of the woods. It was deathly quiet, without a whisper of a breeze. I listened for any sound at all—nothing. My eyelids grew heavy, and my mind fogged in the nexus of consciousness toward sleep.

What? Was that a twig snap?

NAABIA NIIGN
Miles today: 96

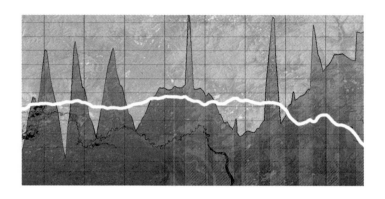

DAY 6
MONDAY, JUNE 25, 2012—NAABIA NIIGN, AK
Miles to date: 387

When I entered Canada, the border agent looked me over, then leaned out his window and looked down. He clearly saw the bear spray in my water bottle holder and didn't confiscate it. I'd tried taking pepper spray into Canada before, but when I declared it, the border agent took it. But that was on a Harley. Maybe it's different on a bicycle, or different when it's clearly labeled for bears. *Cool, he probably realizes it's the only defense I have—except, of course, for the chamois butter.*

The day brought rolling foothills and a lot of taiga, but some of the uphills were pretty long. The distances on the road signs were now in kilometers, so the distances seemed longer. When I saw a sign that indicated a town was 600 kilometers away, it was only 400 miles, but that bigger number was still an initial shock. I did mental gymnastics of converting the distances in my head, which was good for me. *It's always good to be occupied and thinking.*

Beaver Creek in the Yukon Territory is Canada's westernmost community and home of the White River First Nation. *Man, I thought I've been in remote parts thus far, but this is even more remote yet. And, as hard as it is for me to wrap my mind around, I'm told it will get even more remote as I proceed—with longer distances between food, too.* I didn't care where I camped, but I needed to pay constant attention to food.

Decisions got interesting on a trip like this alone. I would like to have gone another 25 miles today, for example, but the next food was not for 110 miles. So, having done 62 miles and reached the comfort of a small community where I could get a hot dinner, I decided to stop and save the next burst for a day in itself. Also, I noted that the roads and pavement were not as good in this part of Canada. *I might not make as good a time from here.*

I planned the next day in my head. *I want to start with a big breakfast in Beaver Creek tomorrow morning and then hammer the 110 miles to the next food. It would be nice to finish by having a couple of brews with my dinner—if it's around.* I bought peanut butter, jelly, and weenie buns as fuel for the crossing. I could have bought bread, but the buns were more convenient to pack, and they'd be smushed in my pack anyway. Only five days in, I was getting sick of energy bars and granola bars, so I threw in a few chocolate milks for variety.

I'd never done a century (100 miles) before, let alone more than that. *But having just completed two ninety-six-milers in a row, I'll just bury my chin and pound it out—should be a piece of cake.* I had no self-doubt mentally and physically, but mechanically? *Now that's a different story.* I was looking forward to joining the Century Club. I should have just plain ridden the four extra miles in each of the last two days to get it out of the way, but my natural stopping points were short of the mark. *Why waste the energy?*

In a momentary bout of self-torment, my head said take a rest day. *I've been cannon-balling hard for the last week.* I also thought rest might prevent nagging injuries, which often occur when you press too hard. *But what the hell, my heart wants to go for it.* Over time, I've found that I mostly make decisions emotionally first and then justify them intellectually—I justify what my heart wanted to do in the first place. *I should let my head win sometimes. But so far, my overpowering heart has made all the decisions.*

Way back in college, after blowing a structural dynamics test, I recalled an engineering professor drumming into me, "Rigidity is not strength, Jerry. You often want structures to flex—instead of snap!" What he said pertains to physical structures that are under constant stresses and strains. Engineers design in flex and give to relieve those stresses, which would otherwise snap rigid structures. I never forgot. And the same went for this journey. I couldn't be rigid on a set course of action or plan. I'd found the same to be true in business: often the policies and practices that originally made a company successful no longer made sense for its customers in a rapidly changing world. But few leaders had the courage to change or kill the past practices. And although planning never was my strongest suit, I'd also found out that I made up for it in quick adaptability. I reasoned (partly as a cover) that by the time I had a plan, conditions often changed and my plan was obsolete. Or, in the structural engineer's parlance, snapped! Besides, I always got the best ideas and advice from customers: they were more valuable than internal thinking. *Follow the money, make business as easy as possible for your customers: find those who pay the bills and follow their lead (need), and be ready to adapt the proposition into a win-win arrangement. It's almost always there somewhere. Throw existing plans out the window if a better option appears.* Variations of this theme played to my advantage on this journey.

So with that in mind, I pondered, *Stay or move tomorrow? I'll see what the morning brings.* But I felt surprisingly good. *Why rest if I don't feel like it? I can't get there if I'm not moving.* I've always had a bias toward action, and it kills me to stop when I can move. *Plus, tomorrow is supposed to have decent weather, while Wednesday is iffy—I should move when the weather is good. I'll make a game-time decision— run and gun, baby!*

The snapped chain had me spooked, though. I was uncertain about the strength and durability of the new link. I'd been overpowering the chain and gears thus far, thrashing and grinding through them. I've historically been hard on equipment—I burn it up pretty quickly. My derailleur was even a little off-kilter now and was skipping in the low gears, which might have contributed to my chain breaking yesterday. *Can I make Whitehorse with the spare snap link? I'd better calm and clean my riding style or I won't make it.* So I became more gentle shifting gears. *I have to nurse my bike to Whitehorse, still about 275 miles away. I just hope everything hangs together until then.*

My new style also became more about efficiency and optimizing the work effort, coasting the downhills to save my legs, picking my bursts, and trying to find the best gear for the riding conditions, whether hills, headwinds, or flats. *I'm not into Zen, but I've found natural rhythms in everything that I do. I'm just beginning to find the rhythm that makes me perform best on the bike.* I wasn't there yet, but I was getting better.

My front tire was also still leaking. *I filled it three times today. Tomorrow, I'll change the tube so I can be more confident. I generally throw away broken things, but I'd better keep the leaky tube—I might still need it in a pinch before Whitehorse.*

My tube wasn't the only thing leaking, I wasn't quite sure, but my air mattress seemed lower this morning. *Was it or wasn't it leaking? It did seem to be slumping under my weight. It's a little thing, but I felt rocks and roots in my back last night—that blows!* Such was the insecure nature of my life at that moment: all mechanical.

BEAVER CREEK, YUKON TERRITORY
Miles today: 61

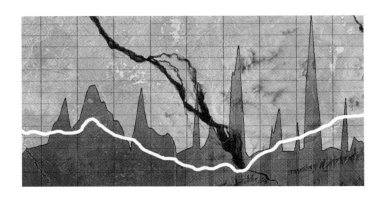

Rain drummed hard on my tent last night, along with continuous lightning and kettle-drum thunder. The storm stalled smack on top of me. A lightning flash followed instantly by an explosive thunderclap blew me out of my sleeping bag. *You just can't prepare for that! Hey, Garth, I have an idea—how about a song called "The Thunder Rolls"! Fuck, that was close! Or better yet, Marshall Tucker, ever thought about a song about "Fire on the Mountain"?* But I loved it—I loved it all as I hunkered down and endured the rage of the storm. *Why is it that wilderness thunder sounds louder, sharper, and crisper? Is it because I'm more exposed, less distracted, and thus more focused on it?* I loved the sound of the booming thunder as it rolled out and echoed in every contour of the distance. Best of all, I stayed bone dry.

In the morning, the exterior of my tent was still drenched, and I hated packing wet gear. Worse yet, my front tire was completely flat. Clearly, I had a slow leak and it was getting worse. *Maybe I should take a rest day, let the tent dry, fix the tire, fuel up, relax, and restart tomorrow.* That was all so logical—except I didn't feel like resting. My heart was still saying, *Get going!*

I wanted my tent and gear to dry out, so I forced myself to just hang around, moving slowly to consume time with menial tasks. I made breakfast, *okay, instant oatmeal,* and sat on a waterlogged picnic table as I ate. Then I pulled the tube out of the leaking tire. Since I couldn't find what was causing the leak, I just replaced the tube with a brand-new one and hoped that solved it.

By 11:30 a.m., though, I just couldn't hang out any longer. If it was raining, I would have stayed put, but while there were low, threatening clouds, the air was only damp with a wafting fog—not rain. *Up here, if it's not raining I should always put in the miles—every dry moment on a bike is bonus time.*

I decided to move. I quickly packed my still-wet gear and took off. Damned if only two miles downstream, it started raining.

It will only last a few minutes. I'll ride through it and hope I don't get sopped. Unfortunately, the rain didn't let up. In fact, it quickly turned into a driving downpour. Once I was thoroughly soaked, I finally decided to stop and put on my rain gear. I layered dry clothes over what I was already wearing, which was drenched. Too late: I shivered, cold to the bone, and my body rattled semi-hypothermic as I rode. I stopped again and added a couple more thermal layers, but by then I just couldn't get warm. And, although I was wearing gloves, my hands were wet and frozen. *Windstopper gloves ain't rainstopper gloves. Frozen hands suck!* I lost all dexterity in my fingers. Still, I never felt in dire physical danger except for a close lone lightning strike. *Pow! So much for Q-Tips—that strike blew the wax out of my ears!* Despite it all, I hated to stop, mostly because stopping kills momentum. In any event, there was no shelter anywhere. The only alternative was to ride.

So I blew what should have been quick and easy decisions! Laziness and procrastination in donning raingear killed me. *It's one thing to be cold, but freezing and wet—ugh!* And before that, I should have just stayed put and rested—the over-aggressive push forward compounded my problems. *Lessons learned.*

Ugh! There's no do over available on those decisions! So, undaunted, I rode frozen in the rain for about two hours before I noticed ever-growing splotches of blue sky, and then the clouds lifted along with my mood. I emerged from beneath the storm system, and as the sun came out I got warm again and peeled layers.

Shortly after the rain quit, I passed a remote cabin about fifty feet off the road with a brand-new, polished and gleaming Bell helicopter parked next to it. Several guys were standing on the front steps, so I stopped.

"Hey, men," I said with great originality.

"Whoa-ho, what do we have here?" one replied.

"I'm on a little bike ride," I said, "heading to Mexico." In their astonishment, they broadly grinned and shook their heads. This obviously was out of the ordinary for them. "That's a beautiful helicopter," I continued. "It must be a ball, shredding full-speed at treetop level in a heli here in the wilderness."

"Yeah, it's pretty amazing, pretty fun—not everyone gets to do this!" another exclaimed.

"Are you Forest Service, Fish and Wildlife, or mineral exploration?" With the new helicopter, I surmised it was one of those.

"You hit it right on—we're exploration geologists."

And so I got a peek into what I had originally intended to be my own career. My undergrad degree at the University of Minnesota was in geological engineering, with a focus on mineral and oil-and-gas exploration. At that time in my life, I thought traveling to the remote and extreme places of the earth sounded exciting. But I had a peek into that lifestyle in college when, for two years of summer work, I was a grunt supporting exploration engineers near the Canadian border in the wilds of northern Minnesota. It started exciting, but I soon found I was starved for more varied human contact. *What a gut check! By the end of the summer, the trees started humming as I slowly went insane in the woods.* As romantic and attractive as it once sounded, I knew months or even years on end in these remote places would ultimately feel too restricting to me.

Plus, I would have been a lousy engineer. If I couldn't even fix a bike chain—and worse yet, didn't have the interest or discipline to learn basic bicycle maintenance before I left—my chance of success in the precision field of engineering wasn't high.

I had a nice tailwind for the last fifteen miles to my natural stop and made great time with an effortless ride down a broad, sweeping, U-shaped valley that could have been the poster picture of glacial carving in a geology textbook.

Due to my late start, I'd only put in fifty miles. But everything is relative: a week ago, fifty miles had seemed impossibly long, but now it felt like a short hop. It also broke up the hundred-plus-mile crossing that I'd originally planned—so much for plans. *I still prefer winging it—it works to my advantage. I'd like to go another twenty-five miles because the tailwind is so good, and tailwinds have been so rare thus far. God I hate to pass them up.* But it was late, and the next food and camping area was still fifty-six miles away. I stopped for the evening.

I arrived at the Lake Creek Campground and met with a surprise. *What? Sarah and her dad are here and have made their camp. How the hell did they get past me?* As I pedaled in, Sarah waved. "Join us for dinner!" she yelled.

"Okay, will do," I hollered as I pedaled past their campsite. "Just give me a little time to set up and clean up."

I picked a secluded campsite about a hundred yards away from them and set my tent. Then I found a private area on the river and dunked myself to clean up. The river was crystal clear, with a rocky bottom. It was also bitterly cold—glacial cold—and thus, extra refreshing. But after my swim I couldn't get warm, even with *all* my layers. I made several cups of blistering-hot cocoa until I finally warmed from the inside out.

Three other cyclists separately straggled into Lake Creek for the evening, and each set up right on top of me. First, Joel from Edina pulled up; then a guy named Peter, an Australian-Canadian from Squamish, BC; and finally, much later, slow Tony from Vancouver. My once secluded part of the campground was now home to a small crowd. *Party time!*

When Tony arrived, he pulled out a brand-new one-person tent that clearly had never been unpacked. Poor guy didn't have a clue how to set it up. I helped him set it up—which was pretty simple. His tent was made to be extremely lightweight and ultrapackable, which was code for zero interior room. It looked more like a coffin to me—and a cramped coffin at that. *I would hate that closed-in tent, so claustrophobic. Especially if you get stormed in for a day. Hey! How about lay in your coffin and read Edgar Allan Poe all day—sprinkle in a little blue sky from Franz Kafka. Friggin' kill me! But it's Tony, and he doesn't seem to mind a bit.*

With the other cyclists, I walked back to Sarah's camp, feeling guilty that I had nothing decent to offer besides PB&J on smashed weenie buns. *So far, I'm just a taker of what Sarah offers—I hate that.* Sarah and her dad shared their carefully prepared pasta with all of us and even gave me a cold beer. "Anybody want smashed PB&J weenies?" I asked, whereupon I got laughs. *No takers.* Of course I knew nobody would accept. Not long after we ate, though, the rain arrived and the party broke up. We all hustled back to our tents.

Deep in the evening and well after dark, a camper trailer pulled in near our collective camp. As they settled, they turned on a gas generator that ground and rattled and broke the pristine silence of the wilderness. Peter, a tiny-framed man, emerged from his tent and strode over to the camper, shouting in his strained high voice, "Hey! Hey, what the hell do you think you are doing? Hey-hey, goddammit, we're trying to sleep! Turn that fuckin' thing off for chrissake!" I cracked up as I imagined Peter out there. *This was the cartoon pipsqueak against all odds, flexing his mosquito muscles, dressing down the brute.* I couldn't contain myself and broke into laughter as I heard Peter crunching through the noisy gravel back to his tent, grumbling loudly about the intelligence and probable ancestry of the camper crew—highlighting key phrases such as *fucking morons.*

There was no outward response from the camper except the sharp crack of the flick of a switch—and the generator ground to a halt. It was a total cartoon scene. *Smallest man, biggest balls! Great material.*

And so, there was silence again, except for the lullaby of rain on my tent.

LAKE CREEK CAMPGROUND, YT
Miles today: 51

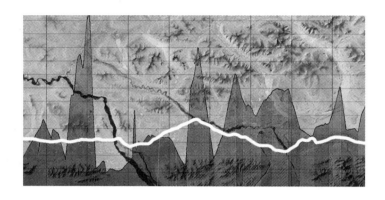

DAY 8
WEDNESDAY, JUNE 27, 2012—LAKE CREEK
CAMPGROUND, YT
Miles to date: 499

I drifted in and out of sleep throughout the night, but was awakened in the wee hours by the cold ground and the outline of a small tree root under my ribs. My air mattress *was* leaking. Although I didn't want to budge from my sleeping bag, I got up and re-blew it full of air. *Uh-oh, another problem. It's a little thing, but another problem nonetheless.*

It was still raining when I awoke at first light, so I rolled over and drifted away for a while longer. I finally got up about an hour and a half later than usual. The rain continued but was intermittent. There was a small, open-air covered pavilion about a hundred feet from my campsite—probably there because it rained so frequently.

I wasn't the only one moving slowly. Joel, Sarah, and I gathered under the pavilion to eat breakfast and fuss with our bikes. Even though I was dry, I couldn't get warm. It was one of those damp, cold-to-the-bone mornings I knew from Minnesota.

What! My front tire is flat again? I replaced the tube yesterday morning! Joel inspected the tire with me. "Because it's a slow leak, you probably have a small wire penetrating the tire and puncturing the tube," he told me. "When truck tires blow, their steel radials delaminate and leave little fragments of wire on the road. You can't even see the hair's-width wires on the road, but those little buggers can work their way into a tire and puncture the tube. Take your tire off the rim, pull your tube, and run your finger along the inside of the tire."

I removed my tire and visually inspected it, but I couldn't see anything. That's when Joel took my tire and ran his finger inside.

"Here," he said, showing me the spot. "Feel right here." I ran my finger on the inside of the tire where he indicated, and true to his prognostication, there was a tiny wire fragment lodged in my tire and piercing my tube. I plucked it out with my small Leatherman pliers, applauding Joel's genius.

But Joel wasn't done. "Do you know how to patch tubes?" he asked me.

"Uh, do I have to answer?" I said. Joel just looked at me in disbelief. "No," I admitted in a slow, sheepish drawl. "I don't know how to patch a tube. Well, it's been so long since I've patched one that I don't remember."

"Well, do you have a patch kit?" he asked. At least I had that in my supply bag, thanks to my cycling gear guy.

"I know, it's ridiculous that I left on this trip without basic maintenance skills," I said to Joel.

But Joel didn't outwardly judge me. "Here," he patiently said, "take this piece of sandpaper and rough up the tube where you have the leak. Then, with your finger, spread this rubber cement over that entire area and let it set for a couple of minutes; when the cement dries, peel the backing off the patch and squeeze it hard over the leak. It's that simple."

Wal-ah! I'm in business!

Once Joel was satisfied that I knew what I was doing, he took off and got moving. I, with my newfound skill, remained under the pavilion and patched two more tubes, one from yesterday and one from the day before. *Problem solved!*

Sarah was also working on her bike under the pavilion. She, her dad, and I chatted while she meticulously cleaned her bike chain and I finished fixing my tire and tubes. By now, the faint, hazy sun started burning through the mist.

"Do you want to ride together?" Sarah finally asked when we were both ready.

"Sure," I answered. "Let's go." It sounded like I was the efficient one who was prepared to leave earlier. In reality, Sarah could have left much earlier but had been busying herself and patiently waiting, probably to ensure that I was properly repaired.

We rode side by side for a couple of hours, talking nonstop in a stream of consciousness about all we were seeing, doing, or had done. As we flowed through the wilderness, we saw a black bear skirt into the bush ahead and also saw a lynx scoot across the road, wanting to beat the coming traffic.

Sarah's dad had driven ahead, and about twenty-five miles up the road we found him in a pullout with three lawn chairs set up. I thought about it, but said, "It's been great riding with you, Sarah, but do you mind if I just press on?"

"Sure, go ahead," she responded in complete understanding.

Sarah and her dad had been so nice, patient, and generous that I felt guilty proceeding alone while she pulled off. But I didn't need rest yet, and I was faster. Sarah just smiled in her calm manner, and the two waved me on as I left the roadside pullout. I hit the accelerator and made time.

By mid-afternoon, the sun was high in a bright blue sky. I welcomed the warmth on my skin. I was on a long, desolate stretch of road. I looked ahead, and that's when our eyes met: the mama grizzly bear with her two cubs foraging on the right-hand side of the road about a hundred feet ahead. I stopped in my tracks. *Whoa.* I was no longer thinking *how glorious a day* or *what a stunning countryside*—I now had bigger issues.

What do I do here? I wondered. *I'm already too close; the easy decision would be to turn around and get away from her as fast as I can. But what can I pull off? What can I get away with?* I snapped a couple photos as I wrestled with the decision whether to pass or retreat to wait her out. I watched her for signs of agitation, but outside of her initial stare she seemed completely calm and unconcerned about me as the three of them ate. *I wouldn't have to cut between any of them to get past.* Still, I watched and waited for about a minute. *This is a big decision. Are the odds in my favor that she won't do anything? I think I'm okay.* Blind optimism, but at the same time, what did I know about grizzly psychology? If I misjudged this moment, it would be catastrophic. I'd be another fleeting, grisly article in the *Alaska Dispatch News.* But the metronome beat of nature would continue without missing a beat. Most people would have a morbid fascination with someone so unfortunate to have been shredded in the wild. And sales of bear spray would go wild as the salespeople cocked their heads and said to the next patron, "Did you hear about the mauling last week?" But, for the most part, the memory of me would quickly fade from the headlines as everyone played to their respective daily drumbeats. I'm not trying to be melodramatic, it's just reality. Poof. Gone. Another statistic. Another Outdoor Channel episode. Everyone else's life continues.

Decision time, impatience, or brains? Impatience got the best of me—I decided to go. With trepidation, I steeled myself, pulled the safety latch off my bear spray, clicked into my pedals—and thrust forward. *My fate is cast—this encounter will be over one way or another in about thirty excruciating seconds. What lies before me, Destruction Bay—or destruction? How ironic, my destination portends my immediate fate—either way.*

I moved to the far left-hand side of the road, into the (nonexistent) oncoming traffic, to get the widest possible separation from them as I passed. I tried to act nonchalant and pose no visual threat—I even deluded myself by hoping I was invisible. I wanted speed but no hasty actions and hit a whopping twelve miles per hour by the time I was adjacent to her. I passed within thirty to forty feet of them. I didn't look directly at them, but I watched them intently through the corner of my eye—constantly accelerating and feeling better by the moment. They just chomped on their food and didn't show the least bit of agitation as their heads swiveled in slow-motion concert with my passing. As awe-inspiring as it was to see bears in the wild, I was relieved to put ever greater distance between us. It *was* over in thirty seconds; I was lucky.

In hindsight, I questioned whether I'd make that same decision again. *What the hell was I thinking? The stakes were too big. That wasn't very bright. Yeah, it worked, but don't do it again! I slid through, but I can't rely on luck. Don't dwell on it—it gives me the willies. Water under the bridge—just accept that flaw and don't dwell on it.* Little did I know it at the time, but my dumbest decision of the journey was still before me.

The headwind was brutal again today, and the wind was whipping harder as the day progressed. *Yesterday, a fifty-mile ride felt short. I was premature. A gale-force headwind completely changes the ride.* Again, I had to pedal during my downhills, in my lowest gears, no less. *God, I'd rather have uphills than headwinds. On the hills, the climb will eventually end and I have the benefit of downhills.* Today's uphills were long but mild, but the headwinds made me work three times as hard.

I was burning tons of energy in this endless battle with the wind. Late in the day, I forced myself to stop at a lodge in Burwash Landing to fuel up. Once inside the lodge's diner, I sank deep into the comfort of something wider than a bike seat—a chair with a back on it! It's not that I was uncomfortable while sitting on my bike, but in a relative sense, I tended to forget real comfort until I got off.

I let myself fall into a dreamy, satisfied stupor, my version of the thousand-yard stare. Happy to have survived a close grizzly encounter, I celebrated by ordering a burger with a haystack of fries and hoped it would take a while for the food to come so I could just veg. *Snap!* I caught myself just as my head bobbed—as though I was sitting in the third row of a late-afternoon business meeting with my manager, Plato, droning through the obvious like it was an epiphany. I dozed right off. When the food came, I ate slowly, which was rare for me as I tried to extend my rest time and savored every bite.

I couldn't help but constantly read my body, so despite the big burger I could tell that I hadn't eaten nearly enough today, or for that matter, eaten enough throughout the journey thus far. My body said, *Dude, you're running a cumulative calorie deficit.* I tended to ride until empty and then try to make up for it with a colossal dinner. *It's probably not the best strategy for optimal power. From now on, I should force myself to eat even when I don't want to stop.*

Burwash Landing is a First Nations community on the shore of Kluane Lake. There was a comfortable-looking campground smack on the water next to the lodge. I considered stopping here for the day. *But daylight is burning, and I haven't put in a ton of miles today.* The siren call of the road beckoned once again. Destruction Bay, my original target, was still ten miles farther downstream. *Ride on.*

As I approached Destruction Bay, I saw two figures in the far distance flailing their arms in the air. Joel and Peter saw me coming and stood in the road to guide me in as though I were a lost pilot trying to find the airstrip. After leaving much earlier than I this morning, the two had been keeping a lookout for me ever since they'd arrived.

Unfortunately, I traded what would have been a great camping site at Burwash Landing for a lousy and uncomfortable spot at Destruction Bay. The banshee wind was shrieking in full fury as I tried to set my tent. *No wonder they call it Destruction Bay. And shit! The ground is concrete: I can't get my tent stakes in even a fraction of an inch!* Finally, I unhooked my tent from its supporting poles, laid it flat on the ground, and placed boulders on the corners. *I hope this son of a bitch is here when I return!* I went to dinner.

Peter, Joel, and I walked a couple of hundred yards to the only bar-cafe in town. Once again to my surprise, Sarah and her dad wandered into the bar—they'd also made Destruction Bay but had grabbed a room in the lone cheesy motel this one-horse wayside had to offer. I hadn't expected to see *any* of my fellow riders tonight, but we all ended up at the bar. I bought several rounds of beer for everyone, happy that I could finally contribute *something*. It felt to me like a partial repayment for Sarah and her dad's previous generosity, Joel's maintenance expertise, and Peter's helpful entertainment with the camper trailer.

DESTRUCTION BAY, YT
Miles today: 65

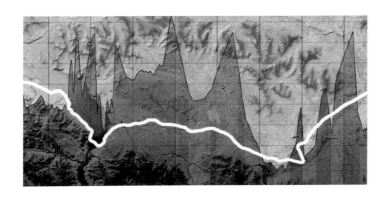

DAY 9
THURSDAY, JUNE 28, 2012—DESTRUCTION BAY, YT
Miles to date: 564

Not only did the wind blow like hell all night, but the temperature also plummeted. For the first time this trip, I zipped my sleeping bag completely around my head like an Eskimo in a fur parka to conserve heat. "Don't knock it, Peter," I said as I described it at breakfast. "It's a great look—and it worked." Joel was already gone by that point. Because I was much faster than Peter, he decided to sit longer at breakfast and sip tea. And who knows where Sarah and her dad were? I took off alone.

The sun rose bright, and the wind had moderated somewhat. I still bucked a headwind, but it wasn't nearly as bad as yesterday's. Soon it was a gorgeous, sunny day: great riding weather, but cold, so I wore several layers of clothing.

I spent much of the morning with the shore of Kluane Lake on my immediate left. Kluane Lake is majestic: 43 miles long, with a surface area of about 150 square miles. Ringed by mountains and fed by glacial snowmelt, it drains into the Kluane River, whose waters flow through several other river systems to the Yukon River and eventually the Bering Sea along the faraway west coast of Alaska, north of the Aleutian Island chain.

At about ten o'clock, something flashed in the corner of my eye just as I pedaled past a large rock outcropping butting up to the road. The outcropping blocked my view into the bush. For some reason I thought of Tweety Bird saying, "I taut I taw a puddy-tat," except that the image in my mind wasn't a puddy-tat. It was a bear. *A big-ass bear!*

The thing was, I wasn't sure. Curiosity got the better of me, and I circled back to see if I saw what I thought I had. *Had I imagined it? People can go nuts out here.*

But there it was: a massive male grizzly lying about a hundred feet off the road, sunning himself on a big rock pile. Just like me that cold morning, the brute was trying to warm up in the sunlight.

That bear was monstrous, with a big broad head and a blondish coat with the classic grizzly hump at the shoulders. *How cool. And thank God he didn't react to me.* Quickly and quietly, I circled back in the direction I was heading and then just poured on the coal. *Sheesh. Why did I have to know?* I accelerated away.

Later on, I saw a mighty eagle being hassled by some pipsqueak bird pecking at its tail feathers in flight. Even the mighty get heckled.

At one point, a bee flew into my face and lodged at the edge of my sunglasses, then slipped behind my glasses and crawled onto my left eyelid. *Stay cool as a cucumber, Cochise—no startling movements that will make him sting.* Without slowing down, I calmly removed my glasses and brushed him away. Thank God I didn't get stung. My brother, Steve, once got stung on his eyelid and his eye swelled shut. He looked like Quasimodo, which to me seemed like a massive improvement for him. Coincidentally, he had to serve as a pallbearer a few days later. "I dare you to drag a foot as you carry the casket," I said to him with gallows humor.

The Alaska Highway paralleled the lake for another twenty to thirty miles, and by the time I reached the far end, the winds had completely abated and I just flew. This was one of those moments of elation—a life moment to be captured and remembered. Near shore, this vast mountain lake mirrored the mountains immersed in the perfect blue sky; further out, huge gusts of wind scraped down the lake and drove whitecaps on the water—*greenies,* in sailors' parlance. The entire lake was ringed by towering, snowcapped peaks, each with their alluvial fans from avalanches and rockfalls. I flew down this road, full of nature and full of motion—exuberant and strong in the pedals, with a driving cadence that constantly changed the landscape's perspective. *It just doesn't get any better than this.* "Yee-haw!" I let out the spontaneous war-whooping battle cry at the top of my lungs. *When was the last time I shouted in complete joy to no one? This is my altar!*

At the far southern end of Kluane Lake, I stopped for a snack on a long, low bridge where the Alaska Highway crossed a large gravel outwash. A pickup truck slowly pulled up, and as the window rolled down, a man called out, "Everything okay?"

"Yeah, all is well!" I responded, beaming from how incredible the morning had been.

"What in the world are you up to?" he questioned, wide-eyed.

"I'm on a cattle drive," I blurted. "Except I can't find the friggin' cattle!" *Shit, no filter between my head and lips—again.* My legs had been powerfully churning all morning, and for some reason Marshall Tucker's song "Cattle Drive" was streaming through my head. *The opening lyrics are perfect for the moment.*

"Where are you headed?" He laughed.

"Mexico!" I replied, hardly believing my own words.

"What? Hey, let me park at the far end of the bridge and I'll come back. I gotta hear about this!"

He was clearly military as he climbed out of his truck and walked back toward me. "Have you ever been in a place so spectacular?"

"Pretty incredible—hard to adequately describe," I replied.

"Man! I'm just in awe of this area—can't get enough of it on my drive." He continued, with his sweeping hand presenting the landscape before us, "I'm Peter." Our introductions were made. "Now, what are you doing?" Peter asked, his eyebrows raised with wonder.

"I'm pedaling solo to Mexico."

"Seriously? Are you kidding?"

"Yeah, well, I wanted to try a big stretch and see how I'd do—see what I'm made of—so here I am!" We went through some natural perfunctory questions—where I had started, where I was headed, how long I'd been on the road thus far, what I'd seen, and so on. My answers were friendly but short. It went silent for a minute as we both casually draped over the railing of the bridge—each mesmerized by the trickling snowmelt carving silty trails through the barren outwash.

Then, emboldened, Peter looked me up and down. "What's your real story, Jerry? What are you thinking?"

"Hmmm, well, where do I begin?" *Should I let him in? Or just have another fleeting exchange and vamoose? Time is burning, and time is distance.* "The short answer, Pete, is that I checked out. But when I really think about it, it's the exact opposite—I'm checking back in."

"How so?" he queried, genuinely interested in a lone stranger's mindset.

"I couldn't continue down the same path I was on—not if I wanted to feel fully alive. I have this strange philosophy, 'If you're not growing, you're dying.' It's become a beacon of sorts for me—like a lighthouse guiding the way."

"Huh, interesting thought. But I'm wondering if you're running away from anything? Or running to something?"

"A little of both, I suppose. Let me try to explain, and you can draw your own conclusion. See, I felt like I became stale—stale competence—doing the same thing every day. Sure, each day had its variations of problems or opportunities to deal with, but the daily patterns became identical—my everyday approach became the same: robotic. Competent replication—I'm running from that! For me, it became a professional conundrum. It was a way to get paid and fund my family, but that doesn't mean I was growing and thriving—or at my best. I had this sinking feeling of being a druid in his hoodie, slogging through the same stuff day after day, year after year—outwardly pretending it meant success and trying to convince myself that I loved it. But inwardly, I felt, *Is this all there is—really?*"

"So you checked out and did this," Peter stated.

"Well, let's be clear, the 'did' ain't done yet! I'm really early in this journey—there's a hell of a long road in front of me."

"Well, do you have any doubts?"

"Sure, who doesn't? But at the same time, I just think I can do it."

"And so you just put them aside."

"Well, it's not exactly that they're set aside, but they're overwhelmed by much bigger forces, like curiosity and the quest to feel alive. I don't have a death wish, Peter, I have a life wish. Hear me out. Using an ice hockey analogy, I asked myself, 'Am I still forechecking hard? Am I still crashing the boards, creating loose pucks, and firing blistering shots—new opportunity, if you will? Or am I now playing prevent defense, dumping the puck in the zone and retreating to defense—playing too safe and hoping to run out the clock?' I didn't like my answer—at all! Running out the clock, just existing so to speak, runs against my grain—makes me bristle. *Only 1,237 more days at the post office.* It's counterintuitive, but in many activities, playing too safe actually puts you in a riskier position. Besides, how do you want to conduct yourself—would you rather be a cougar on the hunt or a hermit crab retreating deep into your shell? I know I'm mixing metaphors, but you get the picture: for me, it was time to get back to offense before it was way too late!"

Peter absorbed my thoughts as though he was internalizing them. "Do you think this will change you?"

"Yeah, I do—how can it not? I just don't quite know how—but I'm really looking forward to seeing what those changes will be."

"God, I'm fascinated—fascinated by what it takes for someone to take something like this on."

"Well, I'm not sure I can specifically define it, but if we played a quick word-association game with this journey, the words I'd scribble on a flipchart would be . . . uh: *twisted, wonder, wanderlust, curiosity, drive, ambition, untamed, unchained,* and *fun*—all jumbled in a turbulent current of a love of travel, adventure, geography, and geology. Somehow, I have to refine that description—but it's the best I can do right now. Do I seem as goofy to you as that sounds? Is it a sign that I've already lost my mind out here?"

"Hahahaha—you're either insane, or the sanest man on Earth, I'm not sure which at the moment."

"*One Flew Over the Cuckoo's Nest*—I'll be the Jack Nicholson character, whatever his name was—you can be Nurse Ratched!" We were both belly laughing.

"Seriously, Jerry, have you ever done anything like this?"

"No, not specifically. Distance cycling is a brand-new experience—I'd never ridden over twenty or thirty miles in an outing before this trip. But in some ways, I've done smaller variations of things that I suppose have led to this."

"Like what?"

"Well, if I flash back to the stone ages of 1972, at seventeen years old, I solo hitchhiked America."

"Whoa—how was that?"

"Phenomenal! Except—and I didn't necessarily know it at the time—you don't feel that way at the moment of standing on an empty road in Lusk, Wyoming for four hours, trying to hitch a ride in hundred-degree heat. But, looking back, it was an incredible experience. I wouldn't trade some of those feelings or experiences for anything. And, there's such great humor—some of the rides were pretty funny."

"Do you actually remember them?

"Yeah, I vividly remember them—you can't forget them." Peter wanted to hear some of the stories as he and I stood on the bridge basking in the glory of this area. I continued, "So, as a set up to the stories—I had to work all summer to save up enough moola to pay for my upcoming year's college tuition and living expenses. But the last few weeks before school started in the fall, I needed *some* sort of break—some fun and adventure. Life isn't work alone! I had a *huge* case of wanderlust—and the notion of Simon and Garfunkel's song

"America" was looping in my mind, inspiring me to see the country. At the time, America was in a period of massive social change, with huge forces in play—torn apart by Vietnam and the antiwar movement, the civil rights movement was in full swing, along with the emergence and independence of women from past traditional roles. I was just getting the view of America through the lens of the nightly news—you know, Walter Cronkite, Frank Reynolds, Harry Reasoner, Huntley-Brinkley, that cast of characters—and of course just a short time later, Jessica Savitch. 'Ahhhh, Jessicahhhhhhhhhhh! Could you do that segment again Jessica? I didn't hear a word!' Sorry, Pete, I digressed." In the stark and magnificent wilderness of the Kluane, we were howling like a couple of hyenas, dying of laughter. "Anyway, I *had* to see America for myself. Nothing ever supplants your own eyes—I don't want someone else telling me what to feel— see for yourself, draw your own conclusions. But, outside of what I'd saved for college, I didn't have any money and couldn't afford a car—I had to be resourceful. Hmmm, I thought, I'll hitchhike."

"Where did you go?"

"Well in the late summer of 1972, I hitched from Minnesota to San Francisco to Seattle and back home—all in about two and a half weeks. And in the late summer of 1973, I hitchhiked east through Canada to Maine and then back home to Minneapolis through the northern US."

Peter was grinning ear to ear and wagging his head. He pressed the conversation forward. "Give me some highlights."

"Well, in 1972, on a blistering late August day, my parents dropped me off about ten miles from home in Chaska, Minnesota. With tears in her eyes, my mom looked at me and said, 'Why do you have to do this, Jerry?' I responded, 'Mom, relax! I'm only crossing America. Let's put it in perspective—it's not like I'm going to Vietnam. And look, Dad hitched America when he was not much older than me, and coming right out of high school, he'd also enlisted in the Army Air Corps in the middle of World War II. America was losing pilots by the thousands. That's risk! What I'm doing is nothing!'

"So, alone and hopeful, I stuck my thumb out on Highway 169 and pointed toward California—thrilled with optimistic uncertainty. Among the dozens of rides to California, I lay in a trailer of grain for a hundred miles in South Dakota, emerging like the Pillsbury Doughboy covered in powdery grain dust; I got picked up by a Bible bus out of Lusk, Wyoming, where about ten religious zealots in their coach spent another hundred miles spreading The Word in withering waves that pinned my ears back. And hitching directly on the interstate is illegal, Pete, but I stood way too long on the interstate entrance ramp in Cheyenne, so I risked it. A six-foot-five, two-hundred-fifty-pound redneck cop pulled me off the interstate and placed me in the back of his squad car, stating in a long drawl, 'We don't like your type around here, *boy*.' I think he was completely bored and was trying to bait me to lip off—it frustrated him when I didn't bite, so, with his head cocked sideways and wagging his index finger the size of a hammer in my face, he concluded, 'I better not find you on the interstate again.' Funny, I didn't feel the least bit intimidated: I felt complete confidence in our justice system. *He's harmless if I handle myself well.* Look, Pete, I'm not against the police at all, they have a tough duty to do the right things in the face of intensely stressful situations—but this wasn't one of them. Look, in any large group, or in many endeavors, you'll find the Barney Fife. I just thought he needed to feel his sense of power—and like deflating a balloon, I just had to let him exhaust himself. *I'll be on my way shortly—in this instance, that's success.* It all resolved itself harmlessly.

"On another ride I was bucking my way down the highway toward Salt Lake City in an eighteen-wheeler when the trucker reached under his seat and pulled up a funnel and hose contraption he'd devised. He glanced at me wryly. I reactively pushed up against the passenger window—*Is that what I think it is?* He admonished me, 'Don't laugh, or I won't let you use it.' He then relieved himself through the funnel while driving at seventy-five miles per hour— all so he never had to pull off the freeway. He'd drilled a hole in the bottom of his cab as a drain. *Ga-ROSS! But funny. American ingenuity? Unmet need?* He then told me a story of a trucking buddy of his who knew about his relief system. At a truck stop, his buddy plugged the hole with gum. A new reality-TV show? *Trucker Wars?* The plugged plumbing backwashed all over his clean clothes. *TMI.* I sat ever further to the right. Beam me up, Scotty!"

Peter mouthed, "OMG."

"I'm not done! Bear with me: you can't make this stuff up!"

"Keep going, I have all day!" Peter shouted between guffaws. "Who wants to leave the beauty of this bridge anyway!"

"I was picked up by a shady character in Salt Lake City who in the course of the conversation informed me that he recently got out of San Quentin for stabbing three people. I thought, *Are you shitting me? But I think I can take him.* He got edgy after we passed a cop—he said, 'Can you drive?' We pulled over and he had me drive. Like a moron—I drove. *Stolen vehicle? Now I'm an accomplice?* Youthful ignorance! Along our drive, the ex-con also picked up one of the last of the classic original hobos—floppy shoes, threadbare suit coat, and trousers worn to a shine, all with a tattered, battered leather suitcase and weeks without a shower—phew!

"I was also picked up in Truckee and climbed onto an open-air truck bed as we ground our way through the Sierra Nevadas, over the Donner Pass. I squeezed in along with about fifteen other riders—all hippies, tie dyed, flowing hair swept back in multicolored bandanas—Jimi Hendrix, *Electric Ladyland,* baby! The guys all wore sunburst-embroidered jeans, and the women had their muted flowing granny dresses—everyone in their uniform. They were heading to the Haight to be empowered by flowers—*Groovy! Far out man!*

"I often had to compete for rides on crowded on-ramps. Once I competed for a ride against a Jerry Garcia–looking guy and his Grace Slick girlfriend, along with their dog and—get this—their goat. *I think I can win this one!* There were numerous other rides with military men, traveling salesmen, and a nuclear physicist. And, in late August 1973, as I hitchhiked into Canada through Sault Ste. Marie, the border Mounties took me into a back room and tore my backpack down to every single item, looking for drugs. I disappointed them: I wasn't a druggie. When I was hitching through Wisconsin on

Highway 8 near Rhinelander, I got attacked by a pack of three stray dogs. I picked up a couple handfuls of coarse gravel, and when they came in as a pack, I scatter-bombed them full force."

"Were you terrified when they charged?"

"Naw, not really, I just reacted—I love dogs, but you can't look afraid. And you have to act decisively and with purpose. They got the message that I meant business and backed off—then barked like hell at me from about thirty feet away until I got a ride."

"Wow, huh, were you ever frightened at all with any of the rides?"

"Nah, I felt pretty tough, like I could handle myself—but in hindsight it was probably more ignorant than tough. Probably not dissimilar from now, really. But I never thought for a sliver of a moment that I wasn't going to make it home."

"Where did you stay at night?

"I had a sleeping bag, a small tent, and a foam bedroll strapped to my backpack. I'd find a lake or river and take a dip, and then at dark, I just slipped a hundred yards off the highway into the woods or onto the open range, plopped down, and went to sleep. There's safety when nobody has a clue that you're there. It was pretty dry, so I never even set the tent; I just slept in the open under the stars."

"What do you think you gained from those experiences?"

"Well, several things. I found out that I could do fascinating things on a shoestring—and along with seeing the country itself, I learned that you can't learn any of this stuff at Harvard! I say that tongue in cheek: I went to the University of Minnesota—it's all I could afford. But the point is, no geographer or sociologist or self-proclaimed expert could ever teach me what I learned in those weeks as a drifter. Just navigating different circumstances gave me an aloof confidence of sorts. It never leaves you. And nobody can ever suppress it or take it away! It's uniquely yours. And now, as I really think about it, that same wanderlust that made me want to see America then, casting my fate to the wind, eventually links to what brings me here now. I never thought about it then, but the small stretches prepare you for the future big."

"Hmmm, I'm inspired, Jerry. I've been in the Coast Guard twenty-seven years. I retire in three more at thirty years. I'll be fifty-two; but I'll still need a little more cash so I have to figure out what I'll do. It's a little scary because I've done this so long—it's all I know. But I also know I need change and will have to change."

"Tough conundrum, Peter—it's the golden noose—you know you need change but have been there too long to not see it through to your pension. Everybody has to reach their own point of impetus to change, but when you hit your point, don't wait for change to just happen to you, or for someone else to pave change for you—you'll be waiting a hell of a long time. Go make your own change."

It went quiet for a moment as the last thought sunk in. But in characteristic fashion, I started flapping again and offered unsolicited advice. "In my view, Peter, I'd start with asking, 'Who do I want to be, and what makes me feel most alive?' Don't just look for a job: try to find your calling. Take an inventory of what you've learned over the years. I'm sure you've gained tons of skills that you take for granted, but that are readily transferable to your calling. Never sell yourself short, don't just settle—settle for *more*, for what lifts you. And then—hit the go button."

"Just like that?"

"Yep, just like that. It may feel risky, but c'mon—what's the *real* risk of venturing out from your knowns, of trying something totally new and different? You'll make mistakes for sure—so what! Just accept that going in and make adjustments. It's part of your evolution. If you're afraid to make mistakes, you risk freezing in mediocrity—you'll never change and grow—and so, you'll never know your best work! Stretching your boundaries beyond comfort is such a tired concept—but it's true. Everybody intellectually knows they should strive for it, but many if not most people don't act on it, they just wallow in and bitch about the familiar—but don't stray from what they know!"

"It's too easy to stick with the known."

"Yeah, I think people think the known is safe—especially relative to their perception of risk—the risks often aren't as great as people perceive. And it may sound like twisted logic, Peter, but in a rapidly changing world, staying too safe is actually an illusion and riskier than movement—motion allows you to evolve. But the biggest risk of all is often overlooked or suppressed. It's a *life* risk of not being invigorated. Above all else, I think you'll find newness, while drawing on your collective experience, invigorating."

"What are you Jerry, an existentialist?" Peter laughed.

"Yeah, Peter, I'd say more a hillbilly philosopher with lily-white legs in spandex bike shorts! Naw, I ain't no Plato or Socrates, I'm twenty-five hundred years too late to beat them to enlightenment. Besides, they'd have burned me at the stake if they knew me then!" We were both laughing at the momentary zaniness. "But seriously, I've reached my own enlightenment. When I think about it, I'm entering the last trimester of my life. Not to be morbid, but I'm as close to the end of my life as I am to when I came out of graduate school. Yikes! Where did that time go? And it feels like time is accelerating. So, in a funky little exercise, I fast-forward to lying on my deathbed and ask myself the question, *Did I live fully?* Which, to me, is the ultimate success."

"Huh, no regrets," Peter chimed.

"Yeah, I'm terrified of regrets! There's that old saying, 'I'd rather regret the things I did than the things I didn't do.' Listen to the elderly in their sunset, Peter—they're full of wisdom, and there's a common lament: many say they settled when they should have tried for more—and taken more risks. You hear it all the time. I fear that lament. And to your point, they're really statements about regrets. Take their words to heart—that's a driver for me. When I think about it, I've already had a few regrets, who hasn't? But what are you going to do about it from here? When I have a chance to try something or someplace new, I rarely refuse. Now I'll try everything—everything constructive, that is. This little bike ride is a part of that notion. And it's funny: I don't quite know what I'm doing, but I'm sure having fun."

The wind whistled across the bridge deck, and I shivered as I reached into a pannier and donned my wind vest.

"So, what do you think you'll do as a result of this journey, Jerry?"

"I have no idea right now, Peter. It's still unclear to me where this will lead. But I have confidence that great opportunities will emerge. Opportunity is everywhere. Peter, I'm fifty-seven—on the doorstep of fifty-eight—but there's a hell of a lot of living left to do!"

"I love it all!" Peter finally exclaimed with a broad grin. "I love what you're doing—the scope, the solo, the career-chucking, lack-of-planning, fearless—even foolish—lack of concern, and the rigor of your ride, especially at your age." He kept shaking his head. "I can't imagine it—I can't wrap my head around making a decision like you have and actually going for it. You've made me think—think about things I should try, or do."

Having lingered way too long and now chilled in the breeze, I turned toward Peter and said, "Time to hit it, Pete! But before I go, I just have to tell you that one of my big regrets is not having served in the military—getting that experience and doing my part for what we all have. Without guys like you, I probably wouldn't be able to be doing this. Thanks for your years of service. Safe travels, and enjoy Kodiak."

"Good luck, Jerry," Peter replied. "Be safe."

I'd had similar reactions from everyone so far. People liked meeting someone face-to-face—live and in person—because it personalized the story as opposed to another impersonal article in a newspaper. They could see for themselves that I was just an ordinary guy out in the wild and wooly. They placed themselves in my shoes, and it ignited their imaginations with what could happen. So everyone wanted to contribute in some little way, even if only moral support—they *all* offered to help, however they could.

Just south of Kluane Lake, the Alaska Highway began a series of long climbs that, despite being easy, slowed me down. I also caught a slight headwind, but I still felt strong. The only inconvenience was a six-mile stretch of gravel due to road construction. There was hardly any traffic, and a couple of drivers slowed to a crawl as they came by to keep the dust down. But there's always that one person who kicks the dog. One driver gunned it and barreled on through, leaving me in a cloud of dust—literally. Every speck of that dust that I didn't inhale stuck to my face. I might as well have ridden through a coal mine.

I approached Haines Junction and was finally rewarded for all my long climbs with a ten-mile downhill. My hands numbed as I gripped tight—"Ride the Tiger," in Jefferson Starship parlance.

At sixty-nine miles into the day, I had to decide whether to stay in Haines Junction or continue on. *Big decision. Haines Junction is a comfortable area. I could stay here and have a good selection of food—but at the price of distance. If I stay, tomorrow will likely be a hundred-mile ride all the way to Whitehorse. However, there's a camp with food about twenty miles farther on, in Otter Falls. After that, there is absolutely nothing for the final eighty miles to Whitehorse. The weather report calls for rain tonight and then crappy for the next few days: I'd better take advantage of today's nice weather and get more distance.* It was 4:30 p.m., and I still had gas in the tank. *Crank out the twenty miles to Otter Falls. That will make it an eighty-nine-mile day today— and it leaves only eighty miles to Whitehorse.*

And so I rode to Otter Falls and set camp. *I've ridden nine straight days without a rest. Tomorrow, I'll ride to Whitehorse, finally have a rest day, and take care of other needs like bike tuning and resupply.* Whitehorse was *the* major city, as towns went in the northland. And it would be the first town with a bike shop since I'd left Anchorage, nine days and 652 miles ago. I'd been nursing my chain for several hundred miles, and my bike was skipping at some of the derailleur settings. Since the next thousand miles beyond Whitehorse would become even more remote, with fewer oases yet, I needed to have my bike tuned and 100 percent shipshape.

OTTER FALLS, YT
Miles today: 89

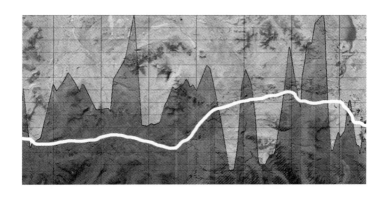

DAY 10
FRIDAY, JUNE 29, 2012—OTTER FALLS, YT
Miles to date: 652

Bad weather moved in overnight, and I awoke to steady rain drilling my tent. *Let it rain—I'll just lay around all day and read.* But then I heard the forecast was for several days of rain. *I can hang around for one day, but not several—I'll go stir-crazy.* Now I was happy to have put in the extra twenty miles yesterday. I bit the bullet and packed my wet gear, including a drenched tent, and headed out into the dreary, steady rain. *It's better to get to Whitehorse and relax where there's warm food and lodging. This will suck, but I'll push through. I'm only doing eighty miles today and the route is relatively flat. At about fourteen or fifteen miles per hour, I'll be done in five or six hours. I can do that under any circumstances when I have to. I'll just be wet and cold. But as long as I'm moving, there's an end in sight. So just pedal. I'll freeze—but I'm not going to die. Get movin'.*

I took off in the steady rain and discovered early on that I'd have to spend the day entirely in my own head. Everything was socked in so I couldn't see any distant vistas. All I saw were trees, trees, and more dripping trees lining both sides of the road for the entire ride. *I hope I can stand myself!*

Riding in the rain slowed me down. I had decent rain gear, but in short order I was soaked from the inside out due to sweat, and eventually the hard, steady rain overwhelmed my Gore-Tex and an even colder wet worked from the outside in. It sucked. *But discomfort isn't danger.*

I knew going into this journey that there would be lousy days. I obviously couldn't change the weather, and I had been pretty lucky thus far; mathematically speaking, this was a regression to the mean, offsetting the better days I'd already had. On crappy days, the challenge was how to mitigate the bad, and it was up to me how to deal with it. *That, I can control.* Thunder constantly rumbled, but never close. Theme songs pertaining to today's awful conditions surfaced in my mind as momentary distractions: "Cold, Rain and Snow" or "Looks Like Rain," both from the Grateful Dead. *Anything to occupy my brain—old trips, old friends, what I've seen thus far, distance and time calculations, and the rawness of this wilderness— anything to distract. This or the office? Hahaha c'mon, Comanche— make it a toughie, that's not even a choice!* Every single pedal stroke was one less stroke to Whitehorse, to dryness, to warmth, to hot food, to civilization. *Just four more, three more, two more, one more hour of this.* Eighty miles of rain.

None—record that!—*none* of the pullouts had shelters. About two-thirds of the way to Whitehorse, I stopped at a pullout to eat and add yet another layer. As I stood chewing in the steady rain, a US Army soldier pulled his pickup truck in smack next to me.

"Pretty miserable, huh?" he said.

"Yeah, sometimes you just have to endure," I replied.

"How are ya doin' on water?" he inquired. "I have a gallon jug for my drive. I could top off your water bottles."

"That would be great, I could use some." *People's goodness yet again—even if only to top off my water bottles.*

I pulled into Whitehorse waterlogged and cold to the bone and got a room for the first time in ten days. My tent was still soaked, so I used every square inch of my room to spread it out to dry. Also, by good fortune, there was a laundromat attached to the hotel. I immediately started a load of wash and cleaned all my clothing of the last few days of grime.

I dressed in warm-out-of-the-dryer clothes. *Bliss! You don't appreciate the normal little things unless you've had some misery. Renewal!*

It was the Friday before a long holiday weekend, Canada's Independence Day. I needed to get to a bike shop before the store closed, or it potentially could be closed until Tuesday morning. I didn't want to get buried in Whitehorse for several days.

I quickly found a bike shop, and since I was on a distance journey, the mechanic was kind enough to prioritize my bike and not put me at the back of the line, though he had a bunch of other bikes stacked up. *Patience isn't on my strengths list—I'm so happy he's working in my favor.* The mechanic thoroughly checked out every part, spoke, derailleur, brake, and cable and tuned them all.

"All in all, your bike looks good," he said. "I see a little wear on your chain and cassette, but not bad—you have a lot of miles left in them."

"Well, I broke my chain five hundred miles ago. I nursed my bike here, and I'm worried about the durability of my snap link. Should I just buy a whole new chain?"

"Nah, don't worry about it. The snap links are durable, and your chain is fine," he assured me.

Thirty-three years ago, on this same holiday weekend, my patience had been challenged not far from here. I was twenty-four at the time and had recently completed my MBA, which, combined with my undergrad degree in geological engineering, made me an attractive hire as an economic analyst for a major oil company. On paper I was the ideal guy. The problem was, the world on paper is not the real world—or, more truthfully, the world that grabbed my soul, where my imagination, curiosity, and performance are sparked. It was an excellent company, but it was the wrong position for me, and thus, I was the wrong employee for them. I quickly realized that it wasn't in my DNA to traipse to my cubicle on the forty-sixth floor of an office building and analyze oil projects all day.

I felt guilty about leaving that company so quickly: it wasn't the problem—I was. But I was restless and unsettled, and I wanted the freedom to drift and explore. I wasn't ready, or mature enough, to settle into the structured world. After I quit, I threw some gear into a four-banger Ford Pinto wagon that one of my brothers sloughed off on me for a couple hundred bucks. That car, with its fake woody decals, became my personal RV. It was also rusted through the floor and the doors, so I could see daylight no matter where I looked—until I put some stylin' shag carpet over the offending holes. And, as if this weren't enough, the driver's side door wouldn't open, so in order to get in and out, I had to crawl over to the passenger door (which once earned me a lively conversation with a suspicious police officer).

So in 1979, I headed for the Alaska Highway in this rusty steed. My Pinto broke down on the Alaska Highway on a Friday afternoon. I was in the middle of nowhere when the car quit and quietly coasted to a stop. I had that same sinking, helpless feeling as when my broken bike chain dropped to the pavement, asking the key question that everyone occasionally wrestles with: *What in hell do I do now?*

I hitchhiked forty miles to the lone auto mechanic's garage, about a hundred miles east of Whitehorse and was dropped off at his doorstep. I had the car towed to his ratty little one-man shop, which also hosted a dirty particle-board shelf full of Ho-Hos, old sponge-covered half-dome cupcakes with the fake coconut frosting, stale Cheetos, two-year-old rotted-wrapper Almond Joys, and other closely related nutritious foods.

Now mind you, it was late Friday afternoon. After looking over the car, the mechanic told me that my timing belt had shredded and snapped (something about chains and drive belts with me). Since it was a holiday weekend, the Ford dealership in Whitehorse would close at noon the next day and also wouldn't ship the parts on a Saturday. And, since Monday was the holiday, a replacement timing belt wouldn't ship until Tuesday. Oh, and it might have taken a day for the part to get to him, and he'd need at least a day to work on the car after he got the part. This meant I would be stuck in his parking lot for four to five days—unless I could somehow get the part earlier. *Crickets! Fuck!*

I knew I wouldn't be able to bear sitting in a sloped gravel parking lot with this tiny, wiry, fiery Scots mechanic and his enormous Canadian wife. What a pair! You couldn't see him, and you couldn't miss her. And they were the community—just the two of them—one gas pump, a shelf of stale treats, and Mutt and Jeff.

No way was I going to wait until Tuesday for that part. A little after ten o'clock that Friday night, I could wait no longer. In a late twilight rapidly turning to darkness, I stuck my thumb out on the Alaska Highway. Around midnight, I was picked up by a US serviceman traveling with his entire family. By then it was pitch black, and their car was packed to the rafters because he was being transferred to Alaska. Still, between the kids, suitcases, and other necessities, they found room for me and dropped me in Whitehorse in the wee, still-dark hours of Saturday morning.

I found the dealership, curled up on a nearby park bench, and slept until it opened at nine. I bought the part and hitchhiked back, and by Sunday, my car was fixed and I was out of there. To be back in Whitehorse over thirty years later on the same holiday weekend was more than ironic—especially because I still didn't plan to wait around.

I've come full circle, away from the structured world and back to the freedom to drift and explore once again. Back to little places that ignite my soul. And again, like thirty-three years ago, I don't know which way the wind will blow—where will this take me?

WHITEHORSE, YT
Miles today: 80

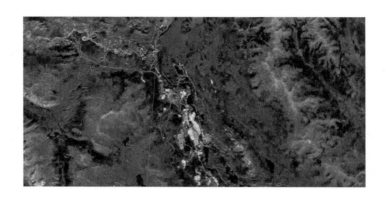

DAY 11
SATURDAY, JUNE 30, 2012—WHITEHORSE, YT
Miles to date: 732

This was my first rest day after ten straight days of riding. Between daily setup, repacking, laundry, personal care, the biking itself, and blogging, I hadn't had a moment's downtime. My in-room shower was not just a pleasure but a true luxury after a week and a half on the road. So was the bed—or so I thought. For the first time in ten days I slept on a mattress—and tossed all night. *It's too soft! Like a dog, I've adjusted to rocks, roots, and dirt—and I'm restless in the comfort.*

I reflected, *I probably have no business being out here solo. But at the same time, I'm having a blast and so far am no worse for the wear. I'm happy as hell because I have the physical and mental sides down. Through the uncertainty each day, what I do know is how to move my legs and press on. That's a big deal: play to your strengths. Sure, I'm challenged on the mechanical, and it may stop me for a moment, but that's a little thing. A good mechanic is a necessity for me. But I can always hire mechanics when needed (as long as there's one around). But no one can pedal for me—if I don't pedal, I'm dead in my tracks. What I want out of this journey can't be outsourced. Mechanics can't get me to Mexico—neither can experts, managers, consultants, or advisors.*

I went to breakfast and another cyclist, a guy in his mid-twenties, suddenly appeared and in one quick motion, slid into the chair opposite me.

"What's up!" he said with a big toothy grin.

"Whoa!" I laughed. "What do we have here, a biking hobo?" He was in a floppy cowboy shirt and baggy gym shorts pulled over long underwear. "Are you out to set the new fashion trend for distance cyclists?"

"Yeah, the cycling version of grunge." He played along amiably.

"What direction are *you* pointed?" I asked.

"I'm heading up the Klondike Highway to Dawson City. Never been there, so I'll just go. And from there, who knows?"

It brought a smile to my face. "You're just adrift with the wind, aren't you, cowboy? Where'd you start?"

"I started out on the southern coast of Alabama and have made my way north to here. I've been on the road for about six months."

"You obviously don't have any obligations, do you?" I half stated, half questioned.

"Naw, I don't have to be anywhere soon. I work in a bike shop for about six months, stack up my money, then I quit, take off, and ride until I'm out of money. Then I do it all over again. Everything I own is on the bike. I don't have a home or apartment, and I have zero obligations. My cellphone is my only bill." He sounded proud—and happier than hell.

"Don't fall in love!" I blurted. We both burst into laughter.

We went through our journeys thus far before we separated. *Total hobo off the grid. Hopping the pedals instead of hopping the rails.*

Meanwhile, I had a looming concern regarding the route I planned to take. The Cassiar Highway (Hwy. 37) is a 500-mile remote stretch that plunges due south off the Alaska Highway a few miles west of Watson Lake. Several people told me just how remote this stretch of the route was. They generally said, "There's nothing there; it will probably be the most remote stretch of road on your entire journey." *I wonder where I can get a little necessity, called food, on the Cassiar? Especially since I'm probably burning 6,000 to 8,000 calories per day. But, I also don't want to carry tons of excess food.*

The Cassiar decision had been lurking in the back of my mind from the beginning of the trip, but I figured I'd cross that bridge when I got to it. *Now, the Cassiar cutoff is only about 275 miles, or three days away—I need to figure it out now—here in Whitehorse.* Enough people had suggested that it was a much safer bet to avoid the Cassiar altogether and instead, go hundreds of miles farther east on the Alaska Highway toward Fort Nelson. I was seriously considering this lengthier detour, which had a little more traffic and food locations. But, like an open hand with the index finger beckoning me, the Cassiar drew me in. *I have to go—I have to see it for myself.*

At the Whitehorse visitor center, after a few pleasantries, the female staffer said, "How can I help you?"

"Well, I'm solo on a bicycle," I said. "I need to figure out food locations along the Cassiar. I'm told there are only a few places. I also need to account for the potential for storms." I said it out loud, but more to myself than her. "Weather can change quickly up here. I could get stormed in and stranded for several days. I'll need enough food to hold out."

She pulled out a map and we pored over it. With a pen, she circled several locations, saying, "There's food here, here, here—and here."

"Ok, that's four places. Can you help me figure the distance between those spots?" We took a string, measured it on the map scale, and then laid it over the Cassiar, estimating distances.

"How about water—do you have a pump and filter?" she asked.

"Yep, I'm all set, and the good thing up here is there's water everywhere! I think the Cassiar stretch works—I should be fine!" I brightened with my new knowledge. "Decision made. Thanks so much for your help!"

"Good luck." She smiled calmly and turned to a waiting RVer.

Next on my set of tasks in Whitehorse was to send home some items that I wasn't using and were getting in my way. First there was a packable and lightweight portable chair. *Huh! I thought I'd be sitting around more. But I tend to move, not sit—and the few moments that I do sit, big rocks and occasional picnic tables are not only fine, but preferable.* Another castoff was my SPOT emergency beacon. This was *the* one item my kids had insisted I take. But all I did was push it around in my bag, and, although it was small, it was getting in my way. Now that I was accustomed to this environment, I was convinced I wouldn't need it. *Use it or lose it.* I rattled that tired maxim in my head. *Man, what I'd give to see my kids' faces when they open this package and discover the SPOT.* A broad smile lit my face. *Yeah, it could be another of the dumber decisions I make because it's the kind of thing I don't need—until I do.*

I circled back to the bike shop. *I'd better grab a couple more snap links, especially for the Cassiar Highway. I have to get them now while I can.* By sheer coincidence, I ran into Sarah and her dad at the shop. I hadn't seen them in a couple of days, and I thought I'd lost them for good. Sarah's dad laughed out loud when he saw me. We'd shared a few ripe stories during the nights we'd seen each other. Although he didn't say so, I could tell that he thought I was a Beverly Hillbilly on a bike, Jed Clampett's lost twin. His whole body shook as he laughed. Watching him laugh was infectious and made me break up too. I gave Sarah the extra snap link she'd given me in Alaska. "You guys have been nothing but spectacular. Take care." We never saw each other again.

Finally, after the evening of restless comfort, I checked out of the hotel and moved to a campsite right on the bank of the wild Yukon River. After ten days on the road, camping just felt better. Not only was I comfortable, I loved the nights outside.

As I settled in along the mighty Yukon, I heard a too-loud yet familiar shrill-high voice through a thick line of trees a few campsites away. *His windpipe must be the size of a straw!* I hiked over. "Peter (from Squamish)! I didn't expect to see you here! Are you going to leave the RVers alone tonight?" We both burst into laughter.

This campground was still within the Whitehorse city limits, and there was a comfortable outdoor patio area and a beer cooler at the campground office. "C'mon, Jerry," he said. "Let's go have a cold one!"

"Twist my arm."

WHITEHORSE, YT
Miles today: 0 — Rest Day

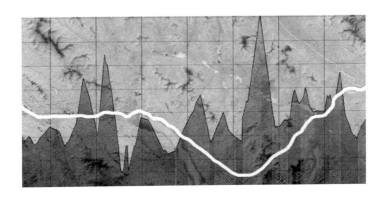

Freezing last night! I had my sleeping bag mummied around my head again. My compact sleeping bag is rated to thirty degrees F, but I was on the edge of frigid all night long. I should have put on my long underwear, but in the middle of the night, I was too lazy to crawl out and dig through a disorganized bag to find my longies and throw them on. Instead, I curled as deep into my bag as I could, found the warm spots, and tried not to move, preserving as much warmth as possible.

When I left Whitehorse a little after 8:00 a.m. it was about forty degrees. I wore a full stocking cap and gloves until around noon. All morning, from Whitehorse to Jake's Corner, there were rolling hills and stiff headwinds. Once again, I had to pedal the downhills in low gears.

I followed the Yukon River and was struck by its size, wildness, and beauty. Its name alone conjures the image of a vast, unspoiled wilderness, exposure, and solitude. Marsh Lake is a thirty-mile mountain reservoir that empties into the Yukon—magnificent except for the stone-cold headwind that funneled between the nearby mountains and ripped across the water, trying to tear my ears off. *I've had massive headwinds on both the Marsh and Kluane, two gigantic mountain lakes—both broiling with whitecaps, each of which stopped me dead.*

I was on a lonely stretch of the Alaska Highway about ten miles out of Jake's Corner when a mama black bear and cub crossed the road about two hundred feet ahead. Mama glanced at me and then broke into an easy trot while her cub double-timed it to keep up. They disappeared into the bush on the far side of the road. *I must be passing dozens of animals just barely off the road and hidden in the bush each day. I don't even know they're there.*

Despite the wind, this was another good day to ride: the weather was clear and the roads were dry. Jake's Corner is another one-gas-pump town and cafe. I pulled in for an omelet and, just as important, rest. Soaked with sweat and a little chilled, I stripped to my base layer and left my biking clothes strewn over the four chairs at my table, drying as I rested and ate. As I finished, I fell into an exhausted stupor and lingered longer than I should have; then I downed an entire pot of coffee loaded with about a pound of sugar. The server, who'd noticed how quickly I hammered each cup, filled me on the run each time she breezed by.

I wheeled another few hours to Johnson's Crossing Lodge and checked into a campsite. "Keep alert, Jerry," the owner said, "a male grizzly has been roaming the camp lately. The wildlife service came by and told us to warn our campers."

"Ok, good to know," I replied. "But really, what's new? Hell, the bears are everywhere!" Anyone could see that.

"Just be on alert," she reinforced.

Johnson's Crossing was located at the western edge of a long bridge that crosses the Teslin River, so I wandered a half mile from my campsite to the middle of the bridge and hung out for quite a while, totally alone, and just stared out to the distant mountains. *I'm not into meditation, but how can you not be transfixed here! After moving all day long, stopping feels good.*

I'd been generally heading southeast ever since Tok, Alaska, and had headwinds every day except for the short twenty-mile stretch heading into Tok, which now felt like eons ago. I wrote my daily blog and jokingly beckoned my three kids, David, Julia, and Justin, to gather all their friends and do a big ol' wind dance for me—to wrestle the wind to my back. *You go a little batty in a good way out here alone, but seriously, a tailwind would be nice for a change. I'm open to anything, and who knows? A wind dance might work. If nothing else, the kids will get a fun laugh out of it.*

I lay in my tent and contemplated. *Tomorrow may be a long day. There are no civilized stops between Johnson's Crossing and Swift River, another hundred miles away.* Despite that, I was content, my spirits couldn't have been better.

JOHNSON'S CROSSING, YT
Miles today: 81

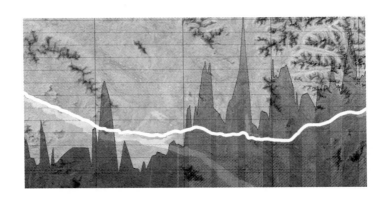

DAY 13
MONDAY, JULY 2, 2012—JOHNSON'S CROSSING, YT
Miles to date: 811

Brrrr, it was chilly yet again last night. I awoke to thirty-seven degrees. But the sun was out, and with the right clothing layers, it was a good riding temperature.

I made my way around Teslin Lake, yet another large mountain lake that's part of the Teslin River system. I followed the lake for about thirty-five miles, into more of the same headwinds, which made the day tough. *Thank God there's no rain.* The terrain was rolling hills with a trending rise the entire day that eventually ended at the crest of the Continental Divide. *I'll probably hit the Divide sometime tomorrow.*

I stopped at a small store to fuel up and saw another loaded bike leaned against a log fence like an old horse tied to a hitching post.

Inside, I met Chris, a solo cyclist from Ventura, California, who'd thus far had a hell of a trip. We were heading the same direction, so we rode side by side for a while, carrying on in conversation.

"I pedaled north from California to Alaska in the early spring," he said, "but I started my ride so early in the season that I got caught riding in some hellacious ice and snow storms."

"You must have frozen!" I replied. "It's cold enough riding now, let alone in a blizzard."

"Well, not only that, it was still so early in the season that many of the food services that had closed for the winter hadn't reopened yet, so there were more than a few times that I was starving and scrounging for food. I rode to Alaska and met up with three friends, and we all attempted to climb Mount McKinley."

"Attempted?" I was sucked into the story. "How far did you get?"

"We made 17,200 feet, but then we got caught in a massive blizzard. It snowed for eight days straight, and we were tentbound that entire time. We ran out of food and stove gas, and coupled with a continued bad forecast—we abandoned our climb."

"Smart," I said, stating the obvious. "I read that McKinley has had extraordinarily heavy snows and storms this season, and there have been six deaths so far. I'm sure you heard about the four-man Japanese team wiped out in a massive avalanche."

"Yeah, that Japanese team was a day behind us. The hell of it was that they were on a part of the mountain that is usually considered a safe spot and never avalanches. We were there a day earlier."

"You never know what fate lies before you." *Listen to my shallow blather, but I'm already committed to the thought, so I might as well continue.* "Many things are so unpredictable, especially for active people. You try to make the right decisions and get to safe spaces . . . " I trailed off and paused. "They were just plain unlucky and got caught by an act of God."

Chris and I rode for a bit in silence. Then I started up again. "These headwinds are brutal! I feel like friggin' Sisyphus." *Push that boulder, bitch!* "I thought I'd have tailwinds going this direction."

"Yeah," he replied. "We're so far north that the polar vortex creates prevailing winds from the east. The winds will switch around for you when you get to central BC." He'd obviously had the foresight to study the wind maps. *Of course, I didn't do any homework on prevailing winds.* I silently reprimanded myself. *Central BC is still so far away—live and learn.*

Chris was on his way back to California and invited me to stay at his house in Ventura when I eventually rode past. He'd done a number of long-distance trips and had this riding stuff down. Traveling light and fast, he packed about half of what I had; all of his gear, including his tent, fit in rear panniers alone. He was a small-framed, wiry racehorse, the picture of fitness tuned for biking, with no excess and unnecessary upper-body weight. By contrast, I was a Clydesdale—a Bud horse pulling a wagonload of shit with my stuffed-to-the-gills front and back panniers, duffle bag, and my tent externally bungeed under the seat.

He showed me pictures of his specially made tent, which covered both him and his bike, though it looked tiny to me. He also used a half sleeping bag. On cold nights he slept in his fleece, with a down jacket covering his top and his bag covering only the lower part of his body.

Because Chris had learned to travel so light, he could chalk up the miles. Best of all, he made riding his business. Chris had dropped out of college several years ago, but it wasn't holding him back. *So much for conventional wisdom.* He figured out how to become a spokesperson for the American Heart Association, extolling the virtues of diet and exercise for a healthy heart, and had formed his own nonprofit organization that was sponsored by the AHA. Chris regularly spoke to schools, businesses, legislators, and anybody else who'd listen to raise money to support heart health. He was thriving. This allowed him to spend much of the year riding—completely funded. *A million ways to skin a cat.*

I'd thought I was taking on a macho trip, but compared to him, *I'm in Wussyville—total, unadulterated Wussyville!* I thought I'd put myself out there in the face of danger and uncertainty—and then I run into Chris, who'd biked up to Alaska off-season in snow, attempted McKinley, packed half as much junk, and rode what felt like twice as fast as me. *I feel totally emasculated here, by someone stronger, faster, bolder, and more clever—and a great guy. I hate that thought; it's rare that I feel inadequate! Shit! At least I could kick the crap out of him if I needed to*—which exposed yet another flaw—a need to find some form of superiority. *Sheesh! Pathetic and immature.* After about twenty miles together, I told Chris to move out and move on; I was going to pull off and refill my water bottles as we came upon a stream. We said our good-byes and Godspeeds.

Late in the day, tired and with no town within reach, I stopped to wilderness camp next to the Smart River. I examined my campsite, looking for evidence of bears, but didn't find any. Only after I got situated did I discover bear scat. *It looks old enough—I'm staying.* There was no getting away from the buggers, anyway.

I skinny-dipped in the river to clean up. *The bears are probably laughing their asses off.* I followed the classic bear-avoidance rules by having dinner about two hundred yards from my tent. *Separate the dining room from the bedroom.* I hung my food off of the short bridge over the Smart River, and finally, exhausted, I climbed into my tent. But for some reason, I had trouble getting to sleep, so I fired up my iPod and swooned to some of my classic country favorites, like Kenny Chesney, Brooks & Dunn, George Strait, and Afroman. *Afroman? Rap music? Someone hosed my playlist!* And I had a good idea of who. My youngest son, Justin, often jammed me by slipping his favorite music onto my playlist. *He got me!*

I was steadily making my way down the Alaska Highway. I looked at the map and could see the significant distance I'd already cranked. *In a micro sense the road seems long at times; in a macro sense, this journey is flying by and will be over in an eyeblink. Savor every moment.*

WILDERNESS CAMPING AT THE SMART RIVER, YT— ABOUT 20 MILES WEST OF SWIFT RIVER
Miles today: 74

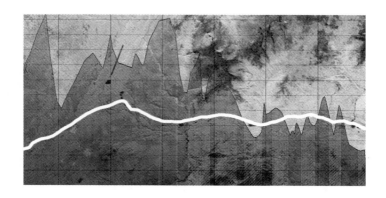

DAY 14
TUESDAY, JULY 3, 2012—WILDERNESS CAMP AT SMART RIVER (NOWHERESVILLE, YT)
Miles to date: 885

Wha? Whoa. Where the hell am I? I awoke in a complete mental fog, so disoriented that I was unsure of where I was and even what I was doing. I just lay there until, slowly, the fog wore off and I put it together. It was so weird to wake up clueless and have to figure out where I was, especially when I was nowhere—off the grid.

It was overcast and a dull cold at forty-five degrees. I was back to the cycle of working up a sweat on the long uphills, then freezing on the downhills. I also had light rain in a couple of places, but no big deal. Despite the blistering, prevailing headwinds, I continued to feel lucky with the weather. But to my amazement, *The wind dance worked: I have a tailwind!*

I burned a ton of energy the last few days as I was generally rising on the regional uplift and also in the face of a shrieking headwind. Finally, during the morning, I made it to the crest of the Continental Divide, a high ridge that separates two of the largest river systems in North America: the west-flowing Swift River and the east-flowing Rancheria River. The wind was still howling, practically blowing me off my bike. If I blew east into the Rancheria River, I'd flow to the Liard River near Watson Lake, then join the Mackenzie River in the Northwest Territories and eventually reach the Beaufort Sea in the Arctic Ocean, a journey of 2,650 miles. But if I blew west into the Swift River, I would flow to Teslin Lake and then northwest down the Teslin River to the Yukon River before cutting across northern Alaska to the Bering Sea in the Pacific Ocean, a journey of 2,300 miles. *But instead, I'm blowin' to Mexico and, symbolic to me, the Great Divide between my past and my as-of-now-undefined future.*

I was having a couple of granola bars at the top of the Divide when two US Army servicemen approached, already laughing and chatting about something before they got to me. They were coming from Oklahoma and being transferred to Alaska.

"Hey! Where did you start?" A typical opener.

"Anchorage," I informed them.

"What have you seen?" they asked, wide-eyed.

"Well, where should I start?" I shared a few of my adventures thus far.

"Is there anything you need?" Again, good people wanting to contribute.

"If you have any extra water, you could top off my water bottles."

"That's simple, we can do that!" They refilled my water bottles from their supply.

We were about to part ways when one of the servicemen exclaimed, "Hey, I want you to have this." It was a small decal that read, in blue block letters, Y B Y A W C.

"O . . . K . . . ?" I gave them a questioning look.

"Y B Y A W C—You Bet Your Ass We Can. We only pass this out to members of our unit—but based upon what you're doing, you're now an honorary member!"

"I'm so honored!" I beamed at them both. "This is my new touchstone. What a bitchin' can-do mantra!" We all grinned. "I'm glad we're on the same side—I'd hate to fight you two nasty dudes!" We shook hands and bade each other farewell.

My reward coming off the Divide was a wild Nantucket sleigh ride downhill to Rancheria. Although I was only at forty-eight miles when I hit Rancheria, it was a natural stop, and the next location with food was too far. I couldn't tell from the map if Rancheria was even a town—plenty of named places up here are just a cafe and a gas pump, and so it was with Rancheria, with the inclusion of a small lodge.

About a quarter mile west of town, the Alaska Highway detoured from clean pavement to a couple hundred yards of rough gravel. A few days earlier, a torrential rain had triggered a mudslide that wiped out the highway and blocked traffic for several days. Rancheria became super busy as travelers were stranded. By now, only the highway construction crews remained. I crossed what was left of the slide. Bulldozers had plowed a temporary lane through the slide area, and workers were reconstructing the highway.

I arrived in Rancheria in the early afternoon and immediately entered the small restaurant and flopped down at a table. Due to long distances between services, travelers essentially *have* to stop here to fuel up, for both food and gas—and so the waitress also gets a look at everybody. She breezed up and blurted, "You look hungry!" as she gazed at my gaunt, wind-burned face.

"Famished!" I exclaimed. "Is it that obvious?"

Smiling, she said, "I'll get you a menu."

"Naw. Surprise me. I'm sure you have your favorite specialty; bring me what *you* like. Don't be afraid to bring me a *big* pile of it." I wanted her to get the message that I was massively short on calories.

A few minutes later, she declared, "Here you go," as she placed a large plate of some sort of goulash hotdish in front of me.

"Does that come with a pitchfork?" Pleased with the size, I had no idea what was in it; it could have been Hamburger Helper, for all I knew. I attacked it as though I were a tree mulcher.

Slow down, she suggested with her glance as I smeared part of it on my face with each shovelful. "You've got time," she politely said. "I'm open all afternoon."

I took the cue and sat back with a big deep breath. After a few moments she swung by again, asking, "Where are you staying tonight?"

"I think I'm going to camp right here, in Rancheria," I responded.

"Are you tired?" I should have known at that point she was angling in on an idea.

"Yeah, I'm pretty wiped, I just came over the Divide, but beyond that, I'm more tired than normal today, and I haven't even done that many miles."

"I'll make you a deal." With my full attention and hollow look of weariness, she offered me an off-the-balance-sheet option. "I have workers' quarters that are separate from the lodge rooms, and I'll give you a room with its own hot shower for $25."

That was especially appealing to me as I slumped in my chair, still wet with sweat. "Sounds intriguing. Can you make that deal?"

"Yeah, I think so," she chuckled. "I own the place." I guessed she probably offered this type of deal to anyone she felt was totally out there and exposed. *Another compassionate guardian angel—and a win-win for both of us.*

I took the sparse room separated from the lodge—no frills here. But to me, frills had been redefined—I now had the simple luxury of a long, deep, hot-to-the-bone shower. Finally warm and wrapped in a towel, I sat on the edge of the bed, and in a fleeting moment my eyes subconsciously slammed shut—as autonomic and involuntary as breathing itself. When I awoke, it was two hours later. I had no idea just how sleep-deprived I was.

As an added bonus, I had use of the staff's laundry. I started my load and went for a walk in the neighborhood along an underused gravel road to a few cabins along the Rancheria River. Oddities turn up in these out-of-the-way places. I found a speedboat sitting with its hull directly on the bare ground—no trailer, no water—and yet the boat was tied firmly to a tree! I laughed out loud—what a juxtaposition! *You'd hate it to get away!*

Early in the evening, I went back to the same restaurant and wolfed down a bacon cheeseburger with gravy fries—cholesterol comfort food. *Marketed by the cardiologists of the world—nothing like building your market!* I entertained myself as I placed my order for pie a la mode.

RANCHERIA, YT
Miles today: 48

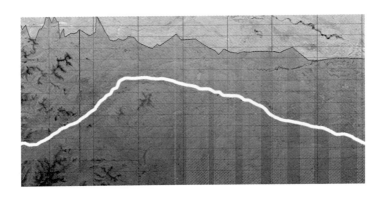

DAY 15
WEDNESDAY, JULY 4, 2012—RANCHERIA, YT
Miles to date: 934

Today, the riding was effortless, as though someone else's legs pedaled. I didn't know where that strength came from. I was explosively strong and exuberant, and I just didn't tire. The first thirty-five miles were essentially downhill as I continued to drop off the Continental Divide—plus I caught a roaring tailwind. *I feel as though I'm cruising on my Harley—but without the noise. Note to self: tailwinds and downhills trump effort and talent.*

I began the day beneath broken clouds and ran into a few sun showers, but no big deal—I just rode out from beneath them. The road followed the Rancheria River Valley several hundred feet above the north bank of the river, so the river was never out of sight. The water was so clear I could see the rocks and boulders beneath, distorted and magnified by the lens effect of the uneven laminar flow. The sun glinted off the waves, and the water's rush through the rapids provided a soothing back-to-nature sound.

It didn't take long to move beyond the mountain range I just navigated. The second half of the ride was mostly rolling gentle hills with pine trees and scrub on both sides of the road. A slight tailwind continued. *I deserve this after all the headwinds I've bucked.* Conditions were so good that I cranked off sixty-one quick miles without missing a stroke. *Get distance while the gettin' is good!*

But wait! OMG! My heart sank when I got my first glimpse of an enormous steep hill in the distance. I was on a high vantage point, still several miles away. *That ain't no mini hill—and it's straight up. Killer coming!* I almost forgot about it after I lost sight of it, but twenty minutes later, I was at its base and digging in.

I geared all the way down to my lowest gear and was cranking full tilt at a whopping four miles per hour when I spotted a large black bear about a hundred yards ahead and right on the edge of the road. I couldn't lose what little momentum I had, so as I approached, I puffed my chest big and yelled at the top of my lungs, "Hey, hey, hey, you big hairy piece of shit! Get out of here!" I thought my volume and aggressiveness would clearly scare her and she'd dash into the woods—but not a chance. In fact, she didn't budge a skinny inch. She stood her ground and just watched me pass within thirty feet. Then my eyes caught more movement in the tree line ahead. About fifty yards farther up, two more black bears were feeding. *The cubs. They're pretty good sized!*

In all my creativity, I yelled the exact same thing as loud as I could. Again, neither bear budged. *What the hell is wrong with my technique?* They just looked at me like, *Seriously, who's this dipshit?*

I pedaled within about twenty feet of the cubs, who watched me with dumbfounded, clownish looks on their faces. Their big open mouths chomped—not chewed—big clumps of grass, half of it falling out with every bite. *They eat with their whole face! There's nothing delicate about it—and that's how they'd dispose of me.* Their heads swiveled, following me at what appeared to be the slow celestial motion of the stars themselves. I, of course, passed as fast as I could: still four miles per hour. *I don't know who looks dumber to whom, me to them, or them to me?* I added these three to the running count of ten bears: four grizzlies and six black.

I stopped for the day at Nugget City—just another wayside gas stop, convenience store with cafe, small lodge, and campground. *I like the name of this oasis: it's an omen of continued good fortune—I've had bucketsful thus far.* And as further great luck, Nugget City had beer! I bought a six-pack of Kokanee. *Canadian PBR—to decorate the picnic table next to my tent site, of course.* For some reason, it took me longer to set the tent for the night.

Watson Lake, an actual town, was only twelve miles farther down the Alaska Highway from Nugget City. But I didn't ride to Watson Lake proper. *Why add another twenty-four miles round-trip when I saw Watson Lake thirty-odd years ago? Time moves slowly up here, so I'm sure nothing's changed. I'll bet they still have the Bee Gees in the jukebox. Art usually follows culture, but in this case my culture follows art—dodging bears in the wild sure has me suckin' 'em in and going falsetto too: "Ah-ah-ah-ah stayin' alive!" Friggin' ridiculous.*

I would have liked to put more miles in, but I had to consider the distances to food over the next several days. I was right at the junction where the Cassiar Highway cuts due south off the Alaska Highway, and the next food was fifty-three miles away. *If I go on, I will end up with less-than-ideal stopping distances along the rest of the Cassiar. By stopping here, I have a nice setup for a natural stop tomorrow at seventy-five miles and then another the following day at about seventy miles.*

I was shuffling across the campground, still wearing my biking gear and carrying the beer, when I caught the eye of two couples sitting on a small porch outside their lodge rooms.

"Want one?" I held up the six-pack. "I share!"

"We're set," they slurred, smiling as they wagged a bottle of whiskey high in the air.

Two BMW motorcycles were parked in front of their respective rooms. "After fifteen days on a bike, a motorcycle looks luxurious!" I was getting more intelligent with each beer, especially because I was fluid-deprived from my ride. "Where ya heading?" I inquired as I stopped in front of them.

"On our way to Tierra del Fuego, mate!" one said in a thick Aussie accent.

"Ahar! Land of Fire! Burn it up, Aussies!" I barked, forgetting to filter again.

"Close, mate!" one said, "But we're from New Zealand."

"Where did you start?"

"We started in Prudhoe Bay."

"How long do you think it will take to Tierra del Fuego?" I asked, jealous.

"We figure it will take about five months total." They nodded to each other like bobbleheads in the back window of a Camaro bounding too fast over a railroad track.

"What a great trip!" I trailed off. *Tierra del Fuego—land's end—continent's end.* I was momentarily lost in my thoughts. *I love that name. Geographic names alone inspire me to see places.* That was certainly the case when Sue and I went to Bora Bora—I simply liked the name. We had to go. I snapped out of my daydream. "I've always wanted to go to Patagonia and see Tierra del Fuego," I barked. "I love raw, harsh places, and you'll be at the end of the earth!"

We talked for about a half hour—they inquired about my journey and I spun my yarn.

"We'd love to have you join us for dinner at six in the cafe," they finally said.

"Done deal, see ya there!" I said in parting.

I traipsed back to my campsite. In the meantime, another man had pulled in on his motorcycle and was setting his tent near mine.

"Hey, man!" I called in full Kokanee accent.

He walked over to my campsite, and the yapping began all over again. He was the chief information officer for the University of Fairbanks and had been implementing an IT system for the university's research facility in Prudhoe Bay. He was now riding his thirty-year-old BMW motorcycle to Santa Cruz, California, for a family reunion. I told him I had a Harley and related a few distance trips I'd taken on it. Big mistake. He unwittingly assumed I knew something about bikes.

"Walk with me to my bike," he said. "What do you think about my front tire—do you think it will make it?"

I assumed the *knowledgeable guy* role, pretending I actually knew jack about his tire. "Looks pretty worn," I said authoritatively. *I haven't been outed by him yet—but it won't be long. First technical question and I'm screwed.*

He proceeded to tell me how he'd taken it all apart before and fixed the tire when he got in a bind. Then he rattled off in machine-gun staccato some mechanical terms and items all about his brakes, wheel bearings, calipers, and whatever—my eyes glossed over, and I gave in.

"Whoa, whoa, whoa, dude! You've just redlined me—I've hit my Peter principle! Full disclosure here: I don't know crap about what you're talking about." I related the tale of my bike chain, and we were both clutching our bellies laughing by the time I finished.

"Good luck and safe travels" was all I could offer. "Join us in the cafe at six."

"Will do."

I went to the cafe, and my new friends from New Zealand were already there. We picked up the conversation where we'd left off. One of the women described how she wouldn't even get on a motorcycle until about a year ago. Then she and her husband did a trial trip around New Zealand, and now this much longer trip was what she called her "stretch." Her husband was the founder of a food company in New Zealand that employed about 190 people; now chairman of the board, he was free to travel. He was also on the worldwide board for Outward Bound. The year before, he and the other member of their crew, a retired professor of education from the University of

Wellington, did a motorcycle trip through India, up through the Himalayas, and into Pakistan.

I love getting immersed in other people's travel—and I get jealous at the same time. The Grateful Dead's "So Many Roads" floated through my head.

NUGGET CITY, YT, AT CASSIAR HIGHWAY 37 CUTOFF
Miles today: 61

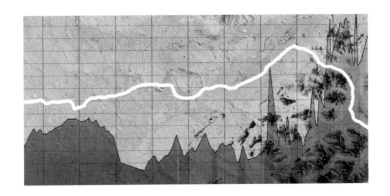

This morning, I left the Alaska Highway and cut due south on the Cassiar Highway. I quickly passed the thousand-mile mark and put the Yukon behind me for good as I entered northern British Columbia.

The Cassiar had beautiful rolling hills and, as I'd been informed, was much more remote than the Alaska Highway—and a rougher, more primitive road surface to boot. I immediately felt more alone and on my own, which made me even more acutely aware of my surroundings, the condition of my bike and body, and most importantly, my mental state. *All in all, I can't possibly feel better, more confident, or more excited about the experiences this stretch promises.*

My sunny disposition was dramatically helped by nearly perfect weather: a clear blue sky, a radiant warm sun, and a high of seventy degrees by mid-afternoon. Still, it was a tough ride as I generally climbed all day—and, to my disappointment, the damned headwinds came back. Like waiting impatiently for a pot of water to boil, I couldn't help but constantly check my odometer, which only made my progress seem that much slower.

Early in the morning I reached a spectacular vantage point from the top of a high hill, from which I saw a faint, snow-capped mountain range far off on the horizon—where the albedo of the glaciers merged with the color of the sky itself. Late in the day, I realized I was in those very mountains and making my way through them. They'd seemed so far away, it hadn't occurred to me that I'd reach them later the same day. *Whoa! I really can ride as far as I can see—if not farther.* It put my daily distance into a rewarding and exhilarating perspective—like carpenters who can see what they've actually accomplished in a day. *I'm actually clawing off the miles.*

My mind was playing tricks on me again. *When I'm deep in a river valley and the surrounding mountain slopes are massive, sometimes it feels as if some unknown force wants to suck me into that mountainside—an illusory gravitational pull, subtly drawing me in.* The perspective had to be just right; I had to both be close enough to feel the mass and far enough away to get the full broad scale of that slope. *What is that illusion? Am I the only one who has ever felt this? Is it an overabundance of natural endorphins? Or am I hallucinating?* It was like a desert mirage, only felt instead of seen. I let my mind run and take me where the illusions beckoned—unconstrained by what I knew was real. It was like simply appreciating the entertainment of magic instead of thrashing about, trying to figure out how the magician did it.

Early in the day, I rounded a blind corner on a steep uphill and a large black bear was suddenly there, only twenty feet in front of me. *Shit! Not a damn thing I can do about it now, I'm at his whim.* I was probably doing a whopping eight miles per hour. Fortunately, like every bear I'd seen so far, the beast wasn't even remotely interested in me. As a result, I became pretty nonchalant about bears; I just hollered at them so they knew I was there. *They've all made other plans for dinner, which suits me just fine.* But in hindsight, I was careless of how complacent I became. *Hmmm, they're more afraid of me than I am of them—I'm golden—I'm bulletproof!* A bad trait, dangerous thinking.

Each day I was running into a few other distance bikers, a cult of people who just rode and rode. I passed a young couple from Holland who'd started in Vancouver and were headed north to Fairbanks, and three young people from Spain, plus another young man from Moose Jaw, all riding to Whitehorse. Then there was the New Zealand university professor who had retired early on a partial pension. He told me he was tired of academia, tired of being institutionalized in a cocoon rife with uninspired groupthink, and now he just wanted to be his own person and do his own thing. In his new life, he rode in a different part of the world every New Zealand winter, which happens to be summer in the northern hemisphere. Meanwhile, according to him, his wife was happy staying put and raising donkeys on their farm. I seemed to be the only one headed south on this highway.

I ended the day on a steep uphill, ten to twelve miles up a mountain pass into a headwind. *Man, that climb was brutal and took forever, but at least I won't have to start with it tomorrow morning.* I stopped at the top in a place called Jade City, named for the company there doing jade mining, cutting, jewelry design, and sales.

I pulled off at a large, green-and-brown-painted structure that screamed "Tourists here!" and went hunting for the inevitable cafe. But there was no sign of one. I found the gift shop counter and asked the clerk, "Is there a cafe? I was told there was food here at Jade City."

"No . . . " she replied slowly, dragging out the word with a look of *Who told you that!*

"The visitor center in Whitehorse highlighted this as a place to get food," I said, as if saying it twice would make any difference in the matter.

"Hang here, let me get the owner," she replied as she disappeared into the back room.

Claudia emerged from the back, and introduced herself before breaking the bad news. "Yeah, we don't have food here, but I can tell you're hungry." She looked me up and down in all my bike garb, exhaustion, and grime. Given the lateness of the day and the long distance to the next town, she knew I was screwed. "I'll tell you what," she said. "Go across the parking lot and into that bunch of trees and set up your tent. Then c'mon back, and I'll set you up with a shower in the staff's quarters. My family and I live above the store; when you're cleaned up, I'll take you upstairs and make you a sandwich."

"Can you make me two?" I queried with my best begging expression.

"Of course," she assured me with a laugh.

So, at around six, I found myself in Claudia's residence with her teenage kids and two huge dogs, wolfing down a couple of sandwiches, potato salad, and chips.

"You won't make it to Dease Lake tomorrow without food, Jerry," she said. "Come back into the store tomorrow morning and I'll feed you breakfast with the staff. My kitchen opens at seven sharp; if you miss that, you're screwed."

"What do I owe you, Claudia?" I asked. "I have to contribute."

Claudia grabbed a donation bucket, placed it in front of me, and simply said, "It's up to you—if you want to, put in whatever you think the sandwiches were worth."

I stuffed her bucket, feeling so lucky to have run into Claudia. I was in a bind, and she saved me. *Another guardian angel.*

I camped in the woods and set my cellphone alarm, *My first scheduled appointment this trip!* I couldn't miss the breakfast bell.

JADE CITY, BRITISH COLUMBIA
Miles today: 77

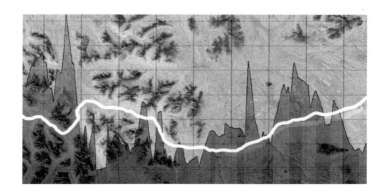

DAY 17
FRIDAY, JULY 6, 2012—JADE CITY, BC
Miles to date: 1,072

For breakfast, Claudia made an omelet wrap and served it with blueberry yogurt. I don't even like yogurt, but everything tastes good when you're that hungry. I ate every lick, knowing that I needed all the calories I could consume. My breakfast companions included not only the jade store staff, but also a highway construction crew working in the area and a Discovery Channel film crew shooting the spectacular landscape for a TV documentary about British Columbia.

It was yet another stunning morning, a crisp forty-six degrees without a cloud in sight. With no wind during the morning, I made good time for the first half of the day, even on the uphills.

Early on I approached a peak that I considered to be British Columbia's version of the Matterhorn. I had continuous views of this peak for about twenty miles as I approached, skirted its edge, and finally put it in my rearview mirror. A classic horn structure, it was evenly eroded on all sides and looked symmetrical from all angles. That simple wonder along with the great weather buoyed my overwhelming feeling of great fortune and powered me forward.

I love mornings and typically started with renewed vigor each day, feeling almost invincible. Despite having ridden over 1,100 miles, I still felt strong and was recovering well at night. The earlier I started, the better, as the weather tended to be calmer in the morning and I burned less energy fighting it. Then convection would take over as the day heated up, and the winds rose. And, of course, the early morning light made everything look so vivid—as though the landscape was lit with neon, shadows highlighting distinct contrasts and colors on fire compared to the muting of harsher midday light.

I rode through a forest fire burn that was so massive that I was surrounded by charred black trees and barren ground for a couple of hours. The fire must have been a doozy, and recent: nothing had begun to grow back yet.

I caught up to a young guy who was also biking solo and going my direction. Out here in the sticks, it was rude to just simply blow by another rider. *Funny, what does speed have to do with it?* I slowed and rode alongside him to check in on him.

"How's it going? You alright?" I asked.

"It's . . . struggle," he replied in a heavy foreign accent. *Interesting how when people don't have command of the language, they tend to end their sentences with an upward intonation.* "I'm three days into my ride—not in shape."

"I know how you feel!" *I've been riding myself into biking shape over the last seventeen days.* "Where ya from?"

"Switzerland." He paused, probably hunting for the English. "I start Watson Lake and head to Los Angeles."

We rode in tandem for a few minutes and talked about our respective rides, the weather, and of course the spectacular scenery. *Spectacular even to a guy from Switzerland!*

Finally, itching to take advantage of the conditions, I said, "I'm moving out, take care and have a great ride!"

For the first time, I saw a couple of small tent communities tucked in the woods, each in a small slice of heaven positioned along the bank of a pristine river. At midmorning I spotted a man sitting in a lawn chair, close to the road just outside his tent. I pulled up close and greeted him.

"What's going on here?" I asked.

"We're squatters," he said, "We come here every season to harvest."

"Harvest what?"

"Wild mushrooms! They're all over the place out in the bush here." He sounded astonished that I didn't know anything.

"Cash business." I laughed.

"Yep." He drawled it into a multi-syllable word.

"Live on!" I gave him a small salute as I clipped back in. *Harvesting? Or sampling the produce? They did appear to be in their own little world.* The people I could see sure looked like they could have been at Woodstock in '69.

I encountered the second jackass of the trip later that day. *Not bad, considering how far I've come.* The Cassiar Highway had no shoulder, so I rode as far to the right as I could: essentially in the right lane tire groove, but still on the roadway. I was on a straightaway with clear visibility for a couple of miles ahead. There was nobody on the road when an RV nearly winged me in passing. *That son of a bitch did that intentionally!* He had plenty of clearance to move over, but instead he closed in and intentionally just missed. And, as soon as he passed, he veered right onto the gravel shoulder and kicked up a broiling dust storm for a quarter mile. I inhaled gravel dust and, with a spurt of anger-driven adrenaline, lashed out at him in my mind. *What a ween—mouse balls—small man's disease—the very worst affliction a man can catch! Really tough from a distance, only tough in groups. Fleeing in the safety and protection of his RV—probably with his mommy. Of course it was a guy: women just don't do that stuff!* But my flash of anger was unconstructive. He detracted from my moment and intentionally brought me into his moment—pissing me off and taking away the glory of this remarkable stretch of road. I wanted to kick the ever-living shit out of him, but of course I wasn't ever going to catch him.

Then I caught myself: anger consumed precious energy, the only thing I really have out here. My rash reaction settled quickly, and I mulled it over for the next hour. Rather than pound him to a pulp, how could I verbally disarm him in a pleasant, constructive manner, yet get the point across? I imagined the conversation like a speech bubble popping out over a cartoon character: "Man, I was worried for you. I know you were momentarily distracted and inadvertently veered off the road. I was so hoping you'd catch yourself before you went over the embankment. I surely would have stopped to help—tried my best to keep you calm and comfortable until real help arrived. See, what's impressed me up here is how manly men are, and how independent, resourceful, and kind the women are—how *everyone* up here has been so unbelievably good. It must be something about the culture of remote areas. Everybody looks out for their neighbor—they have each other's backs. Nobody kicks the dog. What's impressed me is how everyone has seen my vulnerability and looks out for me, far more than I ever would have imagined. I've been looking at any way to repay their kindness. I guess you just extend it to others when you can—everyone needs a break one time or another, and here the person closest to the action just steps up as a manly man or wonderful woman—and so it all works out over time. I just know if you saw me crashed and in a tangle down the embankment—I *know* you would have stopped to help. You people have taught me volumes on how to treat and find the best in everyone. There just aren't any small, shriveled people up here. They all act big, bold, and strong for the betterment of everybody—it's in the DNA."

Of course, that didn't describe the moment I'd just experienced. I've seen far too many people, especially men, who act so strong when they're protected and don't have to show their true colors, but are disappointingly weak when in the action. *Where are the real men these days?* But 99 percent of the people I encountered were nothing short of spectacular. *But this shriveled soul? Hmmm, how would I deal with him? Maybe instead of just calling him a pecker and pummeling the shit out of him, how could I emasculate him in a much more constructive manner that sticks?* If I did it right, I'm convinced that as he was about to fall asleep that very night, those thoughts would rifle through his brain and disrupt his ability to drift away. He'd lie awake all night, tossing in his own stench, asking, "Who am I?" After a truly torturous night, he might come to resemble all the other great people I'd met thus far. *I'm amazed at people with the true skills to disarm, who cool the heat of the moment and make it constructive. Something I need to work on—it's a much greater skill than mixed martial arts. I'm certainly not the toughest man in the world . . . but it still would have been kinda fun to kick the ever-living crap out of him. I guess I haven't evolved very far from the caveman. Neither have any of my friends—cut from the same cloth. Hahahahahaha—get control of yourself, Ahhrrnold!*

I encountered another bear that afternoon. As I came bombing down a hill, I scared him right into the bush. He just took off—this guy rocketed so fast that he looked more like a huge black streak than a lumbering behemoth. *That makes it twelve bears—four grizzlies and eight blacks. How many haven't I seen?*

Thus far, I'd tended to be strong through the first two-thirds of each day and then tire and struggle during the last third. I had to admit that it was partly due to my poor eating habits. Once I was up and moving, I was subsisting on candy and granola bars: the simplicity of tear and eat appealed to me. But I faded earlier than necessary. *I have to eat more consistently while I ride.* But I was just too lazy to dig deeper into my pack to make a sandwich or something with more substance than simple sugar calories. *Motion is distance,* my reasoning went. *I'll just press on, gut it out, and eat well at dinner. Probably not optimal.* I made meaningless calculated guesses: *If I stop for fifteen minutes to eat well, it will cost me three or four miles of distance. If stopping and eating picks up two incremental miles per hour, I have to ride for at least two more hours to break even on the advantage of that stop. Rip, crunch, another candy bar in the gas tank. I'm such a slug.*

Given my habits, it was no surprise that the day's first fifty miles felt easy, while the last twenty-five took longer. With this afternoon's milder headwinds, I still made pretty good time overall, but I was worn out by the time I stopped. *No question, I'm pushing it.*

After I stopped for the night, a couple from a nearby campsite slinked over to my camp and hung around the edge like squirrels eyeing a fallen bread crust, but too timid to run in and grab it. I noticed that they were shy and didn't want to interrupt me but were also too curious to leave. *Boo! Let's see if they jump! I have to break the ice.* I shouted, "C'mon over, I don't bite—unless I'm really hungry! Nice night, where are you guys from?"

"Saskatchewan," the man replied. "We're on holiday."

"Nice RV." They were in a Scamp, an RV so small it can practically be hauled by a bicycle. You'd have to shoehorn two people into it. *Better like each other!*

"Yeah, we love this thing. It's so easy to haul. We go everywhere in it."

"Simplicity sets you free!" I exclaimed. "Funny how you figure out how little you really need out here."

They pointed at my bike, and we all broke up laughing. They just hung at my campsite for over an hour until I finally cut it off. *Do I look like the park ranger with the nightly entertainment program?* I needed to get to the grocery store in Dease Lake and replenish my supplies before it closed. I'd been warned that cyclists often run out of food on this next segment. The next three to five days would be the most isolated of my entire trip, with some three hundred miles with no food or services until Iskut—*Nowheresville itself.* I'd learned my lesson at Jade City: I had to do a better job of being well supplied—plus, I needed to carry safety stock in case I got socked in. So I overspent in Dease Lake. *No freeze-dried powdered food for this dude!* I had enough meat and cheese to easily last me a few days. *The added weight bugs me, but considering the alternative, I'll manage.* The route ahead included two mountain passes—higher than anything I'd encountered thus far—so I paid the price.

Is this normal? I continue to feel so strong; can it really be this good? Prudence suggests that I take another rest day soon, just to pace myself. But I'll let my body be my guide. For the next few days I'll be incommunicado. Even if I had Canadian cell service plan, there were no cell towers in these parts, nor any Wi-Fi.

I'll be on the dark side of the moon.

DEASE LAKE, BC
Miles today: 74

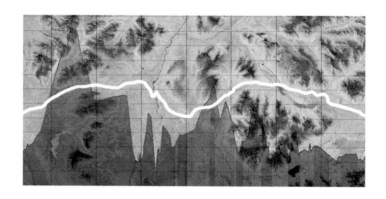

DAY 18:
SATURDAY, JULY 7, 2012—DEASE LAKE, BC
Miles to date: 1,146

Today was overcast, fifty degrees, and threatening rain, so before I left Dease Lake, I swung back into the general store for a final provision run. The store also doubled as the area information center, and I couldn't help but overhear when an older retired couple came into the store and asked about a local canyon that is a natural attraction. The woman running the store adamantly advised against it: "I wouldn't drive down that canyon if I were you; it's tricky driving down there." They wilted. She scared them away. *C'mon, lady! Try suggesting how they* can *see that canyon. Who knows, it might be life-changing! Make arrangements to have their back. Suggest that they could check back with you and maybe pack lunch and stock their car with water before they go, and gee, you just happen to have those items right here in the store! How about that? There surely is a way to make it work where everybody wins!*

Then it was my turn. "What's the weather outlook?" *Can I glean any useful information?* I should have known better.

"I'll tell you what the next fifteen minutes hold, but the weather changes every fifteen minutes," she answered smugly—and loud enough for the whole store to appreciate her brilliance.

I hate that kind of stupid smarminess masquerading as cleverness.

"What direction are you headed?" she continued.

"I'm headed southeasterly toward the Stikine River."

"After coming down a steep, long hill into the Stikine River Valley, you'll come to a bridge that crosses the river. The bridge deck is a metal grate. Walk your bike: it's dangerous. And after you cross the bridge, there's a tight hairpin turn on a steep gravel uphill on the other side. That's trouble too!"

Debbie Downer. Geez, lady! But by then I wasn't surprised. *Get away from her—run, don't walk—she's an alarmist!* She measured activities only in terms of her own capabilities. *What's risky to her is nothing to me. I can't let her fears or lack of ability affect my confidence and judgment about what I can do. Ignore her, trust myself.* Following my own advice, I bolted from her presence and swung into a small cafe for a massive breakfast before I attacked the next section of the wilds.

On these long-distance treks, you tend to run into those traveling the same direction as you more than once. Unknown to me, Joel from Edina, who had been following the same route, was about an hour behind me. As I was finishing breakfast, Joel saw my bike parked in front of the cafe and pulled in, but I took off after a quick hello. Joel is a fast rider but had diverted on a side trip to Skagway, Alaska. He planned to have breakfast and pick up supplies in Dease Lake then continue in the same direction as me. Odds were that we'd run into each other again during this remote segment.

I set off straight into a ten-mile uphill that left me once again drenched with sweat. Next was ten miles of rolling plateau—

with savage headwinds, plus a sideways-pelting rain squall. I was soaked before I finally stopped to put on my rain gear. *Haven't I learned my lesson? Sheesh! How stupid.* With my rain layer, I locked the wetness in.

At the crest of a pass with an eagle's panoramic view of the entire landscape, I felt invincible—on my game. *I'm on top of the world! Jefferson Airplane's "Aerie" fits perfectly here!* In that moment of elation, I caught a glimpse of the truss-style bridge over the Stikine River buried deep in the valley in the far distance. *Like a Tinker Toy—it's so tiny from here.* From there I streaked a ten-mile scorching downhill to the Stikine River—a 7 percent downhill grade. *Hang on, baby!*

I hit the metal grate of the bridge deck over the Stikine at blistering speed—and found that it was wet and slick as grease. My nerves exploded. *Shit! If I go down it'll shred me like cheese!* I snaked like a sidewinder, struggling for control. There was zero traffic; I could have lay in a tangled heap on that bridge for hours. Fortunately, I stayed upright as I slalomed the bridge deck.

That spine zinger gave me an acute moment of reflection. *I'm not as smart as I think! And be a man: apologize to the Dease Lake lady via mental telepathy. She offered a great tidbit about the bridge, and ignoring her almost killed me! Her style prevented me from paying attention to her message, so I wrote her off. I have to learn to look passed the messenger and pay attention to the message. What else have I missed due to my great listening traits?*

Once across, I parked my bike and walked back to the middle of the rumbling bridge, where I stood totally alone. The river ran fast, wild, and unruly, churning and boiling thirty feet below my feet. It was haunting, partly due to just how remote and wild it was, and partly because of the constant, ominous sound of the violent rushing water with nothing but stark wilderness in all directions. *Where would this river take me if I let it? What stories would it bring? I'm sure it would combine the awe-inspiring with the terrifying.*

Still drenched to the bone, I froze in a stiff breeze, and yet something about it all just held me there—I couldn't get away. *It's a powerful magnet, the churning current won't let me go! I'm totally mesmerized, caught in an eddy: each time I turn to go, I swirl back to stay.* I later learned that John Muir likened part of the Stikine River to a hundred-mile Yosemite. It's also considered one of the most difficult whitewater rivers in the world. No wonder I lingered so long, lost in awe.

On the far side of the river, I had a twenty-mile uphill that was pants-splitting steep at the beginning, along with a fierce headwind. While it's easy to read the simple words *twenty-mile uphill* and *fierce headwind*, pushing through these two challenges was extreme beyond description. Making it to the top of that uphill was a victory of perseverance—a pinnacle achieved strictly through willpower. *Christ, will it ever get easier? I'm the antithesis of lightning: lightning follows the path of least resistance—I've chosen the path of most resistance! What if I blew a gasket here in this otherworldly remote? Shit! How much more can I take without breaking?* An hour ago, I'd been on top of the world, and now I was awash in self-doubt about my wisdom. But my lament was short-lived—I snapped out with an old refrain: *Your body can take so much more than your mind! You're on your own, Lone Ranger. Get moving—nobody is going to pedal for you. Y B Y A W C!* In a strange way, the reward was worth the effort. *I'm dead tired— but how alive! What a rush! This is exactly what I wanted!*

Then, as if I hadn't pumped enough adrenaline yet, I scared another black bear. He accelerated so quickly I thought he was on a catapult. When these guys bolt, they appear to fly into the bush. A loaded bike is unstable without two firm hands on it, so, if a bear decided to run at me rather than away, I'd have to take a hand off the handlebars, reach down, pull the bear spray from my water bottle holder, undo the safety one-handed, turn to find the bear, and hope I hit him. *There's no way!* And with the instability of the bike, I'd most likely crash while clipped in. *I'd only have a few seconds to react, based on what I just saw—I'd be so screwed! It's far more likely that I'd end up as biker bear scat, helmet and shoes bracketing my clipped-in skeleton.*

Nevertheless, I was still stupidly casual about the bears. I'd been hollering at and talking to them every single day and found them funny, dimwitted, and clownish. *They're generally more scared of me than I of them. Stay scary!*

I rounded a bend and startled another moose, a large, lanky male who took off in a spirited Clydesdale-style prance parallel to the road, with me pedaling in stride behind him. Then he darted into the brush, which was so thick I lost sight of him by the time he was only a few feet in.

Midday, a guy going my direction in a beat-up pickup truck pulled alongside me and rolled down his passenger window as we both proceeded.

"Hey, bud! You alright?" he shouted through the window.

"Yeah, life is good, no complaints," I responded.

"I just wanted to check, you're pretty alone out here. I'm going to pull ahead and pull over." I figured he was bored and wanted to break up his long drive.

I pedaled up to him and stopped. He climbed out of his truck, and we both gazed over a mountain reservoir to the distant mountains on the horizon.

"Beautiful country out here," he remarked. There was a long pause—he was deep in thought.

Something profound is coming—something life-changing—he's turning toward me—turning more—here it comes!

"I was once on a first date out here—it was dusk, and we were driving in my truck," he recalled. "My date and I saw a bear grazing on the side of the road. My date, mind you, was pretty hot—I wanted to impress her and all. So I stopped, got out of the truck, and ran up and kicked the bear right in the ass! The thing was, I thought it was a black bear—but then he turned his head, and it was a fucking grizzly! I got so scared, I never ran so fast in my life! I dashed back to the truck and dove in!"

"She must have thought you were a true ace—a real keeper!" I was howling. "That's not appealing?" *As though I know jack about what women like in a guy.*

"Oh no, she was sooo pissed!" He wagged his head side to side. "'Take me home!' she demanded. And not in the way I would have liked!" He added in lamenting afterthought, "There aren't many girls up here."

"Well, you took your shot!" I was crying. "Not all shots are a swish!"

"Yeah, but up here they can't be air balls either!"

Here we were, the two of us in the wilderness, waving our arms in animated conversation and howling with laughter. He wasn't trying to be a comedian, but with that kind of personality and style, whatever he said was just plain funny. *Tall tale of the north or true? I don't know. But you can't make that stuff up. Can you?* It seemed true enough to me—but it didn't matter. I was thoroughly entertained.

"Be careful out here." *Pretty funny coming from a guy who'd kicked a grizzly in the ass.*

"Will do, Casanova."

He drove off, waving out the window, and in a moment was gone—from wild conversation to immediate isolation. Like an old Western where the scene fades from Technicolor to the burnt-reddish nests of aged film, accented by the desolate swishing wind—but his story howled in my mind. *He survived unscathed—well, not really*: *she dumped him. Been there.*

I arrived at the Iskut general store on a Canadian First Nations reservation and languished over a five-course lunch: a corned beef sandwich, an oversized gas-station hot dog, a big chunk of cheese, an orange, and a pound bag of BBQ chips, all washed down with a quart of chocolate milk. *Mm-mm, good! Gas tank topped off.*

As I was finishing my gourmet lunch, Joel rolled up to the store. We compared notes and found we were both targeting Kinaskan Lake Provincial Park—still thirty or so miles away.

"Are these the most brutal headwinds you've ever ridden in, Joel?" I asked.

"Yeah," he said. "They're consistently thirty, with gusts to forty."

"I know, and we're straight into the teeth of them. This steep valley is a wind tunnel— and the wind is increasing, the deeper we get into the day."

"Do you want to pair up and work together?" Joel asked. "We can alternate lead and draft."

"Makes sense to me—let's do it."

Riding this way saved energy. My guess was the drafter got about a twenty-five to thirty percent efficiency advantage versus going it alone. Joel knew all about parasitic wind drag because he also was a pilot, and awareness of wind speed and direction in terms of the wind drag and fuel usage are part of a pilot's job. "In a plane, wind resistance increases by the square of the apparent wind speed," Joel said. "It's the same for bikes. Wind drag is the biggest dynamic force working against a biker—creating far more drag than the friction from rolling resistance."

My mind cranked through the math. *One unit of wind speed will deliver one unit of relative resistance or drag, but two units of wind speed is four units of drag, three units wind speed is nine units, and so on. An exponential progression of resistance!*

"And the problem is even further compounded by the large cross-section of our loaded bikes," I stated, as though Joel didn't know jack. "And we're busting through forty-mile-an-hour gusts!" *The math explains why the headwinds have been so difficult—they've been exponentially slowing me down. The parasites have been chewing my ass all day again today—in spades!*

Teamwork made a big difference. The lead biker got the brunt of the drag, breaking through the wall of air while the drafter momentarily recovered for his next big pull—we alternated leads with three-minute pulls and recovery—we were much faster as a result. It also demonstrated why in bike racing, auto racing, or even geese in flight, the contenders all line up and draft behind the guy in front until the last push.

We both thought we would hit the park entrance about ten miles before we actually did. We even wondered if we'd missed it— deceptively farther on, we eventually pulled in. *Whew, brutal—thank God that day is over!*

My campsite was spectacular, right on the edge of pristine Kinaskan Lake. I quickly set camp and skinny-dipped to freshen up. Unfortunately, clouds of skeeters, which hadn't been bad since Glennallen, drove me prematurely into my tent.

With a stiff breeze off the lake, I was cold after my dip. I zipped the tent tight, slipped on my longies, hunkered deep into my bag, and drifted away to the soothing metronome of waves lapping on the shore.

KINASKAN LAKE PROVINCIAL PARK, BC
Miles today: 79

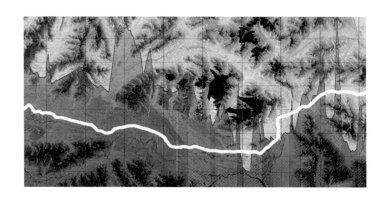

DAY 19
SUNDAY, JULY 8, 2012—KINASKAN LAKE PROVINCIAL PARK, BC
Miles to date: 1,225

Is that the patter of rain on my tent? What time is it? I was half inclined to roll over and go back to sleep. *Do I really want to pack a wet tent?* But from the campsite next to mine, like a nagging alarm clock, I could hear all the zipping and stuffing sounds of Joel packing up. For some strange reason, the sound of tent zippers was magnified in the wild. *How many goddamn zippers does he have? Every zip screeches, "You uncommitted lazy slug, if you ain't movin', you ain't gettin' anywhere!" He's up and moving and I'm just laying here.* Guilt won. *Up and at 'em.*

We took off together in the rain with the Bell 2 Lodge, about seventy-five miles away, as the destination. It would be the only day on the trip that I rode entirely with someone else.

As I rode, I dissected my decision. On the stay side, I had been warm and dry in my tent and could probably have used a rest day. But on the go side, although it was sprinkling, it wasn't raining cats and dogs. You never know if light rain is the leading edge of a much larger storm system that might worsen for several days. But the deciding factor was food: I only had a few days' worth packed for this remote section of the Cassiar. So, go it was.

We started with a long uphill, so within fifteen minutes I was drenched yet again in rain and cold sweat. For the next four hours we rode in a rainy fifty degrees. I can't speak for Joel, but I was freezing, especially on the downhills. I finally donned another layer and got warm, albeit a wet warm. Between my extra rain layers and just being wet, I was dragging a little. *I do need another day off pretty soon. I've gone eighteen days with only one rest day; I've earned another.*

We didn't see much of anything at first because we were focused on pedaling the unending ribbon of wet road socked in by fog and rain. Dripping bright green vegetation as thick as a rainforest pressed in from both sides of the road. I couldn't see ten feet into the bush. At midmorning we passed the first black bear of the day, and an hour later, the second, both only about twenty feet away, putting my running total at fifteen.

At the fifty-mile mark, the clouds lifted somewhat and we started seeing the mountaintops. The pavement even dried for the last twenty-five miles—*Such a simple pleasure.* Even so, I never dried out the entire day.

I became aware of cues I didn't ordinarily pay any attention to. For instance, if I was going downhill and the river was flowing the same direction, I was in for a nice cruising descent for a while. But since rivers flow downhill, when I found myself on a downhill against the flow of the river, I knew it was just a topographical anomaly and there would soon be hell to pay. *I hate these false downhills because I'm just losing ground that I know I'll have to regain—and then some—to clear the next pass.* All too often these brief respites signaled an even tougher climb to come.

After churning uphill for hours, arriving at the crest often presented a whole new set of forthcoming mountain ranges stretching to the horizon. I spent my days climbing, descending, and then climbing again. Sometimes it was straight up one side of a pass and straight down the other. Other times, the road climbed more laterally up a mountainside before crossing a crest and descending into a different river valley below. But once I reached that valley, there was always another mountain to climb, next to another river. Because the mountains were so much bigger and broader than most in the lower forty-eight, the monstrous hills just kept on coming. *How the hell am I going to get through all of this? I just will.*

Joel and I arrived at the Bell 2 Lodge at about 3:30 p.m. Bell 2 was a small resort—a lone oasis in the middle of this vast wilderness. Like arriving at a calm, safe harbor after wickedly stormy seas, I had an immediate sense of safety, comfort, and well-being. There were a couple of shiny new helicopters sitting on the helipad associated with the resort. Bell 2 served as the home base for Last Frontier Heliskiing. *There's something about this place that just feels good! These surrounding peaks are so dramatic—what an out-of-body hoot to be dropped off from a chopper and shred the steep and deep on powder skis.*

When I checked in to pay for my campsite, I found a small refrigerator in the lobby with sandwiches, chocolate milk, and, best of all, beer. I was so hungry that I inhaled a sandwich and chips and drained a pint of chocolate milk in front of the receptionist. She shot me a look—*Come up for air, Hoss!* Then I bought a six-pack of beer to bring to my campsite—*To help me, you know, precisely square the corners as I set my tent.* I made a great discovery along the way. *Get outta here—what a prize! Bell 2 has a hot tub, and it's open!*

I set my camp, grabbed the beer, and hit the hot tub. Famished and dehydrated, I quickly slammed the first two beers—*Whoa! "Eight Miles High," The Byrds! Slow down cowboy!* As an added plus, the laundry was right next to the hot tub, so over the next two hours, while I soaked and polished the brew, I washed all my wet clothes. It rained off and on as I soaked, but the tub was beneath an open-air pavilion. When I did move, it was in super slow motion. *What*

luxury, especially after being cold, wet, and tired from a day of exertion.
I slid into clean and dryer-warmed clothes. *Simple little things—back in the real world, it's too easy to take it all for granted.*

Later, I dined at the restaurant's buffet, if you can call a buffet "dining"—it was more like running laps back to the feed trough! *Note to self: never offer a buffet to distance bikers!* My antics entertained two Canadian ladies, mostly through my wolfing down heaping plates of mystery meat. We jawed back and forth for over an hour and laughed at the strange situations I'd found myself in. These two women were traveling north to see their respective kids in the Yukon but were nervous about their drive due to the remoteness of the Cassiar. They leaned on each other for support and the fortitude to proceed. "Top off your tank at every available stop and you'll be fine," I reassured them.

At late dusk, I returned to my campsite and discovered bear scat near my tent. *Too late now; I'm not moving. What do I gain, fifty feet?*

Laying in the dark, my mind wandered. *What a stretch of road on this magnificent Cassiar. Everyone needs to see this in their life! It hasn't been easy thus far, but I'm so glad I took it. There's a rawness and mystique about it that I can't put my finger on—but once here, I'll never fully leave.*

With bear spray as my companion, my eyes finally slammed shut.

BELL 2 LODGE, BC
Miles today: 73

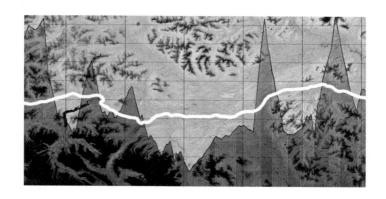

DAY 20
MONDAY, JULY 9, 2012—BELL 2 LODGE
Miles to date: 1,298

Once again, there was light rain as I packed my wet tent. Ugh! Joel was already up, packing his tent and making himself breakfast, when I emerged from hibernation, squinting in the mist like a groundhog. Joel was anxious to hit the road, but this groundhog wanted a nice hot breakfast—so he took off about an hour ahead of me. *He's gone for good: I won't see him again because at Kitwanga, 155 miles downstream, he'll head east onto the Yellowhead Highway and I'll head west.*

I packed and had a big buffet breakfast in the resort. There was nothing like fueling up early with eggs, cakes, sausage, and hash browns, along with gallons of blistering-hot coffee. The two ladies from last night's dinner were there too and wondered what my day would bring, especially as I'd be starting in the rain. "Well, it's a hundred and fifty-five miles to Kitwanga, the next town with services, which to me is food and water. That's too far to for me to make in a day, so I'll just flop in the bush and wilderness camp tonight somewhere at the midpoint—no big deal. Then I'll make Kitwanga tomorrow."

Wide-eyed, all they could offer in good humor was, "We don't want to read about you in the paper—so, good luck and be safe!"

In addition to filling my three water bottles, I bought two pints of chocolate milk and an oversized 24-oz. bottle of water from the Bell 2 fridge for good measure and snapped them all under the bungee cords on the back of my bike. Although I didn't have a premonition of what was to come, thank God I bought extra fluids, because I ran into a water problem. More on that shortly.

After a nice long downhill of fifteen or twenty miles south along the Bell-Irving River, I crossed the river and was met, as usual, by an equally long uphill. From there it was up over a pass and down into the next valley, and up again, over and over and over.

I passed the Stewart-Hyder cutoff, which dead-ended about thirty miles away from the Cassiar at the towns of Stewart, BC, in Canada, and, two miles further, Hyder, Alaska. The classic footage of grizzlies catching salmon in Alaska is filmed there—but it was still a few weeks before the peak salmon run, and if the salmon weren't running, the bears weren't fishing. Since I was seeing bears every day, I didn't need to add a side trip of another sixty miles to my journey.

In hindsight, I regret not taking this side trip. *When will I ever get back there? Sure, it would have cost me another one or two short days of riding, but hell, I wasn't on a schedule. Missed opportunity. I hate missed opportunities. Still, to see all those beautiful beasts fishing the river gives me strong incentive to come back someday—on my Harley.*

About seventy-five miles in, at about the halfway point to Kitwanga, I came out of the highlands. The topography changed to a flattish, marshy lowland, and when I stopped for a snack, I was attacked by bugs. *No stopping or camping here!* I kept riding.

It also became hot—eighty-five degrees—and I was consuming water at an alarming rate. I needed to keep hydrating so my body wouldn't collapse, but I'd gone through more than two-thirds of my supply. *No problem: I have a water pump and filter—and the whole country is lakes and rivers. I'm golden.*

But not so fast. As I pulled along a trickle of a stream to filter water and replenish my supply, my luck ran out. I pulled way too hard on my water pump and—*SNAP!*—it broke. I fidgeted with the pump for about five minutes, thinking, *It can't be fixed. Uh-oh. Catch 22: I can't filter clean water, and I can't risk giardia from unfiltered water! I'm so screwed! I'm also burning time, and time is distance.* With low water and big distance yet to Kitwanga, I might as well have been a bush pilot desperately checking his gas gauge.

What do I do now? Back on the road I went. While I rode, I considered my water situation. *I'm down to twenty-four ounces, with about eighty miles to Kitwanga and clean water. It will cost me more overall water to stop for the night and restart in the morning— not to mention the time it will take me to set up tonight and repack in the morning. The weather is good right now, and I never know what tomorrow will bring. And for the moment, I even have a slight tailwind—riding is a breeze. Why would I set up in a bug-infested bog with a water problem when I can pull off the entire 155-mile ride to Kitwanga? It will be something of a touch-and-go, but doing the entire distance today will solve my water problem—if I can make it.*

I felt surprisingly strong and wasn't tiring as the day proceeded. *Go figure—it doesn't make sense. But I'll take it!* I ran through the mental math. *What's another eighty miles? I can make Kitwanga in another six hours. My body can always take more than my mind. What I don't know is my limit—where my body will hit a point where it just plain runs out of energy and shuts down.* Distance athletes have several expressions for this: "bonking," "hitting the wall," or "getting the bear." Naturally, my favorite was "getting the bear": *A bear clawing into you and dragging you to the ground . . . a real possibility up here.*

The more I thought about it, the more sense it made. *Why not? I've already ridden two consecutive ninety-six-mile days, so I rode nearly two hundred miles within thirty-six hours. Sure, it's long, but it can't be that big a killer, can it?* The biggest ifs were the remaining topography—

and the wind. I couldn't predict either. *Will the lowland give way to rolling hills or big climbs? Will I hit another headwind?*

I had to make the best decision from among two poor alternatives. I quickly made the decision and didn't thrash over it. *Keep going.*

I hit the hundred-mile mark at about 5:00 p.m., and by 7:30 I only had about twenty miles left to Kitwanga, so in my mind, I'd already made it. *Who can't do twenty more miles when they have to? I always have twenty miles in me!* I'd also added five more bear sightings to my running tally, bringing it to an even twenty.

I was pressing to beat sunset to Kitwanga. *It will be nip and tuck, made harder now by a moderate headwind and rising terrain— and I don't have any lights.* In the midst of that last stretch, I saw a long pullout off the Cassiar, a dirt road that descended a couple of hundred yards downhill to the Kitwanga River's edge. I glanced left and through the trees—and blinked.

There's Joel sitting by the river! "Joel!" I hollered at the top of my lungs. He swiveled and gave me a big sweeping wave in response, beckoning, *Come on down!* But I kept on pedaling. "I'm going the whole way, baby!" I yelled at the top of my lungs. Joel knew what I meant. *All the way to Kitwanga in a single day.*

I pulled in and followed signs to a campground. The sun was grazing the horizon, leaving only a couple more minutes of light—*I made it in the nick of time.* As I rode into the campsite, I spotted a few RVers who'd been settled for hours—their occupants were enjoying the evening by their campfires. Overwhelmed with endorphins, I couldn't help but shout, "Does anyone have a can of beer?"

"I think I have one can left," a man hollered back.

"I can't take your last can!"

"How far have you ridden?"

"I've just done a hundred and fifty-five miles," I said as I pulled up, "but seriously, I can't take your last." *What a hollow objection—I'd love that beer!*

With a big grin, the guy dug the can out of his cooler. "Dude, this is yours," he said as he thrust it into my hand.

I'm not about to refuse it. By then, I was bone dry and out of water—my body was craving fluid. I popped the top and shot the whole can like a college kid. *That definitely was the best beer I've ever had.*

The campground office was closed for the night, but luckily, there was a water tap on the outside of their building—and, better yet, a public shower for their campers. I filled my water bottles and quickly set up camp by twilight in a howling wind. *Lights rapidly dimming!*

I ate two packages of Lunchables in the dark and then slipped into my sleeping bag, totally content. With my one-beer buzz, my brain was awash in a rapid stream-of-consciousness retelling of what I'd seen and done today—one thought after another sequencing through my head like a computer processes lines of code. *I'm tired, but not sleepy—I'm still too jacked up by events of the day.*

I lay in the dark, eyes open and swamped with well-being. *I would never have planned to do this kind of distance. But I had to do it. And I made it—155 miles in one day.* This also happened to be my first century ride—ever. My bike calculator recorded an actual in-the-saddle pedaling time of 13 hours, 18 minutes, 35 seconds. *I knew I had strong stamina, but I never knew I had this in me. You can always do more than you think you can.*

I'll be pretty tired tomorrow. I may even have a shorter day due to today's distance. My mind still swirled as I stared at the tent ceiling in the dark, the walls rattling hard and puffing with each blast of the wind. *Slow down, Jerry—close your eyes, try to go to sleep. But I'll never forget this day.*

The Cassiar was over. I threw myself at that magnificent road and came out stronger. But figuratively, I left a piece of myself on that beast. *Once you peer over the edge, you never fully return—and you're never quite the same. What a gift.*

KITWANGA, BC
Miles today: 155—My first-ever 100+ mile day!

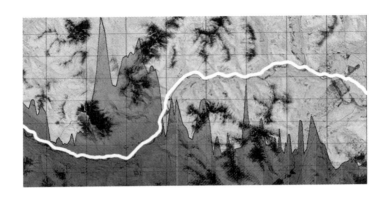

DAY 21
TUESDAY, JULY 10, 2012—KITWANGA, BC
Miles to date: 1,453

Kitwanga is an Indigenous community whose name derives from the Gitwangak Indians—the people of the place of rabbits. *That's funny, I've only seen two rabbits over these 1,500 miles. I've seen ten times more bears. How about a more appropriate name like Frigginbearseverywherewanga!*

My first leg this morning was only a couple of miles, but it included a highlight of the trip: crossing the bridge over the Skeena River. It's the biggest river I've seen so far—broad and churning, milky with glacial silt. *I'm so thrilled, I'll be following it west—downstream all the way to Prince Rupert on the BC coast. Downstream is downhill!*

I hit the end of the Cassiar at its junction with the Yellowhead (BC 16) Highway—another major crossroad. *Take a hard right and head west toward Prince Rupert—don't blow this turn, Pascual, or you're screwed for hundreds of miles!*

The segment of the Yellowhead between Prince George and Prince Rupert is called the Highway of Tears and was highlighted in the July 2012 issue of *Outside* magazine. The author relates, "In the stunning and remote wilderness along northern British Columbia's Highway 16, at least eighteen women—by some estimates, many more—have gone missing over the past four decades. After years of investigation, authorities still don't know if it's the work of a serial killer or multiple offenders."

Still hungry from the big ride yesterday, I needed to juice up on calories. I stopped at a gas stop and cafe at the Cassiar/Yellowhead junction. Posters of several missing persons hung in the front entry of the cafe. I asked my server, a young First Nations woman, "What are your thoughts about the missing women?"

"Well, there are suspicions among many in our community that it's a government authority," she replied.

"Why would you think that?"

"Because there are fifty or so missing people, and there's still no evidence, not one shred—nor has a body ever been found! The only ones who could cover it all up would be someone in a position of authority—a government authority."

Many of the missing disappeared while hitchhiking—it's an economically depressed area and some can't afford cars. So, when they need to get somewhere, they'd hitchhike—they didn't have a good alternative.

I finished off a lumberjack-sized breakfast and lingered for a while, pounding coffee, so I got off to a late start. The moment I turned onto the Yellowhead Highway, a big, bright, in-your-face billboard warned: *IS IT WORTH THE RISK TO HITCHHIKE?*

I noted a road sign showing the distance to Prince Rupert and did a mental translation of kilometers to miles—roughly 150 miles.

My target was Terrace, a sizable town about sixty miles downstream. *I'll take it easier today after my big day yesterday. My body probably needs recovery. Funny, sixty miles is now an easy day!*

As I rode, I did mental distance and time calculations. *If I only hit Terrace today, it leaves Prince Rupert about ninety miles farther—more than I want to have to ride tomorrow, Wednesday.* Still more important, the Prince Rupert Ferry on the Inside Passage runs north on odd days and south on even days. *If I hit Prince Rupert tomorrow afternoon, I could catch the Thursday southbound ferry to Port Hardy, on the northern tip of Vancouver Island.* Otherwise, I'd have to hang around Prince Rupert for an extra day and a half, until Saturday—more time than I'd want. *Hmmm, I feel surprisingly good—I'll ride past Terrace and just wilderness camp, as there's no campground between there and Prince Rupert. I wonder how far past Terrace I should go? Hell, don't thrash over simple decisions, just split the miles into about seventy-five miles today and the other seventy-five tomorrow.*

It was another spectacular day to ride, sunny and seventy-five degrees, and the terrain remained flattish with an ever-so-slight downhill, following the Skeena downstream. The only negative was a hellacious headwind that slowed my progress. *Keep on trucking, one stroke at a time—don't miss the Thursday ferry.*

At one of my rest stops, I was snacking on a granola bar when a guy in an old pickup truck pulled up next to me. "Hey," he called out his window, "are you hungry?"

"I'm always hungry out here," I replied with a laugh. But I spoke too quickly.

A bare, meaty hand emerged from the window, offering me half of a rotisserie chicken, grease from its skin dripping down his dirty wrist. "I just bought this at the grocery store and can't eat it all," he said. "Do you want the other half?"

I tried a laugh. "I'm good for now," I assured him, "but thanks for the kind thought."

To my incredulous relief, he pulled the carcass back into his truck, still licking his fingers and wrist. *Yeah, it's the thought that counts, but yuck! I'd rather eat roadkill.*

At three thirty, sixty miles into the day, I pulled into Terrace, the biggest town that I'd seen since Whitehorse—and bigger than I expected. Despite the gigantic breakfast, I was starving, so I stopped and ate on the eastern side of town. But by the time I hit the western side, I was still hungry, so I stopped and ate again.

With renewed energy, I re-hit the road at about four thirty. *I'll do about another twenty miles, making it eighty total for the day.* Once back on the road, though, everything seemed so right. *Crazy, I'm stronger than strong. What is it? The day after a 155-mile mountainous ride, and I'm not getting tired? This doesn't make sense. In fact, I'm getting stronger as the day progresses—go figure, but don't stop now— don't be the one who stops yourself!*

The road was flat, the winds had abated, and the weather was clear. In the late-afternoon sun, the surrounding mountains lit up stark against the deep blue sky. As I rode into the evening, I passed numerous massive walls, rock climbers' heaven. *Man, I'd hate to miss sights like these. When everything's good, take the gift and push ahead. It's better to ride farther and be tired in great conditions rather than to ride fresh in lousy conditions.*

I passed the entrance to a small summer retreat that prominently displayed a poster warning of a grizzly bear recently seen scrounging in that area. I pressed on, but it was getting late. The farther south I traveled, the earlier darkness arrived.

I'm at 103 miles and could go far longer, but it's 8:15 and the sun is close to the horizon. I need to get off the road and set camp now! I can't be searching for a good wilderness site in total darkness. Get crackin'!

I settled on a spot near a bridge that crossed a tributary feeding immediately into the Skeena River. I quickly set camp and then took a dip to clean up at the mouth of the cold tributary. So close to its confluence, the tributary was swift and I had to be especially careful with the strong current. *Man, would it suck to get swept into the Skeena right here!* There was a tree limb hanging over the tributary. *Grip tight, Grendel. If I get swept away, how in the hell will I get back upriver and across this tributary to my camp—if I could even find it? Especially in the pitch black, without any clothes or shoes, in the thick bush.*

Finally settled, I lay in the dark and listened to the constant, mesmerizing flow of the Skeena. *So beautiful here. But I already miss the haunting Cassiar—whoooooooo oooooo, whooooooooo—so, so cool.*

WILDERNESS CAMP—YELLOWHEAD HIGHWAY, BC, ABOUT 55 MILES EAST OF PRINCE RUPERT, BC
Miles today: 103

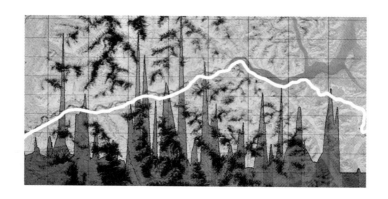

DAY 22
WEDNESDAY, JULY 11, 2012—WILDERNESS CAMP ON
THE YELLOWHEAD HIGHWAY
Miles to date: 1,556

I awoke at six thirty to the sound of truck tires rapidly approaching over gravel. Someone was driving down the small track to the riverfront—right where I was camped. *He'll run me over!* I flew up, unzipped the tent's rain fly, and poked my head out.

"Good morning," said the man just stepping out of his truck. "Did I wake you up?"

"Naw, I was just rustling around in my sleeping bag—delaying when I'd get up." Truth be told, my air mattress was leaking even more now, and though I was up once in the night to reinflate it, by morning the rocks and roots were punching into my ribs again. So, I was up.

"I left Prince Rupert about an hour ago to get here. This is one of my favorite fishing spots."

"Well, fishing's better than working."

"Yeah, luckily I don't work anymore. I did my time," he said. "After thirty-seven years as a longshoreman in Prince Rupert, now I'm free to fish." An old guy, he was decked out in full fly-fishing gear—and selecting which type of fly to use. It didn't look like he even cared if he caught anything; his whole attitude suggested, *Why would you ever want to be anyplace else?*

We chatted while I packed my gear. Not surprisingly, fishing was this guy's passion, and he shared with me many special moments experienced at this very spot—how he saw this or that fish—had cast just right, and reeled it in. *He remembers the specific fish? Fish savant?*

"I had a bear encounter at this spot a few years ago. Right over there, by the railroad trestle, right where your food is hanging."

"What did you do?"

"Oh, nothing dramatic—I just hollered and the bear skedaddled." He flung his hands up as if to say, "whatever."

I finished packing, bade this pleasant old man good luck and farewell, and left him happily in "his" spot.

Thank God I put the miles in yesterday because clouds and fog moved in overnight. If I hadn't ridden as far as I did last night, I would have missed some of the most amazing sights in the Skeena River Valley.

Within a mile of my camp—*whoa whoa whoa, what was that?* I blew by fresh wet cougar prints crossing the road. I doubled back—I couldn't resist. I climbed off my bike to examine them. The cougar had walked through a wet clay area, leaving perfect impressions as well as beautiful, clean, khaki-colored prints on the solid black asphalt road—undisturbed yet by any vehicles. *This guy was just here!* I took my gloves off and laid them next to the big cat's prints for scale.

Another mile down the road, with the cougar fresh in my mind, I thought, *Damn! I should have taken off my shoes as well and positioned them along with my gloves to make it look as if I was tracking the cougar on all fours—that would have made a great picture. Goddammit—another missed opportunity.*

I had all day to make the relatively short fifty some miles to Prince Rupert. Since time wasn't a concern, I felt sluggish and unmotivated. *The less I have on my plate, the more I procrastinate and do even less than I intended. Today is my day of senioritis. Strange, but my worst performances are when I have the least to do. I'm best when I'm overcommitted—go figure.*

I was tired. *Two hundred ninety miles over the last two and a half days is catching up to me.* So, about thirty minutes into my ride, I found a roadside rest area perched about twenty-five feet above the river's edge and decided to catch a catnap on the top of a picnic table—I've always loved to snooze in the wild outdoors. I added a warmer layer of clothing along with my stocking hat and gloves, and, with the cool, foggy wind wafting off the river and the sound of the river itself as a lullaby, my eyes slammed shut—I was out cold in less than a minute. Once in a while, I awoke in something of a mental fog and had to figure out where I was. But then I just shifted my weight and fell back to sleep. Clearly, I was making up for some sleep deprivation.

After about an hour and a half, I jolted awake with what is medically called a hypnagogic jerk. *Wha?! Where in the world am I?* Then the fog in my brain began to clear. *Oh yeah. I'm in a mountain valley along the beautiful Skeena River. Heavenly contentment.* I lay there for a few minutes more, looking straight up at the fog wafting through the pines as my mind sorted out my present situation. *Hypnagogic jerk?* My new non-medical term for it was *time to go!*

The fog made for a cold and clammy ride, but the road remained flat as it followed the Skeena, ever wider and more impressive as it neared Prince Rupert. But after forty flat miles, the last fifteen of the Yellowhead going into Prince Rupert got crazy hilly. *Ugh! C'mon! I can't do hills today!* But of course you have to take what's delivered. All I wanted was to get off the bike and drift into Prince Rupert in slow motion, but those hills meant a final strenuous push. That effort was compounded by my bike being out of tune again.

My gears had started skipping on my long day from Bell 2 to Kitwanga, but it's not like I could do anything about them out in the middle of the bush. Each day they'd gotten progressively worse, and today I couldn't shift into any of the low gears. That made the hills all the tougher. Yeah, relative to earlier uphills, they weren't long, but they were steep, and because I was stuck in higher gears, I had less leverage and power. So I died. *God I'm so exhausted I can hardly ride a straight line—it's all I can do to stay upright.*

But as I pulled into Prince Rupert at about 1:00 p.m., the fisherman who'd awakened me early that morning passed me in his truck. He shouted encouragement out his window while I gave a fist pump, both of us grinning from ear to ear.

Prince Rupert is an authentic seaport—*I love seaports!* It used to be the halibut capital of the world. *This is clearly still a working town—no tourists here.* After so much silence, the activity of the harbor was a treat. The fog had burned off and the sky was perfectly clear, its radiance finally warming me. In a stupor, I sat down in a city park, watching the activity on the water through my binoculars. *After all my aggressiveness, I'm aggressively doing—nothing. Feels good to not be moving for a change.*

What a difference a day made. Last night I camped in the wild, bathed in a silty river, and ate baloney on smashed pita bread. Tonight I had a halibut burger, a bowl of clam chowder, and ice-cold beer at a waterfront pub. I also had a decent room with a bed. Suddenly, like flipping a light switch, I was back in civilization. *In an instant, I've transitioned from the wilderness part of my journey to the maritime part.*

PRINCE RUPERT, BC
Miles today: 54

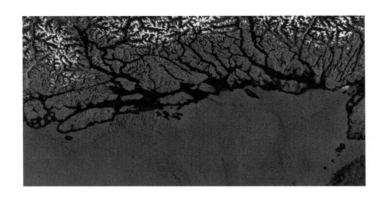

DAY 23
THURSDAY, JULY 12, 2012—PRINCE RUPERT, BC
Miles to date: 1,610

Today was a natural rest day as I cruised the southerly part of the Inside Passage from Prince Rupert to Port Hardy on a BC ferry. The crossing left at 7:30 a.m. and arrived in Port Hardy after 10:00 p.m. in the pitch black of night. I had no idea where I'd pedal to and stay after leaving the ferry. But, in my new world, that was long-range planning. *I'll worry about it when I arrive.*

Loving the outside, I went to the fifth level of the ferry, high above the water, and spent the entire day on the top deck. One of the deckhands told me it was the nicest day by far this summer. The entire Inside Passage was lined with lush green mountains, some snowcapped at the higher elevations. The morning started cold, with a mystical fog bank low on the water creating a contrast with the green mountains and azure sky. There was no wind, so the water was glass smooth in the tight parts of the Passage. Whenever we were exposed to the greater Pacific, the ferry rolled with large swells that had crossed all the way from Japan. I watched it all, sunrise to sunset and beyond—the golds and blues of late afternoon turning to violet grays and finally the black of night. And, of course, I hammered the dining room a few times throughout the day to pound calories—and to avoid the junk I'd brought myself.

I could spot spouts of blowhole spray in the distance from pods of killer whales. I saw puffins, an unusual-looking but beautiful northern waterfowl with a clownish look and an oversized, distended beak. Eagles soared over us throughout the day. Historic landmarks passed as well, including old but still-working lighthouses and an abandoned fishing camp and cannery.

At one point, I saw a solo rower in an ocean dory struggling his way down the Passage. It was his version of my bike journey. I felt an immediate envy—I was safe, sound, and comfortable on the ferry, while he was exposed and self-reliant. *At this moment, who's more alive? Where's the greater experience? I always hate when someone is having more fun than me!*

The ferry arrived in Port Hardy in the black of night. During the ferry ride, I'd learned there was a campground about two miles from the ferry terminal. I rode there in the inky dark—without a light. *Why do I do this? I can't see a damned thing! God, this is, well, wild but brainless!* The shoulder was particularly tricky because I couldn't tell where the pavement ended and the gravel began. In one quick moment, I went off the pavement into the gravel. My front wheel got squirrelly and sent a zinger up my spine as I struggled and fought my way back onto the pavement. *That was close to a train wreck!* I fumbled along and finally made it to the campground.

"Just go up the hill and find an empty spot," the campground clerk said. Outside of the office itself, there were no lights in the campground. Working by camper Braille, I found a spot and unpacked my bike in the dark, leaving my gear strewn all over the ground.

Just then, a car came up the dirt track and stopped. "This is my spot," the driver, an older lady, said. "They just assigned it to me."

Incredulously, I replied, "Ugh, really?" I tried logic. "It's eleven o'clock, and this place is wide open—common sense says nobody else is coming in tonight. Would it be a problem for you to just move thirty feet over to that spot?" I pointed into blackness. "I think you'd be just fine."

"No, I'd like this spot. It's mine. See? Here's the number." She nervously held her ground. *Uh-oh—a rule follower—pretty rigid.* It could have devolved into an ugly case of the inflexible meeting the insensitive. *Don't uncork here, Paco—no Mexican standoff. Rather, get in her world—she's vulnerable, doesn't know me from Adam, probably scared shitless, and we're in an awkward situation—take the temperature down—get her to comfort; it's a better skill than escalating the tension.* I acknowledged it was her site and empathized with her over the awkwardness of the situation—I gave her trust.

"I'll move if you absolutely want—but I think there can be a win-win here. There's a ton of room for both of us, and I can help you if you need it. Can we just work something out?" We did. And once she gained confidence that I was harmless, it seemed like she was happy to not be alone at the site.

After an amazing day on the Inside Passage, I was just damn glad I didn't need to change campsites.

It's 11:45. Close your eyes.

PORT HARDY, VANCOUVER ISLAND, BC
Miles today: 0 (Not including about 3 unlogged miles to and from ferry terminals)

DAY 24
FRIDAY, JULY 13, 2012—PORT HARDY, VANCOUVER
ISLAND, BC
Miles to date: 1,610

It's another perfect day with no clouds, and the temperature is heading for the 80s. I only have about three hundred miles on Vancouver Island. What a great day to bust out the distance. But Christ! Why am I so sluggish? I mean, c'mon, I had a rest day yesterday.

I was starving, but I'd skipped breakfast because food was three miles in the wrong direction, to the town center of Port Hardy. *I'll head downstream; I'm sure I'll hit a cafe soon enough now that I'm back in civilization.* Twenty-eight miles later, and still no breakfast, I was out of gas. *I should know better.* Then I came upon Port McNeill.

In a taunting mind tease, Port McNeill dangled two miles off the highway and a steep downhill to sea level. But I could wait no longer,

I *had* to eat, so I diverted. *This downhill feels great—but crap, it also means that I'm going to have to climb out—plus four miles of additional riding without forward progress. I hate that.* After I'd chowed down, it's as though I downed a cocktail of adrenaline and testosterone—I got explosively strong. *God! I'm no longer a rookie—I should be smarter about my food by now.*

While I was in Port McNeill, I pored over a map with a guide at the visitor center. The northern end of Vancouver Island was hillier and more remote than the southern stretch, so most of my climbing would happen over the next couple of days. She showed me where I'd hit the hardest climbs—the toughest was just south of Woss.

Since I'd started late and then lounged too long at breakfast, it was 4:45 p.m. by the time I hit Woss, a small company town in a logging community of about three hundred people. *The clear-cutting in this area is pretty ugly, but it's what keeps this town alive.* Like most small towns, Woss had its gas station, general store, and diner.

When I slowed down to stop at the diner, I got caught by a bad combination of sloppiness and indecision. I unclipped my left foot but lazily left my right foot clipped—but at the same moment, I complacently allowed my bike to lean right. I couldn't unclip my right foot in time, and the weight of my bike just pulled me over: a funny, slow-motion feeling of *I'm screwed* flashing through my head just before I bit gravel—right in front of a plate-glass window. At least I gave the dining crowd some dumb-ass entertainment. A small girl pointed at me and covered her mouth, laughing—*probably saying that every moron knows how to stay upright.* I saw her mom whisper in her ear—*only laugh when he isn't looking, I'd say. Never get caught in indecision!* I reprimanded myself It was the second time I'd tipped over this trip, giving me and my bike a few dings. *We're no worse for the wear, but how embarrassing!*

Inside the diner, a man approached me. "Was that you I saw on the ferry yesterday?"

"Ahar! Yep, I'm the one," I sassed.

"That must have been a trip riding off the ferry in the dark!"

"Yeah, pretty wild riding blind a couple of miles to a campsite."

"How far have you gone today?"

Gee, Woss is seventy-two miles from Port Hardy. He's at the Woss store, I'm at the Woss store. He started at Port Hardy, I started at Port Hardy. Uh, duh, the same distance you've gone? Having learned—too late in life—that nobody likes a smartass, I was straightforward. "I've got seventy-two miles under my belt thus far."

"Where ya headed?"

"Mexico."

"Well, you're pointed due south, it's downhill all the way from here!" he said with cheesy cleverness.

I knew that was coming—everyone says it in one form or another. So, my new game is, in what part of the conversation do they go cheeseball on me with the downhill to Mexico shtick?

Clamping down on my thoughts, I simply smiled and said, "I'll take it."

"Good luck. Rubber side down!"

As though I needed the reminder. Though I did just wipe in full glory in front of the picture window!

It would have been easy to stop for the night, but riding conditions were just too good. Ever since breakfast I'd felt unbelievably strong—and you never waste a tailwind! *When things are good, don't stop. When I'm flying like hell—ride like hell!*

Just outside of Woss, I hit that uphill for about fifteen miles. When I finally crested, I thought I was done with the tough part. *That wasn't bad! With the tailwind, I flew that thing!* It was followed by a five-mile downhill that I thought would take me all the way to Sayward Junction. Instead, I came upon a series of even tougher uphills. Mind you, I already had over ninety miles under my belt. *Ugh! False optimism on that first climb. Now I just want the day to be over.* But I kept on pluggin' and was eventually treated to a whopping 8 percent downhill grade for the last three miles, my tires singing on the pavement. It was about eight when I got off the bike in Sayward Junction. I didn't intend to ride 112 miles today—I just did.

It's far more civilized on Vancouver Island than where I'd been over the previous three weeks. *I miss the lack of traffic, the remoteness, and isolation of the far north, where I could ride for a long time without seeing anyone and was often totally alone when I camped.* The risks had also changed—now the biggest danger was traffic. In a strange way, I miss the risks associated with the wildness and solitude of the far north. *And bears. Weird. I miss the clownish bears.*

SAYWARD JUNCTION, BC
Miles today: 112

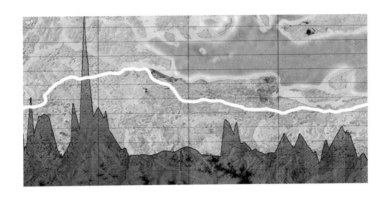

DAY 25
SATURDAY, JULY 14, 2012—SAYWARD JUNCTION
Miles to date: 1,722

With perfect weather once again—no clouds, ninety degrees, and a tailwind—I poured on the miles. *I'm glad I made those big climbs late yesterday—I don't have to start with them this morning and can hump big miles right out of the chutes!*

Big trucks roared past constantly. BC 19 is the island's one and only main trunk highway—and there isn't much of a shoulder. It didn't feel dangerous, but it wasn't as peaceful and fun as the empty roads of the far north. At breakfast I mentioned this to an older couple, who shared some intel. "At Campbell River, about forty-five miles south, climb off 19 and get on 19A: it's the old highway along the coast. You'll love it." I took their advice—and 19A was every bit of what I'd envisioned for the Vancouver Island portion of the journey: small towns right on the water. Plus, the road was flat.

In the early afternoon I came upon a woman sitting alone in a boat, as if it were peacefully floating in a bay and she had her fishing line in the water—except it wasn't on the bay, it was stranded on the shoulder of the road on a trailer with a blown tire. She was lounging in one of the seats. *This is hilarious! I just have to stop and see if I can help her.* I circled back and pulled up to the side of the boat.

"Anything biting?" I laughed.

She cracked up with a broad, toothy smile. "Nothin' biting, but a blown tire bites!"

Great line. We both cracked up. "I see that, and it's not just flat—it's shredded! Are you getting help?"

"Yeah, my boyfriend unhooked the trailer and took off to buy a new tire." *Distances are pretty big here.* "He'll be gone for a while."

"He vamoosed and left you to protect the boat?" *What? The boat is more important than the girl? Hmmm. I guess we all have our priorities.*"

She shrugged her shoulders as if to say, "We all make our choices—he just showed his true colors."

"Would you like some of my water and a granola bar?" I offered.

She smiled a crooked smile. "I'm fine," she assured me, as she lifted her hand above the gunwale to show me an open beer.

"I get the feeling that isn't your first." I was grinning.

"I don't really care when he gets back." She got the giggles. "I'm set."

"Okay. Be good." *Though I'm kind of disappointed you didn't offer me a beer too!*

Late in the day, I stopped to camp at an RV park smack on the water in Qualicum Bay. *Perfect! It has showers and Wi-Fi, and the Crown & Anchor roadhouse is immediately across the street. And, as a bonus, tonight is karaoke night at the Crown & Anchor!* The problem was that the RV park sign said *FULL.* I came to a small porch in front of the office where six elderly people were sitting in the shade and playing cards.

"Any of you run this joint?" I asked.

"Yeah," a man said, "I own the place."

"Well, then, I got the right guy, can you carve me a spot for the night?" I asked.

"Nope, we're full," he said.

"I'm not choosy," I assured him. "You could cram me in an out-of-the-way corner."

"We're jammed up." He stuffed me again. *Maybe I didn't have the right guy! How crazy is this? I thought owners like incremental revenue.*

Then a woman at the table, who I later realized was his wife, asked, "How far have you ridden today?"

"A hundred miles," I responded. "I came from Sayward Junction."

There was a collective gasp at the table, except from the stone-faced owner.

I pursued the deal for a third time, like an obnoxious salesman who through some two-bit sales training program had been brainwashed to believe that *No* is really a buying signal. *I can't understand why he doesn't like me. C'mon!*

"I just don't want to pedal farther if at all possible. All I need is a four-by-seven space." I worked for sympathy.

He took a deep breath and was about to unload on me when his wife thrust her palm into his face with a look that suggested, *Shut up, you crusty old bastard! I've been around your shit too long!* Let's just say that I wouldn't have wanted to be on the receiving end of that look.

"He just did a hundred miles!" She pasted him to his chair with an incredulously raised voice. "Of course he can stay. In fact, he can set up right in front of MY trailer!"

I'd run into she-bears on this trip, but she was the fiercest yet! Thank God she was on my side. *It's no surprise that they sleep in separate trailers.* I camped in front of hers.

So much for salesmanship—you just need a mama bear around.

I was settled for the night but not done! I cleaned up and headed for karaoke night across the road.

I walked into the joint as someone was butchering a song. *Wait! What's that song? The Lion King? Are you shitting me? Timing is everything!* Scrolling up the karaoke monitor at that very moment were the prescient words "It's enough for this wide-eyed wanderer, that we got this far . . . " *OMG, hilarious! The timing!*

When I step forward, it sure as hell ain't gonna be no Lion King! Maybe the Grizzly F'ing King!

QUALICUM BAY, VANCOUVER ISLAND, BC
Miles today: 100

Today was a tough day. Not the pedaling—the traffic.

It was overcast with low, craggy clouds and crappy weather the entire day. I was even hit by sprinkles a few times, but not enough to stop for rain gear.

The first twenty miles or so on 19A from the Qualicum Bay campsite to Parkville were spectacular. I could practically touch the water on my left, and with the tide out, there was that classic smell of sea air over the rotting tidal flats. It seemed as if every bird on Vancouver Island was working the tide pools, providing entertainment as I pedaled. But at Parkville, 19A merged back with Highway 19 and suddenly, traffic was horrendous. It was like biking on a major US metro highway, with all its chaos and commotion.

The farther south I traveled, the bigger the cities, so I started hitting lots of merging lanes, traffic lights, and side traffic. The road itself was good, with an adequate shoulder, but now I had no choice but to ride on the shoulder, which is where all the loose wires, nuts, bolts, 2x4s, and delaminated tire treads came to rest, not to mention the loose gravel spit from the highway. Needless to say, there's a far greater likelihood of getting a flat on the shoulder. The combination of traffic and noise meant I had to stay highly focused and couldn't enjoy the ride as I had in the remote areas up north. It was my least favorite day since I'd left Anchorage.

Late in the day I arrived in a little town called Mill Bay and took a twenty-minute ferry ride across the bay to a town called Brentwood. It chopped out about ten miles of Highway 19 and put me on lonely and winding country roads—an immediate respite from the commotion. *And I'm only eight miles out of Victoria!* From Brentwood to Victoria was steep rolling countryside that reminded me of England.

By then I was starving, so I stopped at a roadside natural foods market that catered to the granola and bark eaters—and, thankfully, also had a deli. I had them whip up a stacked roast beef sandwich with mayo and cheese, along with BBQ chips, a pie-sized chocolate-chip cookie, and a pint of chocolate milk. *So much for Euell Gibbons!*

By the time I finished, it was getting late. *But Victoria is just a scant few miles away. I might as well get into Victoria proper, but I need to beat the oncoming darkness.* It's a good thing I had a GPS snapped to my handlebars. It gave me turn-by-turn road directions and kept me on track through a maze of intersections and potential wrong turns as I approached Victoria's city center. It was misting as I pulled into a hotel about a mile from Victoria's inner harbor area at late dusk. I had been damp and cold all day, but I'd be warm and dry at last.

How about that! There's a Denny's right next to the hotel—time to knock out a Grand Slam! Having just completed over three hundred miles in three days, I practically fell asleep in my pancakes-and-eggs dinner. I knew I needed rest, so I was ready to dial back a bit, at least for a couple of days, and let my body catch up. *Despite the grind, though, I still feel so good. God, this is fun!*

In a response to my nightly blog, though, one of my brothers, Steve, accused me of singing the Captain and Tennille's "Muskrat Love" at karaoke last night. *I'll torture him—he'll never know.*

VICTORIA, BC
Miles today: 94

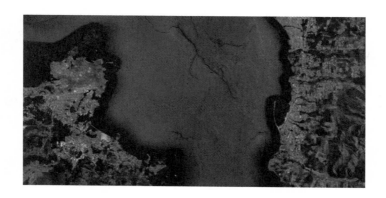

DAY 27
MONDAY, JULY 16, 2012—VICTORIA, BC
Miles to date: 1,916

I planned to spend my rest day just hanging out in Victoria and watching harbor life. Victoria is a charmer of a city. But first I needed to do my laundry. I asked the hotel receptionist, a beautiful young Hispanic woman, about their laundry facilities, and she told me there was a laundry deep in the basement. So I threw an overstuffed load into the hotel's washing machine and then headed back to Denny's for breakfast. *You can't screw up eggs.* When I returned to the hotel, the load had not only been washed, but also dried and folded. In my absence, the receptionist had slipped downstairs and completed the job.

"Thank you so much, you're too kind! What brought you here to Victoria?" I asked. "Well, I married a Middle Eastern man who I met

178

in Mexico, and his work transferred us to Victoria. But now we've recently divorced, and I have a young son. I plan on staying here."

"Well, I'm sorry about your troubles."

"No, it's better now. After we married, he changed, and started treating me like dirt. It's better away from him."

I wheeled my bike out of the lobby, and with my parting words I bade her farewell, "You're very sweet and beautiful—you'll be a real catch for some lucky soul. Carry on."

I rode the mile from my hotel to Victoria's inner harbor, where I came upon a disheveled man riding in front of me on an old bike. He looked like he'd given up too early on life. I'd just caught up with him and was immediately behind him at a major intersection in central Victoria when he suddenly took off to make a yellow light. I wanted to make that light too, so I hit the throttle and followed. But, just as suddenly, he changed his mind and stopped dead. It was a feint! I slammed on my brakes so I wouldn't ram him. My bike screeched to a halt, but I was clipped in and couldn't unclip in time. So I tipped over, again, right in the middle of the intersection—stopping traffic dead. Every car and pedestrian in the entire intersection was frozen in place—just looking at me lying sideways in the street like a warm steaming pile—still clipped in. *Utterly humiliating!*

The man's head slowly swiveled, and he looked back at me. His glasses wrapped wide around his face, and the thick Coke-bottle lenses magnified and distorted his eyes, like an ancient Egyptian painting. In a flash and brash reaction I barked, "Hey, moron—when you go, you go!" I lashed out when I should have empathized with his overall condition. *He's the one who needs help, not me.* I caught myself. *How juvenile—not my best showing.* In momentary introspection—*my words don't mean jack to him, and in any case it doesn't change him or the situation.* But in my humiliation, I was looking for cover— looking to blame when it was totally my fault for tailgating. *Who's the real moron here? I know better than to follow, and I didn't act on it—look where that got me!*

When my GPS said I had arrived at the inner harbor, I didn't see any water. While I examined it to figure out what I was missing, a young woman stepped forward and asked, "Can I help you find something?"

"I'm looking for the inner harbor, and my GPS says I'm here."

"You *are* here, it's right on the other side of this line of buildings," she assured me, pointing. *Back to normalcy from the tip-over incident—another simple act of helpfulness by a complete stranger.*

In addition to all kinds of boat traffic, Victoria's inner harbor was also the runway for seaplanes, and I spent much of the day watching them take off and land. I was content just vegging, eating, and watching harbor life. Then, late in the afternoon, I jumped the ferry across the Strait of Juan de Fuca from Victoria to Port Angeles, Washington.

From the open deck, the Olympic Mountains in Washington State were bright and clear against the blue sky, while to the east, Mount Baker shimmered in and out of the haze. The first time I spotted it, I had to look again, squinting as I looked into the distance. It initially looked like an afternoon cloud formation, but on closer observation, I knew it had to be Baker. I climbed that big beast with one of my best friends using professional guides about thirty years earlier. The entire mountain was glaciated, so we needed to be roped and have full climbing gear, including crampons and rescue devices. Climbing that mountain provided a near-mystical experience: spectacular, surreal views of nearby peaks thrusting above the cloud deck. During the climb and near the top, we also passed an active volcanic vent that had made a permanent melt hole in the plunging glacier. *Don't misstep here, or you'll turn into a hard-boiled egg!*

I didn't know jack about or have any appreciation for mountain climbing until that great experience—and compared to the monstrous mountains of the world, it was only an appetizer. So I also climbed Mount Rainier in June 1998. These were real, yet achievable mountains where a novice can reach the summit in a long weekend—and like most working people, I couldn't take off and do a long expedition at that point in my life. While I couldn't see Rainier from the ferry, I swear I could feel its gravitational pull—it's just that kind of mountain—singular and majestic.

Climbing Rainier was another systemic risk of the type we all take when we engage in outdoor adventures. You are simply at the mercy of the mountain. The day before I climbed Rainier, a young man had died in an avalanche on the exact same route I'd be taking the next day. It could just as easily have been my group the following day. Rainier is a dangerous mountain to be sure—especially for novices like me—but with professional guides and being in decent shape, the statistical odds had been in my favor.

And so it had been on this bike journey. Its systemic risks included animals, frontier bandits, unanticipated crashes alone in utter wilderness, traffic accidents, and illness or injury. Plus, I was flying solo, with no wingman to cover my back. But without any form of actuarial risk analysis, I felt the odds were extremely favorable—*I don't know, maybe about 1 or 2 percent chance of having a disaster?* Stated inversely, my mindset was for a 98 to 99 percent chance of success—*I'll take that bet!* Sure, I could have avoided all the risk by choosing not to go. *But if you're afraid to risk, you're afraid to live. I don't want to just be respirating—I want a rush! To be alive and living!* Rainier and Baker were visual reminders of this powerful desire—the essence of this journey.

Each in their own way, my experiences with mountain climbing and many other weekend-warrior activities set up my chances of success on this bike journey. It wasn't so much that they prepared me specifically for this journey's challenges as that they set up an attitude. *I just think I can do it. Like Santana, "Everything's Coming Our Way," baby! I've pushed through tough moments before. I just have to accept an elevated risk—try to be at my best—and I think I see clear blue sky beyond.* The rewards can be great, even for just a weekend challenge—and, you never ever know where they might lead. *But mostly they're exciting.*

As I watched the scenery slide by, a couple from Colorado traveling by motorcycle approached me. "We saw you on the ferry down the Inside Passage a few days ago," they opened.

"That was a hell of a day," I responded.

"What did you do when you got off the ferry in the dark?"

I gave them the play-by-play, from nearly crashing to groping my way to my campsite to dealing with my suspicious campmate.

"My wife and I wanted to talk to you on that ferry," the guy admitted. "We wanted to know your story, how you came to be traveling alone on a bicycle, gray hair and all. But then, we didn't want to invade your space."

"Salt and pepper silver, not gray—right?" We all laughed as I raked my hand through my hair.

"Well, seeing you here—this time, we just had to come over."

"I get this quite a bit—a loaded bicycle is a pretty good conversation starter."

They peppered me with more questions. I gave them the lowdown on my journey thus far. We talked about related subjects— mostly my mindset, decisions faced, worries, vulnerabilities, what I was thinking—everything. By now a small crowd had gathered to listen, and they blurted out questions like a mini press conference.

"Are you getting tired of the ride at all yet?'

"Not in the least. I've certainly felt physically tired at times, but not tired of the ride at all! In a funny way, all the grueling mountains and effort out here just doesn't feel like work to me. It's too fascinating navigating all the variables and surviving day to day."

"Man! You have some stories. Are you recording this trip? Are you going to write a book? We'll buy it!"

"Hell no! I'm not a writer, I've never written jack! I don't have that skill. I know sometimes people embark on a journey with the intent to gather content for a book or article, but that's not why I took off—that's not my intent in the least. Funny, though, my kids insisted that I write a blog every night—that's hard enough. I didn't really want to do it. I mean, after doing a hundred miles each day, exhausted and lying in a tent, I have to try to crank out a blog? Ugh. C'mon!" *Whoa, I just blurted an unintentional whine—whimper, whimper, where's my binky? I hate sounding that way. How unmanly, how pathetic. Real men don't whine.*

"Yeah, I suppose that's the last thing you want to do!"

"But it has taught me something about journalism. As I

thought about it, I can't just write the same thing every day. You know, 'I got up, rode my ass off, got tired, and went to bed.' So, it's just a simple daily blog, but it's forcing me to be even more observant than I ordinarily would be each day. I have to think, what stood out to me today, why did that stand out, why should anyone care about it, how do I tell that story, can I make it come alive—would an audience find it interesting? Journalism is hard for me. So as I pedal, I'm constantly mindful about what I'm going to say tonight that's different than what I've said the other nights. I've never thought that way before." Momentarily silent in the middle of the Strait of Juan de Fuca, we all looked out at the snowcapped Olympic Mountains in their full glory on the far shores of the mighty USA. I looked at the motorcycle couple and asked, "What have you seen and done that stands out to you?"

"Well, we don't quite have the stories you do, but if you ever get the chance, go to Tofino on the west coast of Vancouver Island by motorcycle. It's the most incredible drive we've ever done—and the most pristine sugar sand beach we've ever seen!"

A woman in her late forties, who had drifted into the crowd with her mother jumped in to say, "I just love these kinds of stories."

"For me, in addition to discovery, it's a form of therapy. I can't really explain it, but it's where I go aloof, where I'm weightless. Sure, it borders on escapism, but it's also when my mind is set free—without the friction of everyday obligations—random ideas just pop into my head. I think they call it a walkabout in Australia. But it's where I go rogue and feel a frontier romanticism."

"That sounds pretty healthy," the woman said with a slight look of wistfulness.

"Yeah, I think so—at least it is for me! I think everybody has their spots, whether it's travel, their garden, their sports court of choice—there's many places. Where are you set free?"

"Well, I live in Missoula—we have a number of great places to hike. But I hike mostly in town. I like to know exactly where I am and what I'm doing. I guess I'm not all that adventurous." *Hmmm, there's a hint of subdued resignation in her voice.*

"Well, you just came out of Victoria with your mom—that's time you'll always treasure and a pretty cool adventure in its own right." *God, what a lame attempt at encouragement.*

"Yeah, but I'm talking about never having done something bold, like what you're doing. I'm fascinated with what it would take, what I would do—what I *could* do."

"Well, just know you can do so much more than you think: that's a baseline attitude. Pick something that intrigues you and then inject it with a powerful can-do steroid where it becomes a stretch. It's a pretty simple formula, really."

"Well, I think I'd be scared to do something like you're doing."

"I wouldn't advocate a solo woman doing what I'm doing. It's not that you couldn't do it physically or mentally—but safety is more of an issue for solo women in the remote areas. I don't advocate danger for danger's sake alone. I just advocate trying new things, but using good judgment and being mindful of when you need support or expertise. For instance, see Mount Baker over there, shimmering in the distance? When I climbed that beast thirty-some years ago, prudence dictated that I use a professional guide—same with when I climbed Rainier, just over the horizon. Conditions can change rapidly on those mountains and become extremely dangerous— beyond mere discomfort—in those cases conditions could instantly place me well beyond my element or my skills to recover. In those cases, I'd need much more training and experience to be self-reliant. So I needed expertise to increase my chances to survive in the event of a mishap. The risks were too great to do solo at my experience level! But I at least wanted the experience and tempered the risk by hiring expertise to supplement my skills."

"I get that—but you didn't hire an expert or even have a buddy along on this journey?"

"It's just a bike ride—you can't confuse the distance of this ride with the magnitude of risk and skills required. Sure there are bears and moose, scant supply posts, and the chance of injury in the remotes, but to me, the risks are worth taking alone. And people often let their fears run wild and loom much larger than warranted. Of course it would be safer to be with a buddy or a group, but I chose not to do that because then I'd lose what I feel is the even greater experience of having to manage strange situations alone. Besides, I just plain think I can pull it off. So far so good, but things may change soon because now I'll be entering prime habitat for—Sasquatch!"

"You're totally downplaying it all—I love that!"

"Well, sometimes obliviousness works to my advantage." We laughed. "In some ways it's a crapshoot for all of us. There's no doubt that I've had some blind luck along the way. Random events could take any of us down, but most of them aren't restricted to remote areas: they exist right on the main street of Missoula or in your home. For me, it's healthiest to just follow my wanderlust, cast my fate to the wind, do the best I can, and try to create new and brighter futures. Although I've been very fortunate, I have this sixth sense that my best days are still ahead of me. Do you ever feel a bigger wanderlust? An urge to drift to wilder spaces or to make a different future?"

"Well I mentioned that I like to hike—but I mostly stay in the populated areas. I'd like to hike the backcountry more, but there's grizzlies out there around Missoula—they scare the crap out of me! I don't like the uncertainties and unknowns. But sometimes I feel like I hold myself back—so I don't have what I'd call big achievements. If I could rewind the clock . . ." She trailed off, forlorn—but there was an unspoken understanding.

I tried to rescue the levity. "Well, truth be told, I haven't exactly set the world on fire either. But listen to the refrain in that Brooks & Dunn song, "Red Dirt Road," speaking to the notion that happiness ain't relegated to high achievers—that resonates with me. Sometimes I lean on a simple song that says so much in so little. Go YouTube the song and lock in the refrain."

"Huh, I'll do that." She brightened.

"Sometimes I need a little beacon of philosophy that points me in the right direction, or occasionally lets me off the hook of failure—often my own self-inflicted hang-up." I tried to keep the moment light. "Yeah, more sophisticated people like to quote deep thinkers. What did Shakespeare say? 'To thine own self be f'ing true, baby!'" The small crowd was giggling—mostly at my cavalier ordinariness. "But, I'm kind of a hillbilly: I catch my philosophy in country western verses."

"I'm still fascinated with what you're doing. It's pretty remarkable."

"Well, I knew I needed change. There's a lot of living left to do, and you're never frozen—there's always a new beginning and a bright future. The trick is following your own path and not letting others dissuade you. "Contrary to Ordinary," by Jerry Jeff Walker, is my personal anthem and has carried me for years. YouTube it!"

The captain of the ferry announced, "Prepare for docking."

"Sorry, I've droned on and bent your ears!" I said. *Whoa! Who put the nickel in you, Tonto?*

"No. No. No. Oh my God," the woman said. She paused in contemplation. "I'm just fascinated with your story. I've been looking for a push to get out and do more. You've inspired me to think—to think bigger—to stretch."

"Well, freeze your fears. Trust yourself. Just simply pick a direction and go—don't worry about reasons, goals, or justifications. For me, wanderlust has always been reason enough—just letting it take me where it will. This bike trip is a grand experiment in curiosity and discovery—I suppose you could call it personal R&D, with a twist of fun. Where it leads? I don't know yet—we'll see how it all goes. In any case, out here I just feel vividly alive—it's very liberating and educational. That's enough for now."

We all jerked and caught ourselves on the railing as the ferry careened into its bundled-log catch. "Shit, the riskiest thing on my journey has been riding with this captain!" I exclaimed as we regathered our balance. "I'm sorry about the extended spew of Tonka Bay philosophy. It's an hour none of you will ever get back!"

"Hahahaha! I for one have enjoyed the stories," the Montana woman said. "I love your spirit and sense of adventure—I'm inspired."

"Well, I'm glad. I normally bore the shit out of everybody and can ruin a good dinner party faster than anyone. I hope you find your stretch. Don't overthink it. It won't be easy-easy—but it's probably easier than you think. Nice talking to you."

"Be good. Safe travels." *Landfall America!* After weeks in the wilds of Canada, I was back in the good ol' USA. *In a strange way, even though the Canadians were nothing but great, it feels good to be home.*

PORT ANGELES, WASHINGTON—AMERICA AGAIN!
Miles today: 0
(Not including about 1 unlogged mile to the ferry)

PART 3

BACK IN THE US OF A

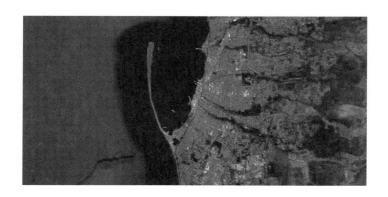

DAY 28
TUESDAY, JULY 17, 2012—PORT ANGELES, WA
Miles to date: 1,916

I took it easy in Port Angeles and allowed myself to linger at breakfast. I hit a bike shop and bought a new bike computer, cleaned and re-oiled my chain, and re-pumped my tires—piddly routine stuff. *I still hate maintenance.* But mostly, I wandered Port Angeles in slow motion—napped, wandered, and napped again.

Until now, I hadn't thought about my route to the coast. I just knew I'd generally take Highway 1/101 to Mexico. Now I had to figure out the specifics to get to 1/101. I bought a map of Washington and charted my course.

Roughing it out using the map scale, I'll be out of Washington in three days if I do about eighty miles each day—easily doable—unless, that is, if Bigfoot intervenes. That's a big *if! I'll ride smack through*

Olympic National Park, the land of Bigfoot—ground zero—on my way to the Washington coast. You never know. I'm easily entertained!

After a couple of days off, I'm looking forward to hitting the road again.

PORT ANGELES, WA
Miles today: 0—Rest Day

The view out my jetliner's window. *I have to pedal through this? What the hell did I sign up for?*

My old life . . .

. . . my new life and all my worldly possessions for the next fifty-one days.

Total time in the saddle today: 13 hrs, 18 mins, 35 secs; Miles: 155.35.
Your body can take more than your mind!

In Alaska, every distance to the next town is huge,
and every sign has bullet holes.

Fine dining. *Rock for one, please.*

Note to self—don't drink the bear spray.

Fresh cougar prints. *Here, kitty kitty . . .*

My own *Planet Earth* episode— bigger than any IMAX screen!

Central Oregon coast. If only it was all downhill from here. No such luck!

My brother Steve and me the night before I tagged the Mexican border.
Turns out I celebrated a little too soon. . . .

Torched! Of course the only time I ended up biting it
was on the very last day of my ride.

Tag! You're it! US border patrol at the Mexican border.

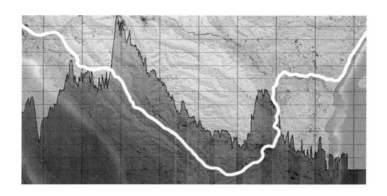

DAY 29
WEDNESDAY, JULY 18, 2012—PORT ANGELES, WA
Miles to date: 1,916

I left Port Angeles this morning and headed due west toward the coast, then followed the highway as it took a ninety-degree turn south late in the day to parallel the ocean. The ride started with an uphill into a misting rain with the temperature about fifty degrees. It didn't take long to break a sweat, however, and the battle between the outside damp and the inside damp soon began. Damp and chilled, I also fought a modest headwind all day.

Rolling hills continued for most of the day, but the rain stopped after forty-five minutes and the road dried. *How lucky am I to ride through the heart of the Washington rain forest without more rain?* In some places the canopy was so thick that sunlight couldn't reach the forest floor, so despite the sun, at ground level I rode in a murky darkness. Some of the cedars were incredibly tall—not giant redwood tall, but through the thick mossy branches, I couldn't always see their crowns. Naturally, I kept my eyes peeled for Bigfoot. I didn't pass a general store today that wasn't selling posters with his picture. *So, I'll recognize him when I see him!*

I was winging it again—not sure where I'd end the day. By midday I decided to shoot for the Kalaloch Campsite, about eighty miles from Port Angeles, so I set my pace based on that. At 6:00 p.m. I was only about ten miles or approximately forty-five minutes away from Kalaloch.

What I didn't figure in was that at the height of summer vacation season, the campground would be jammed full. *Foiled again! Sometimes I pay the price for not doing advance research.* Olympic National Park had signs posted everywhere that no camping was permitted outside of the designated campgrounds, a change from the far north, where I'd just plop down when and where I wanted. So by 6:45 p.m., I had no place to bed down and no clue where the next open campground might be. I felt the time pressure—my GPS indicated sunset a touch after nine o'clock—but I was also hungry. *Sure, I have trail mix and Slim Jims in my bag, but who wants that junk for dinner?*

Fortunately, next to the campground stood the Kalaloch Lodge, where I checked for room availability—and the young summer intern told me it was fully booked. But the lodge was also home to one of those iconic National Park lodge dining rooms. Naturally, I did what every red-blooded American male would do: I ordered a beer—*to help me sort things out!* I also told them to fire up a burger. While I waited for my food, a different guy from the lodge reservation desk sought me out and said, "The Kalaloch campground is always full, because it's one of the few campsites where you can make reservations online through the National Park Service. It's such a popular campground that it was already fully booked six months ago in advance of the summer and peak vacation time. But, only three or so miles farther south there is a primitive campground called South Beach. It's first come, first served. I don't know availability, so you ought to get there as quickly as you can." *This guy went out of his way to find me. The intern must have told him I stopped up front to inquire on a room. Get moving while there might still be space!*

"I'm so appreciative of that info—thanks for seeking me out! I had no idea the South Beach Campground even existed. Thanks so much!" That was enough impetus for me to inhale my burger, chug my beer, and take off downstream. Lucky for me, there were still a few campsites open when I arrived, and I picked a nice one, practically in the ocean itself.

The sun was rapidly diving to the horizon, but it was taking me way too much time to set camp because everyone who walked by wanted to talk. There was something about being the guy on the bike setting up his tent: *Everybody thinks of the exposure, and it fascinates them. Sure, I suppose I'm vulnerable, but I generally don't feel it except for a few select moments. So it's no big deal. But I do appreciate that everyone wants to find a way to aid my success in some small way.*

Another man wandered over to my campsite. "I just had to come over and see what you're doing."

"Well, I'm on a little journey." I went on to give the basics.

He related, "I did a distance ride in the mid-nineties. At the time I didn't have any distance cycling experience either. I just plain took off with a buddy, but we only rode a few hundred miles in Montana. What surprised me most was, whoa, the headwinds."

"Yeah, they put you through the shredder for sure."

"I also remember the sweaty uphills and freezing on the downhills."

"Yea, H-squared, baby—hills and headwinds—brutal! And wet all day!"

"Well, how are you handling it all, are you getting along okay?"

"I suppose I'm doing as best as could be expected."

"Any surprises?"

"Several. It may seem obvious, but I'm constantly reminded that out here I can't change the conditions or terrain, so I have to accept and change for the conditions—or else I'll damn well fail for sure. I didn't know how I'd react to days on end of hardship; that's part of learning of what you're made of, I guess. But I'm lucky in that I've been able to maintain a healthy mindset and good attitude. I know it sounds like psychobabble, but what's most helpful is that I've learned to stay focused on the bigger picture—just how fortunate I am to even be out here and able to attempt this ride. And although I have no idea of what lies ahead, I'm pretty sure I've been through the toughest parts—at least physically. Barring grave misfortune, I'm more confident than ever that I'll actually knock this son of a bitch out! That's a change—I didn't know what to expect a month ago." *Get in his world!* "What did you see or discover?"

"Well, like you, I also went on a whim—somewhat unprepared. But at the same time, I just went without any research or planning. I just got out there. Maybe I could have trained a little better. But just going worked pretty well."

"Yeah, the clichés are so corny, but what do they say—just get in the game?" I laughed. "I especially hate fake business sloganeering."

"I totally know what you mean—how does that shit sell?" he blurted.

"I know! I'm totally confused how people eat that crap up; most people I know just roll their eyes. So cornball!"

"Anyway—" His face momentarily faded to a distant look of whimsy and youth. "I felt a sense of accomplishment after each day."

"What do you think you've learned from your ride?" I pressed.

"I never really analyzed it—never sat back and put it all together—but I do know that I wouldn't trade it for the world. I suppose it has to do with confidence and can-do. I guess, I'm more willing to volunteer or just jump into new things."

"What's cool is all those things lead somewhere, though you may not be able to see it upfront."

The waves crashed hard on the shore like the slow drumbeat of a funeral dirge, wafting the cold after-mist over us. My body had cooled down from the ride, and I felt chilled.

"I see you're wearing a Fridley Police hat—that must be Fridley, Minnesota?" I questioned.

"Yeah, I live in Fridley but I grew up in Hopkins."

"Hell, I'm your next-door neighbor: I grew up and live in Minnetonka."

"I still spend tons of time in Hopkins—I coach girls hockey there."

"That's great! Communities need good volunteers like you. I coached youth hockey in Minnetonka a few years back." And then, as if it was an autonomic response, I blurted, "How about the parents!"

"Unbelievable!" he exclaimed. "Some are a complete *Gong Show*." His eyes widened. "If you can manage the parents, you can manage anything!"

"No shortage of unsolicited advice! Some provided great comic relief—they just didn't know it. Every community has them—same circus, different clowns," I chimed in. "But most of the parents were fabulous—and it's a great skill if you can master keeping the wild ones in the bottle."

"Yeah, the kids are the easy part!" Of course we were howling in our mind meld.

"And the kids weren't stupid: they saw it all. It made for great conversations in the car on the way home from practices and games—and even greater lessons beyond the hockey itself. I have a story related to that if you have another moment."

"Shoot!"

"Well, as you know, hockey being as huge as it is in Minnesota, any group of people includes some with kids in youth hockey. I was standing around in a group of four investment bankers, and three of the four had kids in youth hockey. The one who didn't proceeded to say, 'I hear that youth hockey is so nasty—a huge time commitment and full of politics, backbiting, and some ugly backroom conniving!' He obviously didn't want his kids in hockey because *he* didn't want the commitment and was justifying it to himself.

"'Yeah, it's all of those,' I calmly replied to him.

"'Well, I don't get it, what do the kids get out of that! What can they learn in *that* environment?' he said with a bite.

"'Well, you know what they really learn?' I replied.

"'No, enlighten me,' he retorted.

"'They learn how to be a good investment banker!' The other three guys dropped to their knees howling."

"Yeah, in coaching the girls—between the sport itself and the politics, I've learned most of life's lessons, it's all there when you manage a Minnesota youth hockey team." We were both dying.

We even knew several of the same people. *Here in an unimproved campsite in a rural corner of Washington, I meet a guy who is practically my neighbor. Six degrees of separation—Kevin Bacon phenomenon. Small world.*

I'd lost twenty minutes of campsite setup time, and by now the sun was a big fuzzy silver globe half hidden by the steely gray cloud deck at sea level. "I'd better get moving on my tent!" I finally exclaimed.

"Yeah-yeah, go. Nice meeting ya! Good luck the rest of the way."

But just then, a second couple wandered over and wanted to talk about my travels. When I explained the route, the woman said, "We're from BC, we know your route—we knew *all* the BC roads."

The man added, "We're retired and love Nordic skiing. Our goal is to ski in all ten Worldloppet Nordic ski events. We've done most of them but haven't done the American Birkebeiner in Wisconsin—that's on our agenda for this coming year."

"You'll love the Birkie—I've done fifteen. It's a beautiful but tough hilly course through untouched woods in Northern Wisconsin. It's like skiing through a Christmas card: big, snow-laden pines in a virgin blanket of deep snow. The clods of snow fall off the branches in the breeze and explode into galaxies of air-burst sparkles. The race is so exhausting that I try to distract myself in any way possible. Late in the race, maybe thirty miles in, you'll hit Bitch Hill—you'll know it when you see it—it's perfectly labeled! Just when you don't want a sniff of another hill, this bitch of a hill appears. And every year, at the very top, there are three women dressed in old, tattered, matronly dresses—each wearing a pig mask. They scowl, scold, whine, and bitch at the skiers as they crest. Total hoot! Good luck in that race.

But if you don't mind, I really have to get my tent set." They saluted a friendly good-bye.

But it didn't stop there: yet another couple stopped, this one from Seattle. "Was that you we saw earlier this afternoon buying binoculars in the hardware store?"

"Yeah, I broke my binocs in Prince Rupert and needed a new pair."

"We're surprised to see you here. The hardware store was what—about fifty miles ago?"

"That would be about right. I was there at around two, and I've done close to a hundred miles today, so, roughing it out, that would be about the right distance."

"We thought *we* were adventurous, traveling by motorcycle, and then we saw you!"

"Yeah, but traveling by Harley is a great adventure. It's a fabulous way to not only see the country, but also feel the country. On two wheels, you always go beyond simply the physical sights—unprotected for sure, but also unrestricted by the comfort of a car—you actually feel the heartbeat and soul of the country. You get to greater depths of feeling and wonder."

"Wow! We normally have to try to explain that to others."

"I have a Harley too—I love my trips across the continent. You either have that gene to ride or you don't." I paused and contemplated how much to reveal about my past motorcycle trips. *Try not to dominate the conversation and bore the shit out of them—hard for me.* Electing to shorten the conversation, I continued. "The two-wheel gene just plain makes you appreciate everything more. It's funny, it's similar to coming off a great day of downhill skiing—a great day on two wheels just breeds greater goodwill toward your fellow man—you just don't see many pissed-off riders."

"And it's so cross-cultural and cross-generational. Nobody cares about your background, you meet such interesting people from varied places and perspectives, with great stories. We love connecting with everybody in the parking lot of some no-name motel, or a sunny deck of a dive saloon—all smiles and recounting the day to each other. Just like we're doing here! There's no class distinction, no victims, no divisiveness—you all have a commonality in your shared experience. I've found that riders have such a sunny disposition about what the next day will bring."

"The reality of it all is so different than the public's image of motorcycles forged by outlaw biker gangs. Once you travel on two wheels, you're never the same—and you don't want to travel any other way. And it's so simple, anybody can do it, but many just don't know they can. Yeah, two wheels, rubber side down—I got that gene for sure! I lose myself in the love of it all."

"Well, we're doing just what you describe! We do it every year, it draws the two of us closer as well."

"I couldn't be happier for you. I'm glad you're traveling in an adventurous way—those trips are so much more memorable. How far have you come today?"

"We don't kill ourselves; we like to do about two hundred and fifty miles per day. We stop a lot." They sounded sheepish, as though they felt guilty about their low mileage relative to what they could do.

"Well, daily distance doesn't really matter when you're in great places. It's more about the feeling. Any time you have your head in the wind, you're doing something right! I equate it to a cabin—a cabin on wheels! Enjoy it!"

The sun was down and the sea merged with the sky—I could no longer see the delineation between them. "Be safe on that beast!" I added before I turned and went about unrolling my tent, trying to pay attention to them but working in the twilight.

They took the cue and walked on. "Safe travels—we love your spirit."

I attract kindred souls—people who are in the midst of their own journey—and they love to share. We all wish everyone could feel what we're feeling. And in hearing my journey, they found a kindred soul—which formed a natural connection. These are happy people— living people.

Alone again, I drifted into a dreamy recollection of my Harley trips as I continued my camp setup. *The two-wheel gene. I wish everyone could chase trains on the Great Plains, snake through the Badlands,* or flow past Devils Tower at moonrise—so perfectly eerie!—see the weirdness of Area 51 and the Extraterrestrial Highway, or Highway 50, the Loneliest Road in America crossing Nevada. The majesty of the Tetons scraping the sky or geysers spitting at you in Yellowstone, the silhouette of an eagle against the backdrop of Yosemite's Half Dome, Lake Placid at sunrise, and the Grand Canyon at sunset. Going-to-the-Sun Road in Glacier and on up the spine of the Rockies into Canada's grandeur— to Waterton Lakes, Banff, Lake Louise, and Jasper, where I've been horsewhipped by the elements only to be rewarded with a chilled frosty and Canadian hospitality at the De'd Dog. I'm doing the same thing now, albeit much slower under hillbilly power. Sheesh! Listen to me—I just get dreamy and lose myself thinking about this stuff! "Unknown Legend," Neil Young, baby!

When I'd bought those binocs earlier in the day, I overspent on a fabulous new pair. When I finally completed setting my camp, I took a few minutes with them looking out to sea. They're so much better than the old pair—such clarity! In the late twilight, I saw hundreds of birds skimming the wavetops and occasionally dipping their beaks into the water just in front of a curl at the surf line. A pair of porpoises swam by in the opposite direction, their backs humping in and out of the water as they cruised the wavefront. Man, how cool! I couldn't have begun to see any of this with my naked eye. What else has been right in front of my eyes that I've missed? It's like my entire journey thus far: this trip is its own lens, with its own magnification and light-gathering power—I'm seeing and feeling things I'd never see with the naked eye. A great buy—both the binocs and, more so, this journey.

This campground was primitive—no running water, not even a stream in which to bathe. God, I'm grimy. I'm glad I'd anticipated a night like this and bought Wet Wipes for just this type of occurrence. I'm feeling kind of—brilliant! I'd been carrying them since Anchorage, but tonight was my first luxurious Wet Wipes bath. Yuck! Wet Wipes leave a thin film of dried soap on my skin. Now I'm gummy instead of grimy. So I'm not all that brilliant! I sacrificed one of my three water bottles to soak a small sponge for a rinse. Probably TMI, but I just can't climb into a sleeping bag all sticky.

There were tsunami warning signs everywhere here. If I heard the alarm, I was supposed to get to high ground immediately. Systemic risk, we all live with it one way or another—so just live. *I'm banking on there not being an earthquake tonight. If there is, I guess my tent will need to turn into a lifeboat.*

Past dark, I crawled into my tent, exhausted, but still had to write my blog. *I don't feel like writing, but I have to. I can't fall behind: people are following me and expecting updates. I have to write while it's all still fresh. And if I fall behind, I can't catch up. Ugh.* But as consolation, I was lying about a hundred feet from the Pacific Ocean, the roar of the crashing waves a spectacular soundtrack as I wrote. *Why do I love the white noise of the ocean and hate the white noise of a highway? Oh yeah! I also passed the two-thousand-mile mark today—another milestone. Still strong!*

I eventually drifted off to the pounding of the surf just outside my door. Crash after crash—*I can't get enough of that sound.*

SOUTH BEACH CAMPGROUND,
OLYMPIC NATIONAL PARK, WA
Miles today: 96

DAY 30
THURSDAY, JULY 19, 2012—SOUTH BEACH
CAMPGROUND, WA
Miles to date: 2,012

Today was totally different from yesterday—beautiful, sunny, and warm. And, as the day warmed further, I peeled off layer after layer. The riding was generally moderate rolling hills, and I made good time.

Highway 101 made a wide loop around western Washington, largely inland, except when I finally kissed the beach to camp last night. From there the highway immediately turned back inland for another day in the rainforest. I was hoping for a day of riding right on the beachfront—no luck, and I was beholden to the road.

It's not news to anyone, but the western Washington economy is dominated by logging, and those trucks just barrel down 101. In some places there was a good shoulder, but in many others there was no shoulder at all. *Thank God I'm not a nervous rider, but I do have to be on my toes here.*

Now that I'm back in the populated world, I don't have to think ahead about natural stopping points. The distances between food sources are much shorter. I can afford to be sloppier in my decisions, or better yet, not think ahead at all.

Over the last ten days or so I had typically made seventy-five to eighty miles by about 4:00 p.m. *But it's too early to stop—I may be tired, but I can always crank out another twenty miles. Why stop and sit four to five hours when I can still pedal? That's why I'm racking up the miles: because I can.*

Sometimes, though, I thought that a town twenty or thirty miles down the road sounded like more fun. I'd proceed, only to come upon a bunch of major hills that I didn't know about in that last stretch of the day. Uncanny! This happened over and over, and over again.

And so it happened again today—at four o'clock, eighty miles in, *I got twenty more in me. For chrissakes, where did this hill come from! It's a killer, and I'm dying because I lost my low gear again today.* With only intermediate gears on these hills, it not only consumed a lot more energy but also scalded my legs. *Tackle this bitch and I'll be sledding downhill to a great place at sea level.* I finally reached the crest. *Good! I'm done climbing for the day.* I flew the downhill and thought, *Thank God! Now I can just cruise the flats! Wait! What? You've got to be kidding me! Another climb? Even bigger than the first?*

After that climb, down again I went, only to come up on climb number three, even bigger than the first two. *Jesus!* Worse still, this particular downhill had a whopping headwind that practically stopped me in my tracks. With no reprieve, I had to pedal that downhill. *It's as though someone is pulling a bad prank on me. What again!?! Hill number four? Okay, am I on* Candid Camera? *Is someone filming my reaction? The gods are screwing with me! Is there no end to these mothers?* I was tired back at eighty miles: if I'd known beforehand that I'd hit this series of hills, I'd have stopped. But, ignorance has its advantages—by the time I realized what was happening, I was way too far into the grind not to see it through. *At least I won't have to start with these climbs tomorrow, and I'm that much farther along as a result.* With the benefit of the final downhill, I finally arrived in Raymond, Washington. *Finally! The flats.*

I'd noticed a lot of *Landslide Area* signs as I thrashed through those big hills approaching Raymond. *I'm a prisoner of plate tectonics! My entire journey is tracing the margin of two of Earth's massive plates. The Pacific plate is grinding against the North American plate. The jumbled earth causes these f'ing wrinkles in the land that impede my progress through a little force called gravity. Funny, in physics, gravity is described as a weak force. My ass it is!* Through pedaling, I lifted about three hundred pounds' worth of myself and bike in each climb. I converted kinetic energy during the climb to potential energy at the top of a climb—*the potential of a big-ass screaming downhill!* But I was also converting fresh strong legs into a pair of limp jellyfish and a sore ass! In physics terms, lifting mass against the force of gravity is literally called "work." *No shit! No wonder I'm tired and losing weight. So, note to self: If you don't want hills, don't ride in tectonic zones. I'm caught in the middle of a raging battle of plate tectonics, and I'm the loser.*

Geez! I'm whining about these bumps after torturing myself through the exponentially larger mountain passes of the far north? Funny what expectations do to your mind. I expected killer climbs in the far north and braced myself for them—but once I hit Vancouver Island, I just didn't think it would be so hilly. I had a naïve expectation that I'd ride fifty feet from the beach, cruising easy flats at sea level. *I should know better. False expectations led to false hopes, and they've played mind games with me. Plate tectonics not only wrinkled the earth—it also twisted my brain.*

I continued five miles beyond Raymond to South Bend on a flat road that followed a river estuary near the coast. Riding the flats was relatively effortless, but with 102 miles under my belt, I was exhausted and ready to get off the bike.

As it was getting dark, I came upon a motel in South Bend and pulled in, hoping to stop for the night.

"What do you have for rooms or camping?" I asked the Chinese man in the motel office.

"Motel full and no clamping," he replied.

Clamping? The only clamping I know of is my ass jammed in these way-too-tight bike shorts—and not the best look on this middle-aged body! It would be so easy to turn and slink out of here—but why ride any further if I can help it? "What's your name?" I inquired.

"Chen," he responded.

"Do you own this joint?" I continued.

"Yes!" he said, looking at me with furrowed eyebrows, wondering where this conversation was going.

"Okay, Chen, what would you do if you were me?" I paused and let it sink in. *I need him on my side—set a positive tone—find a genuine compliment.* "You look like a really smart and resourceful guy. Let's be creative. What *can* you do for me?"

Chen thought for a moment and then asked, "Would you sleep in RV?"

"Sure," I told him. "I'm not proud!"

Chen led me to his back lot, where a crusty old RV was parked amid a few weeds. He took me inside and showed me all the amenities.

"How much for the night?" I asked.

"Twenty dollar?" he said, half stating, half querying if that was fair. *The* Saturday Night Live *skit continues. But then again, he speaks English a hell of a lot better than I speak Chinese.*

"I'll take it!" I said, as enthusiastically as though I'd just won the lottery. So, for twenty bucks, I got a full hot-water shower and my own bathroom. And when it rained later, I knew I got a steal.

Chen was a great and accommodating guy. I ate dinner in his roadhouse and paid him tons more for food than I did for the night's lodging. *Smart guy, with a captive audience—capture all the economics!*

We belly laughed as I just kept ordering more food, including spring rolls, wonton soup, a dumpster's worth of sweet and sour chicken, Chinese beer, and pie and ice cream for dessert. The pile of food I ate was bigger than Chen himself.

I appreciated his resourcefulness. *Give people a chance to use their creativity—a win-win for both of us—and as far as I'm concerned, the only kind of good deal is when everybody wins.*

SOUTH BEND, WA
Miles today: 102

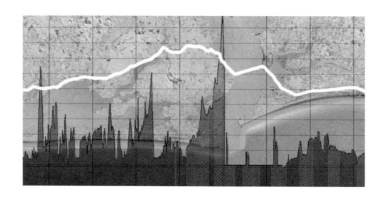

DAY 31
FRIDAY, JULY 20, 2012—SOUTH BEND, WA
Miles to date: 2,114

Take what the day gives you? Today didn't give me much. For starters, I fought another brutal headwind all day. It must have been blowing thirty or forty at the Columbia River crossing—and I was riding straight into the teeth of it. *Hard to make any time, the miles are coming so slowly—my odometer is clicking in slow motion!*

To compound the poor conditions, the day was overcast and dreary, with temperatures in the mid-sixties with intermittent mist and rain, but I never stopped to don rain gear. The ride was relatively flat for the first twenty miles, along a river estuary and salt marsh. The tide was out, so the marsh offered that classic rotting tidewater smell while the shorebirds worked it. I eventually came into some rolling hills, but nothing like the four whales I tackled late yesterday. *I'm so glad I pounded those out last night.*

After about forty-five miles I came to the Astoria-Megler Bridge, which crosses the mighty Columbia River between Washington and Oregon. On the Washington side, a construction zone flag-woman stopped me. Traffic was halted due to the construction on the bridge. Cars and trucks stacked up behind me as I waited for her to wave me on. She queried, "You're gonna brave this thing, huh? You know it's four miles long, right?"

I laughed. "I have no choice."

"Well, be really careful; yesterday a cyclist was having all kinds of trouble and tipped over on the bridge, stopping up the traffic," she asserted, her tone suggesting, *If you have trouble, don't say I didn't warn you.*

Great. That's helpful. What a positive outlook! That solves everything. That gets me across!

Obviously, when this bridge was designed and built many years ago, they weren't thinking about roomy bike lanes for fossilized long-distance cyclists from Minnesota. With the construction going on, it was only a two-lane bridge. They'd somehow worked a compressed bike lane onto each side of the road, but those suckers were a scant three feet wide at best. *There's only so much width to work with on a bridge—cyclists aren't their priority.*

I took my bike shoes off and pedaled in my off-bike shoes. *I don't know what to expect, but if I wipe, I don't want to be clipped in and locked to my bike. Sure, I'll lose power, but if I fall, I want a getaway route!*

The wind howled and buffeted my bike as I concentrated on keeping steady in my narrow lane, while oversized logging and construction trucks lumbered past so close I swear I felt them graze me a few times. *These truckers are real pros, and they know where their fenders are; they're giving me as much room as they can, but they don't have much to give—the rest is up to me to ride a true line.* Still, most passed within a foot of my bike bags, which of course made me much wider than a person on a normal bike. I wasn't nervous, but I had to be at my best and couldn't make any mistakes. *Now I understand what the flag lady was talking about: this bridge could be the undoing of many otherwise brave people—mentally and physically.*

Almost to the Oregon side, there was a strenuous climb to the top of the superstructure—a steep rise that accommodated large ships passing through the canal underneath on their way upriver to Portland. That climb was surprisingly long, steep, and tough— especially without my low gears or being clipped in—and before long, my legs were screaming "Uncle!" at me. I fought back. *I can't dial back, don't blow it here—it's all mental, concentrate and make your legs endure—ride true and let traffic adjust to you—be predictable and consistent, I can't be erratic—stay in your sliver of space—this will end shortly. Y B Y A W C!*

The elevation and view at the top of the superstructure was amazing—although, with the bumper-to-bumper traffic and my intense concentration, I couldn't afford to gawk or stop—so I only occasionally flash-glanced sideways.

Made it! Whoa, that four miles was intense! Hmmm, my new motto: ride true and others will too. I can use that on all the bridges. I loved riding over that bridge. In a simplistic way, it was a *little thing*, but getting over it felt like I accomplished something big.

I was told Oregon would be a flatter ride than Washington. *That's a welcome thought, but I'll believe it when I see it.* And, after riding through the Washington rainforest, I was looking forward to the beach towns of Oregon. *This should be a cool stretch of road.*

I arrived in Seaside, Oregon, and stopped for the night. Since my tent was self-supporting, I could assemble it and then pick the whole thing up and walk it around to set it exactly where I wanted it. But I was also lazy and had never staked it; rather, I just let my own weight hold it down, despite stiff winds.

I set my tent in a large, spongy field and then left to start a load of wash in the camp laundry about two hundred feet away. When I came back out of the laundry area, the winds were howling—and there was my tent in the distance, bouncing and bounding high into the air like a beach ball in a hurricane as it rolled across the grassy field. I took off after it in a dead sprint and chased it down in full view of all the other campers—*Campers who are sooooooo good and waaaaaay too proud of their outdoor skills.* Their tents were all staked, of course, and further affixed with supplemental tie-lines—they stood perfectly erect and taut, even proud, with no wrinkles or sags. After I caught my bouncing baby, I had to take the walk of shame back through the campground in full view of all those know-it-alls—who by then were evaluating my camping skills with pity and disbelief—meanwhile trying to contain their quiet laughter. I could only imagine what their quiet whispers were suggesting: *"See, honey? I'm so glad I married you instead of that tool."* To me, it was pretty funny—a slapstick comedy scene requiring only one stooge—*nuk nuk nuk!* I couldn't contain my grin as I waltzed back through the gauntlet of tents. *How can you not laugh your ass off at yourself over that!* And, when I got back to my site, I staked that puppy—at least for tonight.

By then it was misty and rainy—and getting dark. Fortunately, on my way into the campsite I had spotted a fun little restaurant and pub about a half-mile back. I walked back. *I'll be damned if I'm going to just lay here in my tent!*

SEASIDE, OREGON
Miles today: 67

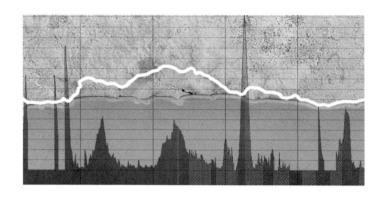

DAY 32
SATURDAY, JULY 21, 2012—SEASIDE, OR
Miles to date: 2,181

When I awoke, I was famished, but last night a woman at the pub told me to ride about eight miles to Cannon Beach and have breakfast there. I was glad I did: Cannon Beach was a great getaway destination. *Yeah, it's a little touristy, but given its setting, it can't help but be.* It's smack on a big broad beach with Haystack Rock as its dominant feature. Haystack Rock is one of the classic sea-stack pictures you see in all of the Oregon travel brochures. *My photo of it is the zillionth plus one.* These impressive sea stacks stand like sentries guarding the entire Oregon coastline.

I arrived in Cannon Beach so early that the restaurants weren't open yet—but a lone coffee shop and bakery was, so I started with a large hot chocolate and a cinnamon roll dripping with icing.

Probably a thousand-calorie starter, but not close to enough—I'm still hungry! So I hung around another twenty minutes until one of the restaurants opened.

Once settled, I ate a big omelet, hash browns, sausage, toast, and a slice of an orange. *Mmmm-mmm!* "You can cash me out," I said to my young waitress.

"Nope, you're not done," she insisted.

"What are you talking about, I demolished that plate of food!" All that was left was the orange rind.

"Nope. You have to eat *those*." She pointed.

"Those? I don't even know what those are? They're just weeds, aren't they?"

"It's kale," she said. "You have to eat it. It's good for your longevity and your skin." She just stood there in front of me. *Clearly she doesn't trust me—she's not leaving or cashing me out until I eat those things.*

"Okay, there! Gone." I punctuated it with a warm smile. "My skin feels better already!" She grinned, and only then did she take my payment.

Just outside of the restaurant, I met an older couple from San Diego. "Which way are you headed!" the man hollered. My whole body vibrated like a shudder from a jackhammer. *Geez, dude, you're killing me—I'm three feet from you, no need to yell! He must be hard of hearing.*

"South," I simply replied.

"We just came from that way. For the next thirty to fifty miles you'll have some killer hills. They'll put you to the test!" Like a reporter with a big ominous scoop, he seemed to relish in delivering the bad news. *Sheesh, man—how about starting with "Good morning, what a lovely day, you'll have a few hills headed south, but you'll surely tackle them in great form"? Try that next time, dude!* By then, the entire street of people knew the topography heading south.

Unfortunately, he was right. I started the day in another misty rain. *Oregon mist they call it.* I didn't don my raingear because I would have been too hot, so I was damp all day. A couple of the early climbs were gorillas, so I was also drenched from the inside out. My glasses were fogged from sweat, and I had only brought sunglasses—so that further darkened the day. The air was so saturated that it just couldn't take any more moisture, so my glasses wouldn't clear, even on the downhills—I couldn't see. I didn't want wet road grit in my contacts, so, straining my eyes through the fogged glasses, I lost all visual perspective and hit a form of vertigo—but at least I stayed upright. Finally, I just removed my sunglasses and put them away. I had no choice if I wanted to stay upright.

Needless to say, I didn't make good time in the morning. But after the climbs the road leveled and, even better, I caught a tailwind. I was finally moving fast—at least for a loaded bike. On the flats, I could consistently cruise at about eighteen miles per hour. Finally, the morning fog and mist burned off and the sun came out. Suddenly, it was a perfect day.

I stopped at a small general store directly on the beach to scoop up a few items for lunch. *Perfect! I'll eat outside on the park bench overlooking the beach.* I was cashing out when the female cashier inquired about my ride. I gave her the general overview, to which she said, "You must be tired!"

"Yeah, a little, but I'll make it."

"Well, you just sit down in that chair right over there and I'll give you a shoulder massage. Let me take care of these other customers. Then I'll be right over."

I stood flat-footed for a moment in stunned silence.

"Go on, hon! Go, go sit down!" She was insistent.

What the hell! Really? How funny is this! I didn't argue—but I could hardly contain myself.

When the other customers cleared, she gave me a half-hour shoulder and neck massage. *I'm just a puddle now. These coastal Oregon women know their stuff.*

I finally felt guilty taking so much from her—I was the one who cut the time off. "Thank you so much. That was awesome—magic fingers!" I said, beaming as I reached for my cash. "After all these miles, I didn't know my head and neck were craving such a loosening." I peeled a couple of twenties and tried to pay her.

"No, no no no—absolutely not!" No matter how hard I tried, she refused.

I left the store all loosened up, shoulders drooped and arms dangling as I ambled out the door—*Rubber Band Man! Wait till my buddies hear about this! I can only imagine their reaction. It'll be—ripe.* Yet another act of kindness from a complete stranger.

I rode through Twin Rocks, so the Shawn Mullins song of the same name echoed through my head. Over and over, it repeated for the next several hours. *I like the song, but enough is enough!* I just couldn't shake it. *Ahhhhhhhh—Help!*

Highway 101 had nonstop traffic, but at Tillamook the bike route split off onto a lonely road that veered to the ocean and paralleled 101 about five miles to the west. *Nice! No traffic, far more the type of road I envisioned on this part of the journey.* But, just beyond the split, and unknown to me until way too late to backtrack, I had to climb over a headland to get to the water—while 101 avoided the headland on the inland side. *That climb torched my legs like a flamethrower, but man, was it worth it!* The Netarts area, with its tidal bay, was a spectacular flat ride on the water, and I watched the clamming and crabbing activities in the estuary as I pedaled. Better yet, I had the empty road all to myself.

However, the tough headlands turned out to be the easiest part—this remote diversion to get to the water also took me to tedious climbs up every cape along that stretch of the coast. I made my fourth climb of the day up the steeps to Cape Lookout. *Does this stretch ever end? Every twist, all I see is more road winding steeply upward.* The grade had to exceed seven percent. And I was again without my low gears, so it was all leg power. *Your body can take more than your mind! But ugh.* Wore me out.

Eventually a long downhill landed me in Sand Lake. *How aptly named!* Dune buggies frenetically peeled around enormous sand dunes. A small general store had a slew of the dune buggies parked out front for the duners to get their next five-hour energy jolt. I entered the store for my own midday sugar spike—chocolate milk and cookies. *Whoa—Bubbaville, complete Bubbaville—accented by oil-company baseball hats and dollar-store tank tops.* The duners eyed me as I breezed through the store—their store, their world. I read their minds: *"Look at* that *dude—Granolaville, complete Granolaville!* So, who was I to critique them while standing in these unbecoming form-fitting spandex bike shorts with a prominent butt pad they might have assumed was a diaper. *I'm as funny to them as they are to me. Funnier yet, I'm not even a granola type, but to them I fit the mold. Appearances can be deceiving. Whatever—live and let live.* A few easy hellos broke the ice. They expounded on their hill climbs and rollovers, and the sand sprays they'd created like jet skis hitting a huge wave. *Somethin' for everyone.*

After another comfortable flat ride along the intertidal marsh, I arrived in Pacific City, a neat little town that was celebrating a dory (fishing) festival. I enjoyed outdoor live music in the public square as I ate yet again from a street vendor's cart—to refuel and recover from that bitchin' Cape Lookout climb.

Decision time. I'm pretty wiped—should I stop here in Pacific City and be content on the beach with live music? I could have a blast here. Or, with too few miles, should I move on? I decided to pound out one more big climb, get to Lincoln City, and once again make it a hundred-mile day. *What strange pull draws me forward? Like astronomers describe the pull of dark matter, I can describe my drive, but I can't explain it—once I have a destination in mind, I relentlessly drive toward it. Well, at least I won't have to start with that bastard hill in the morning.*

I have to remember for future reference just how tough some of these hills were. *The human mind is fascinating—five minutes after I complete each climb, my mind erases it away. Poof. Gone. I forget the burn, forget the pain, and just a few short minutes later will insist it wasn't that bad. I'd do it all over again in a heartbeat.*

That same notion had occurred to me in the American Birkebeiner, a thirty-two-mile cross-country ski race. I didn't specifically train for the Birkie, either; I just maintained good enough overall conditioning to feel that I could gut my way through it. Being competitive, I obviously wanted to do my best, but I never trained for optimal performance. I did a handful of short ski sessions at a local park in the few weeks before the race and then threw myself at the Birkie. *This isn't my livelihood. I just need to be good enough to get through it, but, I do have some pride—I don't want to be a total embarrassment!*

During the races, however, I paid a price for this strategy. I'd have head problems and question myself. *What the hell? Why am I doing this? What is the purpose? What is this proving?* And yet, after I got through the mental strain and eventually crossed the finish line, just a few short minutes later I'd distinctly think, *That was a ball. I'm doing it again next year!* Go figure! But I also realized, *A few short hours of head problems is a small price for the tremendous experience, meanwhile saving all the incremental preparation hours I probably should have done. Know when perfection matters. In the case of the Birkie, perfection didn't matter enough to me; it's only a ski race, it's not like I'm a surgeon with someone else's life in my hands.* An amateur like me simply didn't have to be perfect to get the most out of it. *I win any way you slice it.*

Although I didn't realize it at the time, the mental strength I gained in such weekend-warrior events prepared me well for the mindset needed for this bike journey. I learned that there would be trying times, but they would pass. In my first Birkie, I went out way too fast and was on the edge of a bonk. I was pressing on hills, even at times of racer congestion, which consumed way too much energy for what I'd gained. So when I'd hit easier spots in which to knock out time and pick off other racers, I didn't have the energy. In subsequent races I discovered my own natural pace and rhythm—unique to me—a pushing gentleness that allowed me to pace myself for the distance, yet maintain pretty good speeds. I learned to race that race for my skill level. *Pick your spots to move and capitalize—they happen often during a race, and you have to have the gas to jump them as they present themselves. You can't go full throttle the entire race!* As I learned pacing, my times improved considerably. *Wow—pacing is a useful discovery for every activity.*

And so it was that I was constantly assessing my pacing with the strenuous effort required in all the mountains and headwinds on this journey. Today's effort was no different. At the end of the day I forgot the pain I'd endured just a few moments earlier and just glowed in the exhaustion—a calm stupor. *I love this feeling—runner's high!* There's also a certain dignity, a pride and increased confidence in pushing through the pain and suffering and then distinctly seeing progress. *The freedom to be nimble and decisive relative to my own rhythms is so productive. Nobody is there to second-guess my actions or consume my time or energy in explanations and reporting—it's one-hundred-percent put into productivity. I know where I'm headed, and each moment of time is one pedal stroke closer to my destination!*

You can never learn or feel any of this stuff in a book or in a class—you have to soar and find it for yourself on your own terms. It's uniquely yours. The self-reliance gained in knowing that nobody will pedal for you is so liberating, because as you make progress, it shows your true capabilities in a visceral way. *Shit! I can do this!* What a realization! And I can do more than my head and body want to, or think they could do. I realized that I drew upon this notion every single day. *What a gift! Nobody else can ever give that gift, nor can anyone ever take it away.*

The freedom to experiment, to try new stretch experiences, creates new levels of confidence by default, and better-than-expected personal performance makes you bolder in the face of uncertainty and, just as important, more able to recognize your own deficiencies—but also more readily able to brush off failure. *Hell, it may have cost me time and money, but what an education, a life experience—where else could I have ever learned that! And, it makes you more flexible and adaptable in the face of swirling crosscurrents and change—and, more importantly, empathetic to others' challenges and failures.*

So what the hell: go—try everything! I might faceplant—nothing is assured—but I also might soar! But I'm not there yet: I'm still a long way away, but moving well. So far so good.

Even though I didn't have a set schedule, I was pushing hard. I was starting to feel some time pressure to be in Napa Valley by next

Friday because my wife was flying out to meet me there for a few days in wine country.

Sue had been watching my distance calculations and knew I was averaging ninety to one hundred miles a day. Based on that, she'd googled the distance from southern Washington to Napa, which was about eight hundred miles, snapped a mental chalk line on the map, and calculated that I'd reach Napa in about eight days. She texted me her calculations, and we agreed on a date that she'd fly to San Francisco and rent a car to meet me in Napa. *But God! To make Napa by Friday, I need to hammer the miles to make it in time.*

I pressed on. With my throttle stuck at Hammertime—a verifiable personality disorder—I had the appetite of a Tyrannosaurus, and when food was easily available, I pounced! For example, the fuel for this ill-fated day was:

- Large hot chocolate
- Pie-plate-sized bakery cinnamon roll
- Ham and cheese omelet
- Sizable fruit portion
- Toast
- Six cups of sugar with a splash of coffee
- Three granola bars
- A six-inch meat lover's sub sandwich
- Big bag of chips
- Quart of chocolate milk
- Three large pieces of string cheese
- Another pint of chocolate milk
- Big chocolate-chip cookie
- Bowl of clam chowder
- Cheeseburger and fries
- Three lite beers—*to keep the calories down?*
- And kale—whatever those weeds are—*for my skin, of course*

So there I was, on Saturday night in Lincoln City, Oregon, sitting in the biggest dive bar you could imagine—called The Oregon. It was the only place in town with live music, and I was loving it. *This band is hilarious—more of a garage band than a bar band. I wonder how this group of four burned-out seventies types came to call themselves the Water Brothers. They may be butchering Clapton's rendition of the Bo Diddley song, "Before You Accuse Me," but these guys are hilarious.*

Really, can life get any better than this?

LINCOLN CITY, OR
Miles today: 98

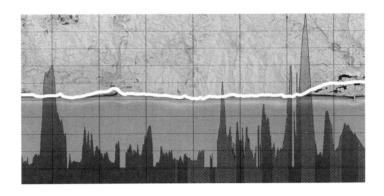

DAY 33
SUNDAY, JULY 22, 2012—LINCOLN CITY, OR
Miles to date: 2,279

The stretch of terrain I covered today was one big sand dune. I talked to a young guy who had spent his entire day dune-boarding: the equivalent of snowboarding, except on the sand. "I'm stoked, man!" he enthused. *I'll have to break out The Beach Boys glossary of terms.* He was a free-spirited type with a big, sunburned grin. "Total gas, dude," he assured me.

The weather was high overcast and cool. I had gentle rolling hills, including a couple of decent climbs, but it was much easier than yesterday. I rode up and over Cape Foulweather, a massive basaltic head named by Captain Cook after he hit horrendous weather here on one of his around-the-world journeys. The cape rose only about five hundred feet above the sea, but it provided spectacular views of the rocky coastline and open ocean.

Still, even that minor elevation gain was challenging without my low gears, so when I pulled over at a parking lot, a couple of guys advised me how to get my derailleurs back into tune. "Tighten this cable, loosen that," they told me, pointing as if it were straightforward. I knew they were just trying to be helpful, but they don't know how mechanically impatient I am. I needed to find a bike shop as soon as I could.

I rode into the early evening and checked into the Honeyman State Park campground. I was directed to the hiker/biker section, which was in a small circular enclave formed by a grove of tall trees. I was the last to arrive, and the perimeter was already ringed by the tents of other travelers. Everyone stopped their activities and watched me warily, hoping I wouldn't crowd their space. *I feel like the last person walking down the aisle of an airplane as every passenger hopes I don't take the empty center seat next to them!* My crappy campsite was wedged into a tiny sliver of remaining space. Due to lack of room, I infringed on the young couple next door, Kevin and Stephanie, but they were more than welcoming.

"Hi there," Kevin said. "Let me move some stuff and you can share our picnic table." They had two bicycles leaned up against the picnic table, and it was jammed full of their gear because they weren't alone. Attached to one of the bikes was a trailer for toting small kids. At the moment, Stephanie was mixing a bottle of baby formula for the one-year-old girl she was clutching in her other arm. Kevin was tending to their three-year-old boy. They cleared a corner of the picnic table so I could lean my bike and lay out a few items. "Hey, want a beer?" Kevin asked. *Are you kidding? Not only are they toting two small kids, but they had the presence of mind to pack beer on their bikes. I'm such a slug—they're the ones overcommitted, and I have nothing to offer!*

"I'd love one," I responded. "But that's a precious resource, and with your hands as full as they are, you may need it all for yourself!"

Meanwhile, Stephanie fished in a small cooler and handed me a beer. Not to be outdone, she was sipping on her own Mylar flask of wine.

"Everyone's covered." I laughed—Kevin and I with beers, Stephanie with wine, the infant with formula, and the toddler sucking on a juice box. "Where did you guys start, and where are you headed?"

"We're from Nanaimo, just north of Victoria. We started there and are headed to San Francisco."

"I'm impressed!" I said, astonished. "That's a hell of an undertaking with an infant and a toddler. You have your hands so full! How far do you ride each day?"

"We're doing about thirty miles a day—with lots of stops. They get restless, so we need to stop about every hour. We find a park and let the kids run around."

"Wear them out so they fall asleep as you drill the next stretch, huh?" I said. Traveling with my own three young kids didn't feel too long ago.

"Yeah, we just do what we can each day—we don't have any set time limits."

"You guys seem so flexible—I love your spirit. And you're starting them early."

"We both decided we don't want to grow old not knowing our kids. So we quit our jobs and decided to do this trip," Stephanie remarked.

"Well, I'm awarding you two the Parents of the Century Award!" I handed them a couple of chocolate-chip granola bars—it was all I had to offer.

Kevin and Stephanie are probably the friendliest people I've ever met. And they're always smiling. Man, I can take a page out of their book on how to live and, better yet, how to welcome and treat total strangers who've just invaded your space. They're amazing.

Looking around this small circular enclave, I noted that every male had a beard, ponytail, tattoo, or piercing. A couple guys even topped it off with a man-bun. Here in this micro community, I was the oddball. *So this is what it feels like! In this group, I'm the alternate lifestyle—the nonconformist.* I was pretty sure I was the only male in this part of Oregon without a single one of those brand markings. In a funny way, they were all conforming. Still, they all warmed to me as I circled the camp and briefly chatted with each group.

This enclave represented a microcosm of what I generally observed in the greater Pacific Northwest. Unfortunately, I also saw a number of guys who also had a faraway look—they'd worry about tomorrow, tomorrow. *I can relate: that's my new long-range plan too! I probably have my own faraway look—from big distance, too little sleep, and too few calories.*

It got dark, and the activities of the enclave wound down. I climbed into my tent and onto a deflating air mattress. *That's progressively gotten worse—how many times will I have to blow it back up tonight?*

HONEYMAN STATE PARK, FLORENCE, OR
Miles today: 85

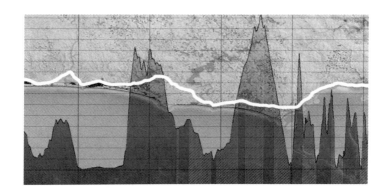

DAY 34
MONDAY, JULY 23, 2012—HONEYMAN STATE PARK,
FLORENCE, OR
Miles to date: 2,364

What a day! It had three completely different segments. It was cold early, but clear of the usual Oregon mist as I rode a few miles inland through tall pines and sand dunes. By midday I was several miles inland, in rural ponderosa. In the afternoon, I rode the final segment along the most isolated beautiful beaches where I could practically make a motorboat wake dragging my right hand in the ocean. I again rode rolling hills all day, with a few decent climbs and flying downhills thrown in.

Someday when I'm not as much on the move, I'll spend more time in Coos Bay and Brandon—great small towns to just hang in for a while. I passed a street in Coos Bay named Slaughterhouse Blvd.

Let's see, women make most real estate decisions—how easy do you think it would be to sell a house on that street? Or better yet, "Hey darlin', c'mon over to my place for dinner: 13 Slaughterhouse Boulevard." Of course it's probably a historic street of stockyards and meatpacking—but would you like that as your address? Creepy. I didn't stop to find out: because of the time of day and the few miles behind me—not to mention a shredding tailwind—I kept moving.

The tailwind was such a screamer that I was determined to ride it as long as I could and as late into the day as practical. *Take this gift! It's going to be a big-mileage day.* Out loud, I mutilated a few lines of Marshall Tucker's "Running Like the Wind." Completely out of tune, thanks to my tin ear. *Who cares, I'm flying!* The wind howled so hard that at one point, that sucker was actually pushing me up a steep uphill. *Put your spurs on cowboy, and kick it! Giddy-up!*

When I stopped for a snack, a guy came over to chat, and as we talked, I told him that I needed another bike tuning. He seemed to know a lot about bikes and told me what to do with each adjustment. Then he left. *What the hell, I'll give it a whirl—I can't make it worse.* So, despite not trusting my mechanical instincts, I tried what he suggested.

Well, my efforts made it worse. I'd been looking for a bike shop for the past several days. Just my bad luck: when I passed through Newport yesterday, the only bike shop in town was closed because it was Sunday, and when I passed through both Coos Bay and Brandon, the only bike shops in those towns were closed on Mondays. *The first open bike shop I see, I've got to get another professional tune-up. Although I've ridden this puppy almost 2,500 miles, I don't quite know what I do that thrashes its tuning.*

The ponderosa portion of the ride was like a scene from the old Western show *Bonanza*: rolling hills of burnt amber–colored grasses in sheep, cattle, and horse country. Berry-picking and a bunch of artisan-type businesses dominated this segment. Clouds of turkey vultures and buzzards circled high above the trees waiting for something to die. *Not me, baby, I'm alive!*

Cruising along this segment at about twenty miles per hour, just hoping the tailwind would continue, I constantly calculated and recalculated just how far I could get. *I'm at eighty miles, but given the time of day and my speed, I don't see any reason why I can't crank off another fifty.* And, in fact, I did.

About ninety miles in, I hooked up with the coast again. I could tell I was tiring, but since I was still riding on the wind, I wasn't about to stop. I had stripped down to one layer at midday, but near the coast, the temperature dropped significantly, and because I simply didn't stop to don another layer, the cold bit to my core. The stiff tailwind shoved me onward, pushing me up the rolling hills but also adding to the chill.

Despite the big miles I was clocking each day, something was nagging at me. *There's no way I can make Napa in time.* I started hinting to Sue via text that even though I was working like hell, the chalk-line method didn't account for the twists and turns of smaller roads, or the headlands and foothills I'd have to cross to get to Napa—and which I would then have to re-cross to get back to the coast.

I pulled off in Port Orford, with its dramatic sea stacks starkly silhouetted against the shimmering late-afternoon sun—a setting befitting a high-end travel brochure—to call Sue about our Napa plans. "Sue, there's no way I'm going to make Napa in time."

"But I have reservations at a great place," she protested.

"Cancel them," I told her flatly. "I can't make it."

"No. No. No." Sue wouldn't take no for an answer. "This place is the best—we wouldn't be able to get it again!"

Here I was with that howling tailwind, standing behind a windbreak, but my sweat starting to freeze while we talked. I didn't want to waste any more time discussing Napa, and I wanted the benefit of the tailwind while I had it. "Sue, I'm freezing and I gotta go. You have to cancel Napa; we have to meet someplace that I can get to!" I cut our conversation short and, with intense silver sparkles flashing off the waves, kept on pushing.

I'd already clocked a hundred miles by Port Orford. By 6:00 p.m.—the air getting cooler yet—Gold Beach was still another thirty miles down the road. Although the sun wouldn't set until 8:45, I was now racing sunset to get there.

A few miles out of Port Orford, I rode into a valley just off the immediate coast and lost my tailwind, which immediately slowed my progress. *Time to recalc and refigure where I can stop. I'm definitely running out of gas. Ophir looks like a good target.* It was only seven miles away, and it looked as if it was right on the water. Gold Beach was still eighteen miles away.

I made Ophir, but rode wondering, *Where the hell is the town? Am I blind? There's no sign of anyone anywhere!* There was just a sign pointing away from the coast, essentially saying Ophir was thataway. I took the road thataway for about a quarter mile, but looking ahead I couldn't see anything remotely like civilization, I turned back. *That-a-sucks! I've just wasted a precious ten minutes trying to figure this out— and the sun is dropping fast!*

Gold Beach was still eleven miles away. *I could squat right here on the beach, but I don't have any food except a pint of chocolate milk. If I want to eat tonight I have no choice: I'll make the final push.*

I shot the chocolate milk for a quick jolt and took off. To my good luck and joy, I not only hit a flat stretch but also veered back to the coastline and my shrieking tailwind. By now I was just off the water and cranking along at about twenty-two miles per hour—even getting bursts to twenty-five—constantly recalculating time and distance via mental math. *Get me there—I want off this bike pronto! But this last stretch is also dramatically cool—I can practically feel wave mist on my face.* Like punching the accelerator, the wind blasted me forward with its heady gusts.

By now the sun was grazing the horizon, casting a bronze hue off the darkening blue water. Lighting changed by the moment as the sun rapidly disappeared, and the ocean on my right became slate gray, rapidly heading toward black.

I think I'm losing! But it's kind of fun racing the sun—a game of chicken. We'll see who wins. I can't let that son of a bitch beat me! Yet again, I was playing it too close with no place to stay. I was pushing it, and I knew it.

When I pulled into Gold Beach, the sun was down and it was late-late dusk—more dark. The first thing I saw was a Motel 6 sporting a red neon *No Vacancy* sign. *Uh-oh, trouble: if even they're full, I'm screwed!* The wind was winding up to a mild cyclone by now, and the temperature was downright cold without the sun's heat. I still hadn't stopped to layer up and was freezing. *I need to pedal while I can—while it's still twilight. I'm rapidly running out of time and options. Keep going and see what's over the crest of that hill.*

I cranked up a steep hill farther into town. That's when I spotted the Oregon Trail Lodge and pulled in. "What do you have for a weary traveler?" I inquired.

"I have one room left." *Relief!* I slammed down my credit card.

While I was checking in, a guest named Bobby passed through the lobby and asked me, "How far have you gone today?"

"I've just clocked a hundred and twenty-eight miles." I spoke softly, out of breath and portioning out the last vestiges of my energy.

At that, he pulled a can of coconut water out of his backpack and handed it to me. "Drink this," he said. "It has more potassium than a banana." He went out of his way to be helpful—a great trait, but he also had the look of a zealot. *A wild-eyed health-drink zealot.* I examined the packaging—*it's a branded product, professionally packaged and in a sealed can, so it's not a homebrewed concoction*—so I opened it. "Thank you so much, Bobby. It's awfully kind of you." As I walked out the door and toward my room, I took a big swig. *Y U C K! Spew!* I spit it out, splattering the parking lot. *Gaa-R O S S!*

But Bobby meant well—so generous.

When I checked my phone, a text from Sue was waiting. "I canceled the hotel in Napa. I know you're busting hard—I see your miles every day. Maybe you should relax—even take a day off. Don't worry how far you get—I'll get to you." Heartwarming and understanding. *"I'll get to you." Love you, Sue!*

GOLD BEACH, OR
Miles today: 128

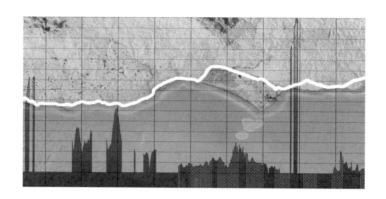

DAY 35
TUESDAY, JULY 24, 2012—GOLD BEACH, OR
Miles to date: 2,492

My room in Gold Beach was pretty cheesy. *Hey, it was a bed, and I'm not choosy.* I slept until 8:15 a.m. *God, that felt good. I just plain need more sleep.*

Before I'd left on this trip, I thought I'd be pulling off the road in the middle of each day in some little remote slice of heaven to grab thirty-minute catnaps on picnic tables or comfortable rock piles. *It's never too late to start, and catnaps would probably be good for me.* But I just kept pressing on instead.

It was a crisp, cold morning, but at least the sun was out. I put on an extra layer and headed out. *I'll be starting with a tough climb right out of the chutes: that'll heat me up.* Which was true—until I climbed into a dense fog. Then I froze once again in my sweat.

Fog was the day's theme. In Brookings, the last Oregon town before I hit California, I caught fleeting glimpses of sheer coastal beauty through the fog, and I could hear the crashing waves of the Pacific, but I couldn't see it—I knew I was missing a great seascape. *Man! The cars instantly disappear into the fog, which means I'm invisible to them too. Be hyperaware and attuned to the sound of cars coming from behind. Stay as far right on the shoulder as possible.*

After days of looking, I finally found an open bike shop in Brookings. I showed my chain and derailleur problems to the two middle-aged mechanics, but it was as though they didn't hear a word I said. Maybe even more so, they didn't need me explaining something that was so obvious to them. It was no surprise to learn that my bike was completely out of whack and horribly out of tune. One of them proclaimed, "We're going to mount your chain on our wall of shame." The other added, "In all our years, that's the dirtiest, grimiest chain we've ever seen."

"Well, at least I'm first in something." *Proud, when I should have been embarrassed.*

"You've also worn your sprocket cassette due to the miles and the road grit that's fused to your chain."

"Makes sense, I never clean my chain."

"Alright, here's the deal: you have to buy a new chain, or we won't work on your bike." Half statement, half ultimatum—all with a broad smile.

After they made the necessary adjustments, one of them asked, "How are you doing your downhills?"

"Like a runaway train—clear the track!" I boasted.

"Well, look at this back tire," the other one said. "See how it's flattened out due to wear? Compare it with this new tire. See how nicely rounded it is? Plus, it actually *has* some rubber. You need a new one. We don't have the right one in stock, though. Doctors' orders: no more freight-training downhills until you replace that back tire."

Their directive was quickly supported by a young woman who'd just stepped into the back room to rent a bike. She was going to ride the Oregon coast while her mother followed in a car. After a quick look at my tire, she shook her head. "I wouldn't ride that—you better replace that tire," she said. "You don't want to go down." *Of course I don't. Nice pile-on! Funny how it became a community issue.*

I gave them all a look of topic overkill. "Okay, okay, I got it. Sheesh." In my defense, I hadn't been oblivious to my back tire's wear. *I recognized it, I just couldn't fix it.* The bike stores either weren't open or didn't have an equivalent to the Continental tire that came with my Surly Long Haul Trucker. Most shops had a thinner tire, but with my load, I didn't want a skinnier tire. *Now it's become a real problem—I'm worried.*

When I continued, I could distinctly tell the difference with their adjustments and the new chain. I was amazed at how much easier the pedaling was. The lack of routine maintenance, even simply cleaning my chain, had led to atrocious inefficiency. *And that, even I could do. But will I? Meh. I'll be done before it gets this bad again. But those two mechanics? Really off-color funny guys. The best. The very best!*

Just south of Brookings I entered California, where the road headed somewhat inland and flattened as I proceeded to Crescent City, situated right on the ocean. I was at sixty miles and I could have stopped for the night, but Crescent City was cold and in the fog. At around five o'clock I spotted a visitor center, so I stopped in for a change to find out what was down the road. "You may want to hang here for the night," the expert stated. "There's a big climb from sea level to twelve hundred feet in the next few miles, and Klamath, the next town, is twenty-plus miles away."

"Okay, sounds good. Thanks so much for your info," I responded. I didn't waste time in indecision. *Twenty miles is nothing.* I climbed back on the bike and took off for Klamath. *He advised the most conservative action. I know he's trying to be helpful, but in his view, it's better to be conservatively right rather than potentially flameout wrong. But the flameout zone is where you have to dig in, become creative and resourceful—it's where change and growth occurs. And c'mon, what's my downside, really? More tired?*

I moved on. That stretch of Highway 101 is called the Redwood Highway because it passed through colossal redwoods, so tall and thick that they blocked the daylight from penetrating to the base. It was late in the day, so traffic was nonexistent: it was just me. Only the occasional squawk of a raven broke the dead silence. The visitor center guy was right: the climb was long and steep.

Later yet, on a shadowy, lonely stretch near the crest, I came upon an unkempt and disheveled-looking backpacker walking the road. I could have easily ridden past, but curiosity compelled me to stop. *Who is this guy? What's he all about?* He had long, wild hair and a full, bushy, dirty beard, and only his eyes and nose were visible through it all. *Is his father half buffalo? A hippie chimera? Jeez!* Like a hobo, he carried everything he owned in a humongous black garbage bag slung over his shoulder. *This guy looks exactly like Charles Manson. Helter friggin' skelter!*

This is so surreal, deep in the shadows of the redwoods, fog wafting past us. Just the two of us, about eighteen inches apart. This guy is looking right through me.

"How ya doing?" I asked.

"I'm hungry," he answered.

"What have you eaten?"

"I've been finding mushrooms in the forest."

"Are the mushrooms hallucinogenic?"

This got a little crooked smile from him. "Uh, I don't think so, but they are big, juicy, luscious, and delicious." I cracked up. *That's a lot of adjectives.*

Still curious, I kept on. "Where are ya coming from?"

"Uh . . . upstream." He said it slowly, with a drawn out *uh* and the *upstream* punctuated with a rising intonation.

"Where are you headed?"

"Downstream." *Of course.*

"Where are you from?"

"Uh . . . heaven," he answered.

"Is heaven a town I missed?" I slowly drew out my words. "Or do you mean heaven, heaven?"

"You know." *I, of course, didn't. But I'm on a dead-end tack.*

"How long have you been traveling?" I pressed. *Who am I, Sam Donaldson confronting a president?*

He paused to consider before he answered, "About twenty years."

Why do I keep talking to this guy? He's fried, there's nothing there. Trying for anything, I said, "That's a pretty big pack."

"Yeah . . . well . . . it's mostly blankets."

I looked at him as he stared pasted me. *Awkward silence.* Finally, I reached in my pack and gave him my last granola bar. It's all I had. "Here, dude. Eat this." I paused. "And take a break from the 'shrooms!" He wolfed it down, barely getting the wrapper off first.

When you pedal, you have all the time in the world to just think. As I continued upslope, I couldn't help but think about Manson. My original question, *Just who is he?*, went unanswered. My gut said there wasn't anyone there to connect with, but in any case, he didn't let me in. Although his answers were nonanswers, I had a sense that he wasn't stupid. *I don't think he's mentally ill, but has he just given up too early on life? Has it been so long since he's had to formulate a coherent thought that now he can't?*

But then I caught myself—I was focusing on Manson's deficiencies. *What about my deficiencies? Was my approach the wrong one to really find out who he was? Huh, maybe I've unconsciously defined my journey as pounding the miles and seeing the sights. And although I have to make miles, the bigger adventure might be slowing down and trying to figure out how to connect with these souls. What could I have learned from him? Get in their world!* I'd certainly missed with Manson. *In hindsight, is my impatience and quest to move—to get to the point—really a hindrance? Does it actually set me back due to missed opportunities? Is my personality such that I just pound shit out and miss the little things along the way? Is the rough and tumble masking vulnerability and sensitivity? Do little things that don't matter to me—things that I blow off—matter to the other party? I'm better than that—or am I?*

Back to Manson—*Was he just that burned out? Or did I fail? Fail to give him the time and space—the trust—to reveal to me who he really was? Just how flawed am I? Can I get deeper with people? Can you really change a leopard's spots? Does every enigma need explanation? Aw, fuck it, I hate self-analysis—too complicated—it feels more like self-destruction. And I ain't no Bhagwan, anyway, so I don't struggle with this shit. It just feels like clutter—throw it away or step around it, but don't wallow in it—it buries you.* I breezily let myself off the hook. *Just pedal, Pedro.*

I climbed above the fog and crested into beautiful, clear, warm sunlight at the top of the headland. I came to an open area, and although I couldn't see the ocean, I could hear waves crashing on the rocks far, far below. I was alone, barely above the clouds—a pure white, billowing fog-deck extending far to the horizon, but I was now in the warm sun among towering redwoods—priceless moments.

I streaked back into the cold and dreary fog, only to come out from underneath it. *This is a phenomenal downhill!* With the ocean to my right, I bombed into big, beautiful turns along the edge of a canyon. I could look straight down onto the water, with my perspective rapidly changing as I super-cruised through the broad, sweeping turns. My tires sung and whined, complaining as they clawed to hang on as I rolled and swayed, the wind whipped through my hair, I felt the heat of the sun and the cold of the ocean, all of it so raw and close. *How do you describe this?* I was totally attuned to the sounds, the fluid motion, and the beauty all around me. *I'm totally alive—and yet the visitor center guy advised me to stay put. I'd have missed all of this—including Manson.*

At about 7:15 p.m., I found a campsite with a shower and a small diner nearby, so I stopped for the night in a thickly forested campground four miles shy of Klamath.

I entered California today. How fast is this going? Tomorrow morning, I'll hit another killer climb of 1,500 feet pretty quickly. At least I have my low gear and a clean chain again. And, for every grueling uphill, there's a scorching downhill. Despite the warning on my worn back tire—I think I hear a freight train comin'.

Soon I was lying in my tent, freshly buffed and clean—well, at least by camping standards. By 9:30 p.m. it was dark and everything had shut down—nothing was stirring. It felt eerie. A month ago, in

Alaska, it would have still been bright daylight at this time of the evening, with all the birds and animals still working. But now I was much further south and a month past the summer solstice. I plugged my earphones into my iPod and selected random play. *What? The Grateful Dead's version of "I Know You, Rider"? Could a more apropos song have come up first? How funny!*

Brrrr, it's cold, even deep in my sleeping bag! I might need my longies tonight, but I'm too deep in my bag already and way too lazy to pull them on. Slightly chilled, I drifted in and out of sleep. *Deathly quiet, pitch black, and with a ghostly white fog wafting through my clump of redwoods—this is kinda mystical.*

CAMPGROUND 4 MILES SHY OF KLAMATH, CALIFORNIA
Miles today: 75

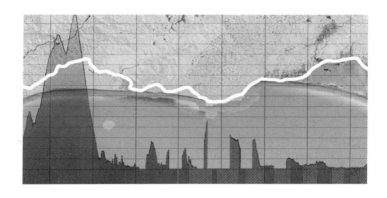

DAY 36
WEDNESDAY, JULY 25, 2012—CAMPGROUND NEAR
KLAMATH, CA
Miles to date: 2,567

Okay, somebody get me a beer! I struggled today. The short version: tons of hills, no momentum, and for some reason, I couldn't get warm.

As I packed up my camp, though, I met an interesting guy who wandered over to my campsite and lingered, obviously wanting to talk. "Good morning," he sheepishly opened.

"Hey," I answered. Seeing my bike with all its packs, he wanted to know my story, and I quickly filled him in—for once careful not to bore the crap out of someone. Then it was my turn. "What brings you here?"

"I'm on a motorcycle trip with a few friends, we're headed to some motorcycle races further north."

"Vacation?"

"Sort of, but I'm retired, so I can take off anytime I want."

"Nice!" I affirmed. "What did you do when you worked?"

"I was a physicist. I have my M.S. in physics from USC and worked on the nuclear weapons program at Los Alamos Labs for twenty-seven years."

"Wow. Impressive. What parts of the program did you work on?" *Trying like hell to carry an intelligent conversation with a campground Stephen Hawking!*

"Well?" He broke into a quirky mad scientist's smile. "My specialty had to do with the nuclear trigger mechanism—the initial explosion that gets the massive nuclear chain reaction going. I specifically developed an expertise in photographing the first few milliseconds of the nuclear trigger in action, using X-ray video— until the entire instrument is destroyed in the triggering." *Talk about specialized!*

"How could you leave that!?!" I knew it would draw additional reaction—and I wanted to know more.

"Well, after twenty-seven years, it was time, and the government retirement program and benefits made it easy."

"Easy street sounds good. So now you can just loaf?"

"Well, you have to do something. So after retirement, I went to law school for kicks."

That's the best you could do, Chief? Did you get your head in front of the X-ray machine a few too many minutes? Maybe a couple of rads, huh?

He continued, "Now I do pro bono work on water rights issues for New Mexico's Hispanic communities. In New Mexico, water is such a limited resource and there are so many interested parties— ranchers, municipalities, indigenous people, and downstream users. So, water rights are incredibly complicated—between the Native American tribes, the Hispanics who've been there for four hundred years, and the more recent Anglo arrivals—it's always a battle."

"That's a hell of a change in direction!" *I'm playing the shallow morning talk show host—about an inch deep—but I can hit enough connecting statements to keep the show going.*

"These Hispanic communities don't know the water rights they have and how to exercise those rights. The water rights are tradeable—I help them get good deals."

"I can tell you feel fulfilled!"

"I love it!" He beamed. "It's opened up an entirely new world that I didn't even know existed. I love the little out-of-the-way enclaves it brings me too, and they need the help. It gives me real pleasure to bring them value."

Maybe he did check his rad badge. Talk about remaking yourself! "You're a good man! Have a great time at the motorcycle races. I have to pack my tent and boogie."

Once I was packed, I bopped a quick four miles downhill from my campsite to the town of Klamath. *I have an enormous climb coming out of Klamath: I'd better stop to get a chocolate milk and some trail mix just in case I need a sugar spike on the climb.* But when I fished in my pack for my favorite credit card, I couldn't find it. *Christ! I had it at breakfast at the little wayside cafe four miles ago.* I was so deflated because I hated the thought of riding four miles back uphill to get my card. *These miles are so hard-earned. I just want to lay down in the fetal position and suck my thumb!* I *never* backtracked. I contemplated canceling the card, but then I did one more pocket check and there it was. *Relief!* If I'd had to ride back, it would have been eight wasted miles all told.

Just out of Klamath the grueling climb began. The road went from sea level to 1,500 feet over the next five miles. I climbed uphill for an hour and a half. There wasn't anything to be done—I had to just accept it and keep grinding. *All tough stretches eventually end—but goddamn!* Finally, I climbed out of the fog into warm, radiating sunlight.

Regulating my temperature was tough. The morning started cold and crisp, but I was quickly drenched from pushing uphill. I rose above the fog, hit sunshine, and overheated. I even had to put my sunglasses away as my face flowed like a river and the stream of sweat down my sunglasses distorted my view. *Sopping wet again— and all day long!*

But in a repeating cycle, I froze on the downhills as I reentered the fog; for the rest of the day, I just couldn't get warm. As for my worn back tire, I cast my fate to the wind and let the wheels fly. It wasn't the brightest move, but I couldn't help myself. *I'm bulletproof—bad things only happen to others. Don't they?*

I hit a continuous series of hills, but there was never enough momentum from one hill to carry the next. The one bright spot was some amazing redwood country. Beyond that, the lack of momentum turned the entire day into a struggle. *Even the easier sections feel hard.*

I eventually rolled into Eureka and decided to belly up to the marina's bar and treat myself to a frosty beer and burger. That's where I met Matt, a guy in his early thirties with a sunburned face and broad, toothy smile. Matt opened the conversation with a good-natured complaint: "I was onshore, fishing off the jetty today, and a commercial fisherman motored right into my space and tangled my line in his prop. Here he has the whole fuckin' ocean, and he comes right into my space and hooks my line!" Matt's hands waved expressively.

"What did he do when he realized he hooked you?"

"Well, he apologized and offered to buy me a new line."

"Did he park the boat and follow through?"

"Naw, I waved him off! But, it's forty dollars' worth of line that I can't afford."

"Let me buy you a beer, Matt. That will be your pain pill." I signaled the bartender with two fingers.

"Worst of all, the fish were really hitting!" Matt clearly lived for fishing.

"Bummer." *To each his own. I don't have any patience for fishing—I can't sit and wait for them. Besides, I've never been able to outsmart a fish enough to catch one.*

Thus far, my first two days in California had brought nothing but cold fog—literally a river of white clouds, like a dry-ice fogger blowing over the road from the ocean. *But no complaining—what would I rather be doing? I'm so lucky: many disadvantaged or disabled people would trade everything for just one tough day on the bike. So although I still haven't warmed up—and couldn't seem to make time today—it's such a small thing compared to real issues.* I usually put things in perspective with a very simple test: big deal or little deal? *That usually shuts me up pretty quickly.*

All right. Tough day. I have to rest up. God willing, I'll be hitting the Avenue of the Giants tomorrow. That should be a hoot!

EUREKA, CA
Miles today: 72

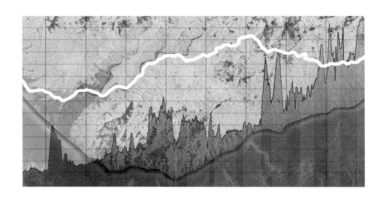

The Avenue of the Giants is thirty-plus miles of road through the enormous redwood groves. *Riding through these giants is an out-of-body experience, and I feel especially small and insignificant among them.* I felt like I was in Lilliput or a fairy tale. This area inspired the haunting, spooky trees in *The Wizard of Oz.* I was so immersed and entranced that I nearly crashed more than once while craning my neck, looking up instead of watching the road.

People tend to get quiet and talk in hushed tones in places like this. There's a natural reverence that overtakes everyone; nobody wants to disturb the magnificence of the moment. They ought to call this place the Cathedral of the Giants—I'm not even religious, but this stretch feels just that sacred.

The day started overcast and foggy, but I was moving well. It was flat for the first twenty miles south out of Eureka, and I was flying. When I hit the Avenue of the Giants at about forty miles, the fog burned off and it turned into a warm sunny day. The terrain was gentle and rolling. *This is a tremendous ride for anyone looking for a doable out-of-body experience! It's amazing how quickly the miles click by when I'm lovin' the ride, even though I'm not going all that fast.* Despite the gap made by the road-cut, the trees towered overhead and formed such a mammoth arboreal tunnel that my GPS couldn't even get a satellite reading. The road followed the Eel River for miles as it snaked through those trees.

These small towns in Humboldt County, dotting along the Avenue of the Giants, are cool as hell. They feel like authentic throwbacks to the Old West—or, at least, two generations back—and it would be a kick to spend more time here.

It was campaign season for the 2012 US presidential election, and in one of the towns, a long-haired local with a big, white, handlebar mustache blurted to me, "The president better not come here to campaign. We'll shut the town down." It reminded me of the old Charlie Daniels song, "Long-Haired Country Boy." *It was tailor-made for Humboldt County. I don't think Charlie Daniels inspired this guy: quite the opposite, he could have inspired Charlie Daniels.*

Whoa—did my back tire just slip in that turn? It felt a little squirrelly! Or, is it me—have I gone psychosomatic? My rear tire was several hundred miles beyond the point where it should have been replaced, so I was extra conscious of it. I'd stopped at two more bike shops today to try to get a new back tire, but neither had the right tire. One tried to sell me a skinny substitute, but I wanted bigger and beefier. I held out and traded the risk of riding a bald rear tire for the risk of the wrong replacement.

I'd clocked about seventy miles by the time I exited the Avenue. *Oh man! I lollygagged a little too long among these giants. Where did the time go, it's six o'clock!* I looked at a map and targeted Leggett, a small town where Highway 1 forked off from Highway 101, marked with a black dot the same size as the other cool small towns I'd just passed.

The size of the dot indicated the relative size of the town, so I figured this would be a significant enough community to find some ratty, rustic place and get a good trucker's dinner. *Given how I'm moving, I'll hit Leggett at about seven thirty.*

But I hit the classic late-day series of long hills, which slowed me considerably. *With my new calculations, I'll be lucky to make Leggett by sunset. Goddammit! Shouldn't I know better by now?* Racing the sun, the last twenty miles took forever, and when I finally arrived in Leggett, it was twilight.

What? My GPS says I've arrived at city center, and—nothing! There's no sign of a town whatsoever. The only thing I saw was an RV stopped on the side of the road; the owners were letting their dogs out to relieve themselves for the night.

"Is this it? Is this Leggett?" I asked the RV driver. "Is there a town center or something that I just haven't found?"

"I don't know, but I'm pretty sure that what you see is what you get," he replied. He continued, "Where have you come from? Where have you been?" *Some people just don't have a clue of the moment. He's fat and happy in his large RV, set for the night and wanting to chitchat like I'm his evening entertainment.*

I cocked my head with a look of disbelief. "Dude, I don't mean to be rude, but I can't chitchat right now. It's dark and I have to find a place to squat." I blew him off and took off in the dark.

I found an empty, overgrown field nearby and settled in. But it got worse—I had just ridden close to one hundred miles, but because there was no town, there was also no food. *All I have in my bag is—an orange. One measly orange.*

Well, I peeled that orange and ate it ever so slowly—savoring every little lick on each individual slice. *Huh. I'm not so far removed from an ape.* When I'd been to zoos, I was always fascinated by the ape house—*To better understand my two older brothers, right?* Anyway, I'd noticed that the great apes often *play* with their fruit as they eat it. It's in their mouths, it's out of their mouths, it's sideways in their mouths, and then, after a while, it's gone. *Well, after I've just ridden a hundred miles and only had an orange, I'm not too different.*

Being down in the "real world" made me sloppy. I didn't think I needed to carry food like I did in the wilderness. *Live and learn. I'm starving to death tonight—and uncomfortable. But in the big picture this is another little thing, it's only discomfort—discomfort isn't danger. Don't confuse them. I'll survive.*

To distract myself from the growls of my empty stomach, I whipped out my iPod. The first song that came up on shuffle was Roberta Flack's "The First Time Ever I Saw Your Face." *For God's sake! How did that get on my playlist? I mean, c'mon, this ain't the type of song guys have on their iPods—as my lower lip quivers and tears stream down my face. I crack myself up! I'm punch drunk. Ridiculous!*

So there I was, lying in my tent in an overgrown field, having just ridden a hundred miles and eaten only an orange for dinner, listening to Roberta Flack, having taken a lovely Wet Wipe bath, my air mattress noticeably deflating toward the rocks and roots. *Pathetic—all of it.*

But pretty funny, really. What a terrific day.

LEGGETT, CA
Miles today: 96

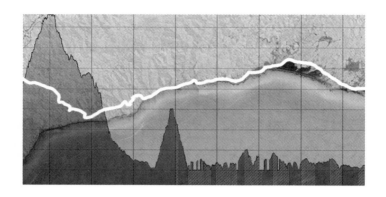

This was a short day by design. Sue flew out from Minneapolis, rented a car, and drove north so she could get to me. When Napa didn't work out, we'd decided on Fort Bragg on the Mendocino County coast.

Since I'd only had an orange for dinner last night, I was naturally starving this morning. After a restless night, I packed and got moving early—I wanted to boogie before I had to explain myself to some authority. I found a minimal gas station nearby as the attendant was opening it at 6:00 a.m. I scavenged a stale wrapped muffin and a chocolate milk from a crusty old fridge. "How old is this stuff?" I asked the attendant. *Can I trust this snack?*

"No idea. But it should be alright, it's been in the fridge." *Yeah, since 1972.*

"I guess I have no choice, I need fuel—badly! I'll take anything I can get my hands on." These provisions needed to get me at least the thirty miles to the next town.

"Which way are you headed?" the station attendant inquired.

"Toward Highway 1, the Pacific Coast Highway, to get right on the coast."

"Ouch! You have a steep seven percent grade uphill for the first five miles coming out of here—it's a tough, windy road, even in a car. Where did you sleep last night?"

"I squatted in that open field a few hundred yards back." I pointed to the field as I spoke.

"It's a good thing the owner didn't come around. He's a total ass!"

"Well thank God I didn't run into him—I only had an orange for dinner last night, and I don't quite know what dealing with an ass on just an orange might have unleashed!" We both laughed hard. I wheeled out of the station with a "See ya."

"Be safe on that road. It's a toughie," he warned again. With that, I took off.

God! My teeth are chattering—it's midsummer in California, and it's freezing! I can see my breath—I thought California was supposed to be warm! Once again, I was drenched and simultaneously sweating and freezing during the five-mile climb. The road wound higher in leg-numbing steeps. *Hills have to end sometime, don't they? Shut up and just pedal.* I thought I'd never crest the top.

On the subsequent downhill, I was numb from the cold and mentally struggling to hang on. I wasn't at my best: my mind was processing information way too slowly and my cryogenic body was late in responding. I could hardly feel the handlebars in my frozen hands. I went through a series of rolling hills and then another big uphill and downhill—a grueling traverse over the headlands to get to the coast. I struggled, especially on so little fuel. At about twenty-five miles, I finally made the coastline and pulled off at a scenic viewpoint.

An RV was parked at the pullout, and a couple of guys were admiring the natural beauty of land's end at the coastline. They both walked over to me and asked about my trip. I gave them a quick rundown and then finished with my story of last night and lack of food. "Oh my God, are you okay?" they exclaimed. They couldn't fathom a hundred miles on only an orange. *Shoot, now it looks like I'm begging for food, not my intent at all!* I just thought they'd find the predicament entertaining—I sure did!

"Yeah . . . it's not *that* big a deal," I responded, trying to take the urgency and emotion out of the scene.

"Can we make you breakfast? Would you like a sandwich? We have bananas! Do you need juice?" they offered generously.

"I'll just take a banana, if that's alright," *It's peel and eat, no other work or prep.* "It'll get me to the next town about five miles south—piece of cake—then I'll eat a big meal." *Food is right around the corner now; I don't want to inconvenience them.*

But when I arrived in that town, I found a general store and a hotel, but no cafe. I went into the hotel, where the woman behind the counter said, "I'm sorry, we don't have a breakfast, but you can have all the coffee you want." As an afterthought she continued, "I can try to make you something."

"No worries. I'll just see what they have at the general store. But thank you for your offer!" *Can people get any better?*

Finally! Food! I refueled with off-the-shelf donuts and milk in the general store. I now only had fifteen miles left to Fort Bragg, where I would meet up with Sue.

Those last fifteen miles were spectacular—right on the coast in the morning sunlight—but it was tough, too, due to steep, rolling hills and several stream crossings. Every time the road met a stream, it veered inland and descended to the streambed—essentially sea level—leaving me to crawl out in a steep, winding rise back to the seaside cliff height. It took a lot longer than I expected. In the meantime, Sue was making her way north from San Francisco in her rental car.

As I pulled into Fort Bragg, I immediately hit a burger drive-in, wherein I ordered the half pounder works with fries and a chocolate malt. Just as my food arrived, Sue called. "Hey, where are you? I'm about five miles away."

When she arrived at the drive-in, I was tearing into my food. She took one look at me and cracked up, laughing so hard she couldn't get her words out in one breath! Her head swung away from me and then back. "Okay, honey. You're going to eat your burger, and then we're getting a room and you're going to sleep. I'll do your wash, and when you get up, you're going to eat again."

While I ate, she stepped away and almost melted her phone exchanging texts with the kids saying how skinny I looked. She wouldn't tell me what she was writing, and I didn't press. *I know I look like hell from no sleep.* But I didn't fully realize how skinny I'd become. Since she hadn't seen me for so long, I was practically unrecognizable to her. Every time I looked her way, she shook her head with an ear-to-ear grin.

"I haven't seen myself in a mirror lately. Is it that bad?"

"In all of our years together, I've never seen you this thin!" She couldn't contain herself. "Okay, here's the deal: no buying any clothes until you put your weight back on," she bantered. "You look European!" Mind you, there's nothing wrong with Europeans, but she preferred me with my regular American heft.

As I awoke from my nap, I heard her talking on the phone with her sister in a hushed tone. She was *still* amused, shaking her head and waving her arms as she spoke. When she saw I was awake, she said, "Okay, honey. It's time to go eat again. We have to pork you up!" We headed to a microbrewery, fired some brews, and ate, and ate—and ate some more. We had a blast catching up and just couldn't stop laughing.

"Someone Like You," by Van Morrison, floated through my head. *I didn't realize how much I missed her.*

FORT BRAGG, CA
Miles today: 50

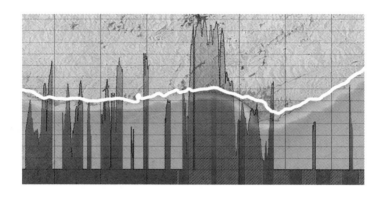

Adrift, Sue and I worked our way down the California coast from Fort Bragg to Mendocino to Elk to Gualala. We'd get up and have breakfast, and then I'd climb on my bike for the hour or two to the next town, casually drifting southward, averaging an easy twenty miles per day. Sue would drive ahead and get us checked in somewhere, and when I arrived, we set out to explore. We went to wineries, a redwood grove, and beach walks, and we just caught up. It was a relaxing, low-key break, and it was just plain nice to spend time with her again.

In the meantime, I bought a new air mattress. *Sticks and stones may break my bones, and midnight blowups suck!*

GUALALA, CA
Miles the last three days: 60—R&R,
about 20 miles per day

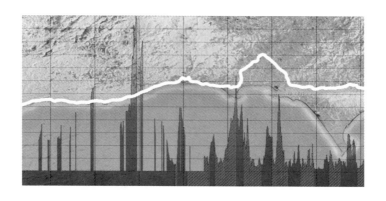

DAY 42
TUESDAY, JULY 31, 2012—GUALALA, CA
Miles to date: 2,845

Sue and I had breakfast and hung out until about eleven o'clock, and then she headed back to San Francisco to fly home as I climbed back on my steed and continued my journey in the saddle.

With such a rolling road and steep coastal hills, I couldn't gain a steady momentum and pound out the miles. I was often in my lowest gears, which reduced my speed to five or six miles per hour, and the numerous streams forced me again and again to wheel inland, drop to the streambed, and climb back out on the other side. *I'm just not making any time today—but the seaside views are killer and more than compensate for the slow going.*

Many stretches of road along the entire Pacific Coast Highway, from Washington State all the way to Santa Barbara, are treacherous.

In many areas, there was no shoulder or guardrails. Steep drops of hundreds of feet—if not a thousand feet or more—plummeted immediately off my right side straight to the ocean; I often had a bird's-eye view of the sea directly below. And so it was on the stretch between Gualala and Jenner. *This is no place for the fainthearted—at all!*

The danger of this section was compounded by traffic from large logging, petroleum, and construction trucks because the truckers had zero room for clearance. I paid close attention to the sounds of the traffic coming from behind; I couldn't make it tougher for them. *If I get bumped here—look out below! It's a thousand feet to the ocean.*

Sometimes I wanted to stop for rest on the steep and ever-rising incline. *Shit! I can't get unclipped!* I was straining so hard in the pedals, my feet would get locked into the clips due to the intense friction. *My legs are trembling with fatigue, but I can't stop here! I have to be smarter and think further ahead on my moves. Next time I see a flat stretch, I need to rest while I still have control—before complete exhaustion.*

At one specific moment, I stopped on a steep uphill and needed to start again. With traffic coming immediately behind me, I misjudged the starting thrust and didn't get enough momentum on the first stroke. I tried to clip in with the other foot to continue my thrust, but it wasn't clipping, and I pawed at the pedal like a buck scraping for food in the winter. Unconnected and without forward momentum, I wobbled left into traffic and then, in a knee-jerk reaction, weaved hard right to the drop-off—catching myself just a couple feet short of an unplanned BASE jump! *Whoa, Nelly! Pull the ripcord—that was a scary moment! Total spine zinger! Shit, my heart's racing. I can't put myself in that position along the cliff edge again!* From then on, I let traffic clear before restarting on the steeps.

Despite the danger, this section was thrilling, with killer views looking out high above the endless blue Pacific. Fishing boats plied the water off-coast, and further out, the pure white sails of yachts sharply contrasted against the deep blue. I watched the patterns of wave swells far out to sea build and break in the shallows with thundering crashes on the shore below. Despite my altitude, the rhythmic crash of the surf far below carried clearly. It was sensory overload: all my senses redlined with the blast of input. *I had no idea about the magnificence of this region before now—but I wouldn't want to miss this for the world!*

Because of my late start, I was only at the fifty-mile mark when I arrived in Bodega Bay at around 5:00 p.m. I grabbed a needed burger to fuel up, as I still wanted to knock off the thirty or so miles to Point Reyes Station. The waitress exclaimed with amusement, "Wow, you braved that stretch? That's nasty!"

I also had a text waiting from Sue, who'd driven the same Gualala to Jenner route as she headed back to San Francisco: "Did you make it through that stretch? I can't believe the exposure! If that's any indication of what you've been doing, it's probably a good thing I don't know the roads you're riding."

My back tire was now acutely ill—on life support! *I've gone way too far on it! Hopefully I can get a good fit in San Francisco tomorrow.* My confidence waned on the downhills. *I swear my bald tire slipped again on that corner. The risk of a crash and injury now probably exceeds the speed and thrill gained from bombardier downhills. Crap! I love flying the downhills. But for now, c'mon, Jerry: be smarter—safety vs. speed—good judgment vs. exhilaration—head vs. heart. Decisions, decisions.*

I didn't know what the terrain held south out of Bodega Bay, and so, yet again, I got into steep, rolling country where it was tough to make good time. I was again riding later than I wanted, so I hoped to find a room. As I neared Point Reyes National Seashore, the sun was low, a stiff wind was blowing off the water, and I was getting cold. I had no idea of what motels, if any, were ahead in the small town of Point Reyes Station.

Just as I rode into town, though, a small B&B with a blind driveway flashed past. I quickly doubled back to check for vacancy, and although the owner had no rooms available, she asked, "Do you know a Jerry Holl?"

That threw me. *Is she clairvoyant or what?* "Uh, yeah," I told her. "I *am* Jerry Holl."

"So, did you call me a while ago about a room tonight?"

"No . . ." I responded slowly.

"Well, a Jerry Holl called. He asked if I had a room available tonight. He told me that a cyclist would probably stop and ask for a room." *Bizarre!* The five chimes of *Close Encounters of the Third Kind* rang in my head!

I was totally confused, but then I figured it out. My uncle's name is also Jerry Holl—he and my Aunt Bonnie live in Berkeley. He's lived in the Bay Area forever and knows this entire area by heart. By following my blog, Uncle Jerry was tracking my daily progress. He even sent me an e-mail saying that he and Bonnie wanted to catch me coming over the Golden Gate. *Now it's making sense. I tried calling him from Bodega Bay and left him a message saying what town I thought I'd make tonight.* I was trying to give them a sense of how close I was to San Francisco, to help them judge their timing to catch me on the bridge tomorrow. And given that it was prime vacation season, he knew many of the rooms in this area would be full. So, unbeknownst to me, he'd made calls and tried to find me an available room tonight. *What a great guy!* And, it was a pure coincidence that I'd even spotted this particular place.

I wonder if Uncle Jerry tried to book a room for me in other motels? The woman at the B&B broke my trance: "There aren't any vacant rooms in the entire town of Point Reyes Station. I know because I've checked for other travelers tonight. But hang on," she continued. "Let me call a friend in Olema." I listened to her side of the phone conversation. From her desk, she looked up at me and asked, "Do you have three more miles in you?"

"Absolutely, piece of cake!" I told her.

So, now I had a room for the night in Olema, which was only thirty-five miles or so north of the Golden Gate Bridge. *I'll cross it tomorrow.* Best of all, there was a nice little pub attached to my motel in Olema. *Nothing like the first slurp of a cold craft beer in a frosted mug after a grueling day.*

OLEMA, CA
Miles today: 85

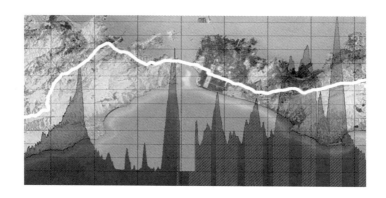

I set out in the cold and fog on a modest uphill for the first six miles, followed by a downhill to Dogtown, and then a flat run to Stinson Beach, where I grabbed a snack. "Brace yourself for a bitch of a climb," a stranger blurted when he learned where I was headed. *Nothing like brutal honesty.* He was too right! There was a giant headlands climb from Stinson Beach to the crest of Shoreline Highway (Hwy 1) in the Mount Tamalpais area. *Up, up, up, and surprise, more up!* Yet another of the Pacific Coast Highway's treacherous uphills: no shoulder, no guardrails on the ocean side of the road, Bay Area traffic, and thousand-foot drops to the sea below. *Oh, and also some mind-boggling vistas!*

Finally cresting, I peeled off a snaking downhill all the way to Muir Woods. *Easy on the back tire big boy—be good here!* I thought I was finished climbing, but no such luck. I immediately had to climb over another equally large tectonic wrinkle from Muir Woods to Sausalito under the same conditions. *Where are David's* (my son) *giraffe-sized heart and youthful stallion legs when I need them! Shit!* The second climb was as brutal as the first.

As I pulled into Sausalito, I saw a huge bike shop and immediately diverted to it. *Fab! They have everything here! Back tire solved—renewed confidence!*

Earlier in the morning, I'd called Jerry and Bonnie and estimated when I thought I'd hit Sausalito. *I totally underestimated the time and effort in the headlands.* My tire replaced, we connected and caught up over lunch at a sidewalk cafe near the water.

Jerry gave me specific instructions to get to the pedestrian and bike entrance on the bay side of the Golden Gate. Then he and Bonnie drove to the far side of the bridge to catch me riding across. The bridge was packed with pedestrians and casual cyclists, including numerous schoolkids and tourists riding across on rented bikes. There wasn't much room. Most of the other bikers were inattentive amateurs who were lousy behind the handlebars, and more than one almost pasted me. It was foggy, with the wind shredding like hell across the nearly 250-foot-high bridge deck. *I never get tired of the Golden Gate vantage—the view of the entire bay, the whitewash hue of San Francisco, the world-class city in the distance through the haze. Alcatraz and its storied past; the huge container ships passing under the span, heading to or arriving from distant shores, stacked with containers of goods; sailboats heeled over at forty degrees and weaving through the commercial traffic lanes—this whole area abuzz with constant activity and motion—all viewed from high above on this marvel of engineering. Look, look, look—I love it all!*

Snap out, Francisco, and get moving! Jerry and Bonnie met me on the far side of the bridge, where we took our photos then said our good-byes. Bonnie generously gave me a package of cookies and Nut Goodies to fuel me forward. *So sweet, and important!*

Once off the bridge, I rode through parts of San Francisco that weren't on the tourist checklist. *This is what's neat on a bike. Sometimes I just can't easily avoid questionable areas, and they're often some of the most authentic and interesting places—although, at times, potentially nasty.*

I had another long climb to Daly City—all in a dense fog that relentlessly broiled over the road as though from a sorcerer's cauldron. In Pacifica, I rode through a street festival in a Hispanic community alive with celebration. Finally, late in the day, I had one last long climb from Pacifica toward Half Moon Bay. *I just can't adequately describe all these climbs! How do I do them justice? My words take seconds, but the climbs take hours, steel nerves, and thousands of calories! Can my body really take more than my mind? Shit!*

When I arrived in Half Moon Bay, I asked a Hispanic woman standing on the street with her six-year-old boy for directions. She turned to her little son and asked him something in Spanish, and the little kid became our interpreter. I'd ask him a question, and he would translate to his mom. She would answer him in Spanish and he would translate back to me in English. His brows furrowed with concentration as he did his best. *Cute as hell!* By the time we were done, we were all grinning, and then I got to use the full extent of my Spanish vocabulary by saying *muchas gracias* to both of them. We all burst out laughing. The little boy was the star, beaming over his performance, and his mom was rightfully proud.

By end of day, I was famished; I'd burned so much more than I'd eaten. At a Mexican dive restaurant, I ordered the carne asada burrito. Normally, these dives have the best food, but when I stuck my knife in the meat, it wouldn't come out. *This makes jerky seem juicy! But I'm going to eat it all—I need the calories.* I didn't have the heart to tell the cook that this plate sucked. *But for now, please pass the diamond saw to cut this last piece of horsemeat!*

Crossing the Golden Gate felt like a major milestone—the gateway from northern California to the Central Coast. *This trip is flying by—and given my pace, Southern California and the Mexican border are just around the corner.*

I'll have another significant milestone first thing tomorrow morning: I'm one mile shy of three thousand miles.

HALF MOON BAY, CA
Miles today: 69

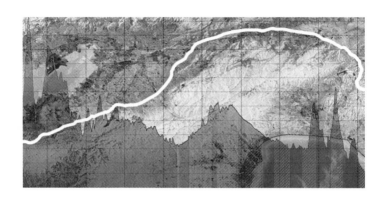

Another wet mist escorted me out of Half Moon Bay, damp, but not enough for rain gear. I caught a tailwind and, with a relatively flat terrain, cranked out some decent miles. The road moved in and out from the coast with a couple of long uphills, but nothing like the headlands I'd been riding. *I trust my back tire again—full throttle, baby!* I hit forty-five miles per hour on one long downhill. *Super Fly—without the oversize sunglasses!* Plus, I had a normal four-foot shoulder and great pavement, so I quickly cranked out the forty-five miles to Santa Cruz. But then things changed.

Highway 1 becomes a freeway in Santa Cruz, and the California Highway Patrol doesn't allow bikers on California freeways. I had to find a southbound side route. Coming out of the city, I could see the whole of Monterey Bay: all I needed to do was circle it. It *looked* easy, but by road it wasn't. I couldn't simply follow the shore, and because of the terrain, the roads weren't in a grid pattern. Somehow, when I lost sight of the ocean, I got turned around. One moment I'd be going south, and the next the road would wind around and head north. *The freeway is so straightforward, but I just lost an hour or more trying to find a side route.* The GPS both helped and hurt: it kept directing me to the most efficient route—the forbidden freeway section of Highway 1. I tried the compass function instead, which pointed me in the direction of my target city, but whenever I found roads that went in that general direction, they ended up weaving around to the opposite direction instead. *So frustrating!*

My southward non-highway effort took me inland a few miles from the coast, and at one point I came to a T in the road and made a directional decision that led me about two miles out of the way to a Not A Through Road sign. This was my first real backtrack of the journey, and not a fun segment because heavy ag machinery had left big clods of packed mud all over the road—*tooth chattering!*

I'd seen most of the trendy California coastal towns before, but one of the benefits of getting off of the main road is that you see the working areas that you wouldn't hit as a tourist. On these back roads, strawberry and artichoke harvesting operations were in full swing, and the fields were swarming with huge trucks carrying the harvest. Small crowds of migrant workers were scattered throughout the fields. *I've seen these workers from a distance in earlier travels, but it's so different and more personal when I'm up close. God, that looks like thankless, tedious work—but I have to admire them making their way. I'm glad I detoured into the thick of this area—it's a firsthand education on the productivity of the California ag community, and the grueling nature of migrant farm work.* I also noted that the area's modest homes and towns are not highlighted in the California travel brochures.

The weather went from fog in the morning to beautiful sun in Santa Cruz, and then back to fog and dreariness later in the afternoon near Monterey Bay. At about five o'clock, the clouds thickened and it became storm-threatening dark. *Uh-oh. I'm about to get drilled!* I saw a standalone motorcycle shop just ahead and stopped. The woman who ran the store was tattooed to the sun and pierced to the moon. *Whoa, no more skin estate!* "I know Moss Landing is just a few miles ahead. Where do the Harley guys stay?" I asked.

"They don't stay in Moss Landing, it's too expensive," she replied. "They go on to Castroville, just about two or three miles farther and inland from Moss Landing."

"Cool. I don't need the frills!" I stated. Off to Castroville it was.

As I passed through Moss Landing, I saw a big, floating dock crowded with hundreds of seals. I was downwind from them as I crossed a bridge near the dock. *Wow! Phew! God do those seals stink!* Most of the time I love my face in the open air—you get the natural smells and mostly fresh air. Not here! *You'd think the sea would constantly be washing those beasts. God—they make an Iowa hog farm smell like fine French perfume by comparison.*

Castroville, The Artichoke Capital of the World the sign read as I pedaled into town. It was clearly a heavy ag town, in the heart of the farms. All the signs were in Spanish, many for payday lending and money transfers. But Castroville was clean and authentic. The proprietors of my motel didn't speak English, so I registered using hand signals.

I waltzed into a small Mexican cantina for dinner and bellied up to the bar next to three honchos. The jukebox was rockin' full tilt and only had authentic Mexican music. *Am I in Mexico City? I haven't heard a word of English spoken in here.* The young female bartender came over and asked, "Puedo ayudarle?"

What? My eyes crossed. "No comprendo," I replied, with my palms up and drawing on the last of my Spanish knowledge. She didn't speak a lick of English—she didn't have to, it was Castroville, the artichoke capital of the world and the center of a Mexican migrant worker community. In sign language I consulted with the nearest of the three honchos next to me and, with his help, I ordered a Victoria beer. It was the chosen beer of the joint, imported from Cerveceria Modelo, Mexico. *I'll exercise a little goodwill and community relations.* I signaled the bartender to fire up a round of Victorias for the three honchos on me.

The honcho closest to me, Ivan, didn't speak English either, but we fumbled through a conversation in pidgin. He was from the Yucatan and had been in America for seven years. He was a roofer and business was slow—he'd only worked two days this week. He was thirty-one, had gotten married two years ago, and had a two-year-old boy and a nine-month-old girl. He was planning to take them back to the Yucatan in December so his parents could see them. *Super nice guy!* He showed me pictures of his family and the grottos of his hometown. One of the other honchos at the bar happened to be his brother, and when they left, they got into a brand-spanking-new Chrysler 300. *Business is slow? Brand-new hot car? Flashy hubs, smoked windows! I must have missed something!*

Well, I missed even more than I realized because when I got up to pay my bill, unbeknownst to me, Ivan had picked up the tab for my couple of beers before he left. This was well after I'd told the bartender to buy a round for the three honchos on me. I realized Ivan had told her in Spanish to put the beers on his tab. Then I had a brainstorm. I asked her if Ivan and his brother came to this cantina often. She got someone who could translate because she didn't have a clue what I was trying to say; through our "interpreter," I learned that they came into this cantina all the time, so I forward-bought two rounds each for Ivan and his brother—and left them a note. That got a big smile out of the bartender. *Just wait until they get their surprise. Wish I could be here to see it, but I'll be long gone.*

After I ate, I walked Main Street home in a dark mist and watched a few muscle cars slow crawl the main drag, occasionally peeling rubber. *Testosterone: don't leave home without it. Too funny— light 'em up!*

CASTROVILLE, CA
Miles today: 85

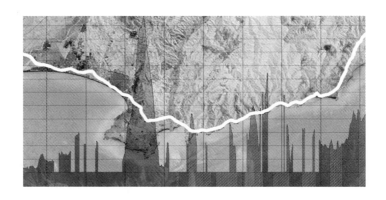

DAY 45
FRIDAY, AUGUST 3, 2012—CASTROVILLE, CA
Miles to date: 3,084

Relatively speaking, I didn't make many miles today. There aren't many towns along the Big Sur coast, so I had to pick my stops as carefully as I did in the far north. My final stop today was too short, but given the terrain, the next stop was too far.

I arrived in Monterey at about 10:00 a.m. My nephew Peter was enrolled there in the US Navy's graduate school. He knew I'd be passing through at some point, but because I never knew exactly where I'd be when, it was hit and miss whether I'd see him. Luckily it worked for us to meet on the pier, and we hung out for about an hour. I'd never spent that kind of one-on-one time with Pete; for me, there's a tendency to think of nephews and nieces as still little kids. *Are you sure you don't need my advice anymore, Pete?* And then you have an adult conversation with them. *Stand down, Einstein: he's navigated some great accomplishments without a stitch of your advice and counsel—including a couple stints as an officer on naval subs! Explosive growth. Amazing how quickly kids grow up when they leave home.* It was just plain good to see him.

After I left Peter, I got trapped in Monterey, trying to obey the law again. Denied access to Highway 1, I tried my best to point south, but yet again the road twisted and turned, and before I knew it I was somehow heading in the wrong direction. *Screw it! I've wasted an hour!* In frustration I climbed illegally onto Highway 1 and rode the direct and straightforward route to Carmel—the northern boundary of the vaunted Big Sur. I fueled up on the finest cuisine of the Chevron station, wolfed it down on the comfort of the roadside curb, and mulled, *I've been looking forward to this section—this will be amazing.*

After an afternoon of riding in sensory overload, I rolled into the town of Big Sur at about five o'clock feeling bushed, having completed an exhausting climb on a beautiful, but grueling road full of drop-offs. *If I don't stop here, I'll have to ride another thirty miles or so to where there's food and camping.* Unfortunately, it was the height of vacation season, and every campground and motel in town was booked full. Luckily for me, a guy at a private campground directed me to Pfeiffer Big Sur State Park, only three or so miles farther. "They have a hiker/biker section," he said, "and even if they're crowded, they'll always squeeze in another tent." *Thank God they know that when we bikers stop, we really need to.*

The redwood grove where I pitched my tent had other hikers and bikers scattered throughout the trees. These guys were classic campers, all stirring their noodles and munching trail mix at their sites. *Not me, baby, there's a slab of lasagna waiting for me back at the lodge dining room!*

I was just finishing setting my tent when I spotted him walking toward me from about fifty yards away. The man carried a large garbage bag Santa-style, slung over his shoulder. He was scrounging aluminum cans. "To clean the environment," he explained. "And to sell the aluminum for change." He was camped in the next site over. *My lucky day.* He dropped the big bag next to his tent and wandered over. I straightened to receive him at my small plot of dirt. "Hey, man, how's it going?" I opened.

"Hi, I'm Barney!" *Whoa, meet Barney!* "What a great bike and tent!" he exclaimed as he circled my gear and lusted over my equipment.

"Yeah, it's okay—standard off-the-shelf stuff." *Good gear, but not that special—it's all relative, I guess.* I warmly welcomed him, and we small talked for a couple of minutes as his character unfolded. Barney was in his late forties, and while originally from upstate New York, he was raised in California.

"I'm on my bike trip too," he went on. "I've ridden my bike to here from Monterey." *About thirty miles away, but what the hell, good for him.*

"How long have you been here?"

"I've been here three days—I'll stay a few more and then ride back to Monterey." He paused, then slowly continued. "I want to bike to Oregon someday, but I'd have to ride thorough San Francisco, which scares me. The city is so big, confusing, and easy to get turned around in and all." *Stretches are relative, but stretches nonetheless.*

"That would be a good trip, Barn," I encouraged him. I started walking toward the park's lodge to grab a quick bite. Barney, pushing his bike, fell into step beside me.

"I take my bike with me wherever I go, because it's the best bike I've ever had. Aren't you taking yours?" he asked me.

"Naw," I told him. "I'll take my chances." I'd lost my bike lock about a week ago.

"That's good!" he exclaimed. "The wind blows the chaff away and clears the way for goodness." *What?* That's when I realized Barney was a kind of, well, the nice term would be an eccentric philosopher. *Okay, truth is, he's a nut, but a harmless nut who means well.*

As we walked toward the lodge, I was treated to other Barneyisms.

"People are drawn to the sea because the salinity of the ocean is the same as the salinity of your blood. The salinity allows you to have a clearer head. And that's why we're drawn to the sea and not to the mountains where there's bears and things.

"Kids don't need cars. It makes them want to chase dollars instead of life.

"People shouldn't drive until they're thirty, so they can live first. That's what I'm after."

Barney also told me that he had been a quarterback in high school, and his coach awarded him a letter. "But now I wish I would never have received that letter and jacket because it branded me."

There were so many more, but I couldn't get them all down. I hardly spoke—I just listened. *Fascinating the way Barney's mind works! But he's obviously not rational. He wasn't dealt a good hand and he looks so vulnerable. I hope to God nobody takes advantage of him. But he appears to be doing the best with what he has.* He told me he'd had trouble holding down jobs. *I hope some employer can carve a role for him where he can perform, feel worthwhile, and be fulfilled. But for now I'm in a minor conundrum: how do I bridge empathy with the need to kindly get away before the restaurant closes—but leave him feeling good?* After a few more Barneyisms, I simply stated, "That's all really good stuff, Barn—keep refining it. And, don't hold yourself back! I believe in you—attack Oregon, and you'll get through the city. It will give you a big lift and some extraordinarily beautiful country. You can do it."

"Thanks, man," Barney said. "You've made me grow so much because you're so positive—you welcomed me from the moment I walked up. You're like a big tree, full of growth." The funny statement caught me off balance. I warmly giggled. *So, okay, I've got that going for me.*

I didn't have much to offer him at the moment except encouragement. But before we parted, I gave Barney my four remaining granola bars—*I just sort of think he could use these.* He thanked me profusely.

I never expected to meet a Barney on this journey—he was thrust upon me by random circumstance and threw me off course for the evening. He wasn't in dire straits, but he wasn't thriving either—

he was merely trying to survive day by day. I wrote him off as the town nut. I helped him a little, but I felt I should have done much more—at least give him a boost to get through this day. He had no expectations and was completely satisfied with our encounter—in his mind, I made a small difference. But in hindsight, I could have had a much bigger impact. I was too blinded by the quest to achieve my own goals for the evening—feeding my famished body and knocking out my blog. Thus, I was too inflexible to adjust to that circumstance. *I made a mistake, as nutty as he was, I should have bought him dinner at the lodge. It's the least I could have done. An unexpected dinner for a lost soul is more important and human than a damn blog. Empathy is a virtue—many people pretend, some people do. How do you really make a difference? I just got a C, at best. Grade inflation.*

The outside deck at the lodge was packed full of diners, but I found a spot. I ordered dinner and then slipped off to the men's room to wash up. I was fortunate that this park had showers, but there weren't any mirrors in the shower room, so I'd just combed my hair straight back, knowing, in my best Billy Crystal impersonation, that I'd look just *mahvelous.* When I freshened in the lodge, I glanced in the mirror. *For God's sake!* "The horror!" Taken aback at the sight of myself for a moment, I laughed out loud. I looked gaunt and tired, and my hair splayed in all directions: *Red Skelton Clownsville!*

I returned to my table and pulled out my iPad. I owed my new-found blog following an update. My lasagna came, and I wrote as I ate. I then topped off that delicious slab of Italy with a big-ass American hot fudge sundae. As I sat on that outdoor deck, late afternoon slipped into dusk and eventually pitch dark. Even under the portable deck heaters, wearing all of my off-bike thermal layers, I was chilled. *But it's too cool to not be on this deck in the Big Sur redwoods—I'd be out here, heaters or not.*

It was dead calm, without a breath of air, a wispy fog wafting high through the redwood branches looming above the deck—I was lost in my thoughts and writing. Then—"Is there anything else I can get you, sir?" the server asked. *Sir? Who's he talking to?* I looked up, and I was the only one left.

"Yeah," I replied jokingly. "It would be nice to have a flashlight—how the hell am I going to find my campsite in the sea of tents in the pitch dark?"

PFEIFFER STATE PARK, BIG SUR, CA
Miles today: 56

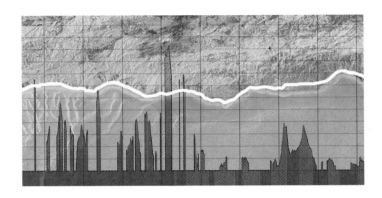

DAY 46
SATURDAY, AUGUST 4, 2012—
PFEIFFER STATE PARK, BIG SUR, CA
Miles to date: 3,140

Last night, some people at a campsite near me just wouldn't go to sleep, until Bigfoot (me) gave a razor-sharp "Hey!" They immediately went silent. *I'm the first to want people to have a good time and party, but after 2:00 a.m., and not slowing down, c'mon!* That one simple word—short, loud, and curt—did the trick.

When I set out this morning, I never thought that I'd knock off ninety-seven miles today, especially with a thousand-foot climb right out of the gate. As usual, it was foggy, and it remained that way for about two-thirds of the day. But it was actually good riding weather. The coast road terrain through the entire the Big Sur had some grueling climbs, with rolling topography between the larger climbs.

It's not a fast road on a bike, and from the outset I was drenched with sweat. I plunged back to sea level, hit rolling hills for a while, climbed to eight hundred feet, back down to sea level, more rolling hills, back up to eight hundred feet, down to three hundred, and then immediately back to seven hundred . . . Welcome to the Big Sur. A killer physically, but even more killer in terms of beauty.

Each time I reached the top of a climb, I pulled over to rest a few moments and take in the view. Even though I couldn't see them, I could hear seals yelping on the rocks far below. Below me I saw flocks of big California brown pelicans cruising in formation, riding the cushion of air along a wavefront, smooth, effortless, and perfectly in tune with their environment. They looked prehistoric, like a barely upgraded pterodactyl. Although I attempted maximum speed, I traveled slowly enough to see the twitches and adjustments as the pelicans flew, or when little birds pecked their tails. *I miss these little dramas when I'm driving. But when I'm riding I see it all. Glorious in its small, wondrous ways. And when I'm entranced, where does the time go?*

I came upon a solo woman also pedaling south along the Big Sur. "Hey! Wasn't that stretch a bitch? If it wasn't for the beauty, I'd be suicidal!" I exclaimed. We both broke into laughter.

"Yeah, I could have done without that," she responded in a distinct, heavy British accent.

"Nice accent—welcome to America! I'm Jerry." *Who am I? The ambassador?* "Where are you from?"

"I'm Catharina, and I'm from London."

"Where are you headed?"

"Cabo San Lucas; I started in San Francisco!"

"Nice! What a great ride! What allows you to do that?"

"I'm an assistant principal at a school in London. The long summer holiday gives me the time."

"You're like me? You have no friends so you have to go solo?"

We laughed. "My boyfriend has to work. He gets so jealous when I can just take off for the summer!"

"Have you ever done something like this before?"

"Quite a bit, actually. I'm forty, so I've had a lot of long summer holidays. I've been able to do a lot of distance bike touring over the years."

I rode with her for a few miles. "Are you hungry?" she chirped. "Are you going to have lunch? My map shows the town of Lucia is just ahead."

"I'm starving! Sure, I'll stop." And so we had lunch together at a cliffside cafe.

"Where else have you ridden?" I asked.

"Well, many rides in Europe, Greece . . ." Her voice tailed off. *Her face just changed with a look of consternation, some dark thought?* And then she slowly continued, "I got into a bad situation riding solo in Turkey and Syria a few years ago." She paused again; I didn't talk. "I was on a particular road in Turkey, and I got this bad foreboding feeling. Predatory men are an issue there—my instincts were right." *Don't press her for details; it looks too painful and personal. If she wants to say more, she will.* She didn't.

She changed subjects. In a lighter, funnier mood she went on. "I'm four days into my ride. Every year I have a big cry at day three—and yesterday was no different. I don't know what it is, but I just break down, sobbing, all alone—then I gather myself and get on with my ride."

"You okay now?" I asked, amused. "Is it all out of your system?"

"Yeah, I'm fine now, I just think it's a combination of being alone, uncertain, and tired by day three, and it all breaks."

"That's pretty funny, really. It's good to know yourself and be able to re-gather your wits. How far will you get today?"

"I like to do about sixty miles a day—I'm planning on staying in San Simeon State Park tonight. I hear it's a great park if you're looking for a place tonight."

"That's a nice target from here. I'm not sure where I'm staying; I usually read my body late in the day and see what I have left—and spring forward if I still have gas. Let's get moving."

A couple of miles later, I felt the usual call and said, "Catharina, I'm going to press ahead and put the hammer down."

"I totally understand!" she replied. "I know it's tough not riding at your own pace." Although she chose to ride her journeys solo, I felt guilty leaving her to ride so alone and exposed. And while I never saw her again, I'm sure she did just fine. *As for me, I've been saving up my sobbin'. I never know when I might need it.*

In the late afternoon, I rolled out of the hills of the Big Sur and onto flat terrain at sea level. Just before San Simeon I saw a beach packed with sunbathing elephant seals, grunting, flopping, and poking their neighbors, using their flippers to toss sand on top of themselves. They were hilarious to watch because they'd smack their neighbors right in the face with clods of sand as they tried to cover themselves—and the neighbors just lay there and took it with no more reaction than a dull, "Duh, what'd you do that for?" look. Humans could learn a thing or two about patience from these guys.

I passed the San Simeon State Park campground at about five o'clock, but I was only at seventy miles and the weather was too nice. I decided to knock off another twenty-five or thirty miles and get to Morro Bay. I knew from senior intelligence officials (i.e., I'd asked someone a question for a change) that the Morro Bay campground had showers and a marina restaurant just outside the gate. I pressed on.

As I rode along the main drag of Morro Bay toward the campground, loud music was blaring out the open front door of a lively corner pub. *It's calling my name—my kind of place!* I like loud music, so even though it was late in the day and I felt sunset pressure to get to the campground, I pulled in. I must have looked like hell: the female bartender took one look at me and said, "Whatever you're havin', it's on me!" Never one to ignore free nourishment, I fired down a pint. "I think I can get you a room right here in town if you'd like; let me call one of my girlfriends and see if she has one." *What a sweetie! She didn't have to go out of her way to be helpful.* But it wasn't to be: she couldn't reach her friend, so she gave me final directions to the park campground—still a few miles away. I had to get cookin', so I gave her a nice tip and zoom! Two miles later, at about seven thirty, I pulled into a tight grove of trees and quickly set up as the sun plunged below the horizon.

From there I went to investigate Saturday night at the Marina Cafe. *I know I'm not drinking enough; whenever I stop at a store and buy chocolate milk, or one of those big cans of Arizona tea, they go down the hatch in a single gulp like I'm at a college kegger.* And again tonight, my body was a sponge, craving and absorbing fluids. I fired back a few ice-cold beers and a couple carafes of water. Simple pleasures. *Doesn't take much to make me happy.*

The Marina Cafe was cookin', first because it's a fun spot, and also because it's just outside the gates of the jam-packed Morro Bay State Park. I had fish and chips, one of their specialties—I ordered the jumbo plate rather than the small one. But I had to force down the fifth piece of fish and gagged on the last few bites—*I need the calories,* but *I just can't keep up.* Then my server came with boysenberry pie a la mode. "It must be for someone else," I said. "I didn't order that."

"There was only one piece left," my server said. "I just thought you'd want it. I'll pick it up if you don't like it." *Smart woman and great server.* She spotted a sucker, and a slob, because when she brought the check, she also brought me a Wet Wipe. "You have boysenberry smeared over half your face. You can use this to tidy up." She laughed.

Once again, I found my tent in the dark and lay back. *I'm off the Big Sur—that ride from Carmel to San Simeon is dramatic and magnificent. I'll to do it again someday. Everyone should.*

MORRO BAY STATE PARK CAMPGROUND, MORRO BAY, CA
Miles today: 97

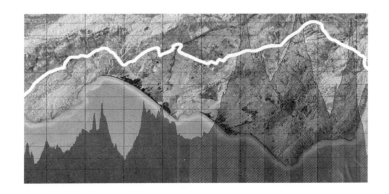

DAY 47
SUNDAY, AUGUST 5, 2012—MORRO BAY STATE PARK, CA
Miles to date: 3,237

The day started with light rain in Morro Bay. Despite the pile of fish I'd eaten last night, I was starving by morning—but I didn't have any breakfast because when I reached into my bag to get my pie-sized chocolate-chip cookie, it was gone. *Where the hell did that cookie go? I swear it was in the flap of my pannier, and it has to get me to San Luis Obispo!* I was groggy and confused, but like a detective, I eventually pieced the story together. A squirrel had swiped it from the loose lower side flap on my pannier. I found the wrapper ten feet away. Earlier, around five, in a fog of semi-consciousness I'd heard squirrels chortling just outside my tent, but I didn't put two and two together. *Those little bastards!*

So, fuelless, I struggled thirteen miles in a drizzly rain to San Luis Obispo, where I stopped for breakfast. As I ate, the sun came out and burned off the fog; the day warmed up, and with a big breakfast under my belt, I regained power and immediately sped up.

I was bombing down the highway when I heard a quick *whoooop-whooop* and then a loudspeakered CHP voice barking. "Pull over!" With a heaving chest and sweat-soaked face, I looked at Smoky as though I thought I was legal. "Climb off the highway and jump back on the bike route," he nonchalantly told me as he pointed the direction. *He gave me the benefit of the doubt—good guy.*

By Pismo Beach, about ten miles beyond San Luis Obispo, the sun was high and burning, the ocean was glistening, and the wavefronts were smooth. *Perfect surfing waves with a nice right break. Huh! I've left the Central Coast, and for the first time it feels like Southern California.*

But I didn't see much of the ocean. Highway 1 veered inland, and I was back to passing through agricultural towns like Guadalupe. Not surprisingly, it was heavily Hispanic. Everywhere I looked, migrant workers toiled in the fields. It had to be 90 degrees. *I'm boiling, so it must be blistering out there in the fields. I can't imagine doing that day in and day out.*

Fifty miles downstream, I got to Orcutt, a small, out-of-the-way town. I was starving and had to fuel up. I picked up a chocolate shake and a sandwich, but then, as I looked up the street, I spotted a small, funky bar called Elmer's with a line of Harleys parked out front. Some of the bikers were outside and smoking, only wearing sleeveless leather vests over their bare beefy torsos. *I just have to go in—with my bike shorts and canary yellow shirt, the setup is just too good to miss.*

As I walked into Elmer's, those bikers looked me up and down. "Hey, guys!" I called out. Finally, one spoke up in a low growl. "Where ya comin' from?"

"Anchorage!" I said, short and punctuated. There was a collective *yeow!* "Can we buy you a beer?"

"Yeah!" I replied, fitting multiple intonation changes in that one word. "But I'll only have one because I'm fifty miles in and still have fifty miles to go today." That got me another collective *whoa!* I fired down a pint of Bud draft in one shot, slammed the glass on the bar like an outlaw in an old Western movie and declared, "Gotta go, boys," and slow-walked out with the proud strut of a bullfighter in all his glory—half-dragging my feet, ass tucked under like I'd just dodged a horn up the keister, a Neil Young scowl on my face, and the pathetic extended bobbing arms of a banana republic tyrant seeking adulation in the square. I knew the walk: I'd run with the bulls in a festival in Spain—*you never forget it.*

I could hear them laughing their asses off behind me. *Don't look back—it will kill the moment.* Then they started shouting, "Good luck, dude!" and "Be safe, dude!" *What a kick! Total movie scene!* The Anchorage shtick took them right out of their element. It redefined the moment as, in their eyes, I walked into their lair as the wimp and came out the tough guy—with them even cheering me on. *I didn't expect that. Hmmm. How can I tilt the axis in my favor in future dealings? I'm sure there's always a way: find it.*

Coming out of Orcutt, I climbed a long hill to the main entrance to Vandenberg Air Force Base, an expansive base that hosts the US Air Force's Space Command. Over the years, I've read about satellite launches from here and was hoping to see a rocket cork off as I rode by. I once saw a space shuttle launch at night from Cape Kennedy. *What a burst of energy—billowing flames lit the night as bright as day, and even from five miles away, it sounded like a hundred freight trains bearing down—definitely one of the most dramatic moments I've ever witnessed.* I felt overwhelming pride in America's prowess in science and engineering, and passing Vandenberg made me remember that night. I'd even made my wife and young kids stay up until four in the morning to see that drama. *When will we ever get a chance to see this again? Carpe diem.*

In Lompoc, I stopped at a cheesy Chinese buffet and pigged out. I had seventy-five miles logged and could have stayed put. There was even a Motel 6 advertising $45 a room, but it was only five o'clock, and I knew I could easily knock off another twenty-five miles to Gaviota State Park. I also learned that there was no food near the park or anywhere else between Lompoc and Gaviota. *I'll be hungry when I stop—I'd better stock up here.* So I bought two gas-station sandwiches and two oil-can-sized Arizona teas and took off.

I wasn't sure about the terrain between Lompoc and Gaviota, but looking west I saw the ever-dreaded headlands. There were about two miles of flats out of Lompoc, then eighteen straight miles of uphill—although not steep, and I had a nice tailwind. But I was also partly fueled by an image that will forever stay with me.

Halfway to Gaviota, about a quarter mile off the road, proudly alone in colorful contrast to the amber sunburned grasses of the empty ponderosa—stood a lone American flag. The image was so powerful. *God! I've taken it for granted. Freedom! That flag represents my precious freedom, our freedom—the envy of the world. I never really think about it.* But out here its meaning pierced like an arrow. I let my mind go, and romanticism took over. *Look at that beautiful symbol, waving opportunity.* The flag snapped in the wind like a whip, stridently reinforcing its message: *I am here. Your sentry. Standing guard over your freedoms. This is America! Don't mess with me. And don't squander what I offer. You actually* can *follow your dreams. Go! Soar! Get moving! You're not stuck. You're never stuck. There's always new beginnings, and you can do* anything. *And you're forever under my protection!* I'd never experienced this feeling in formal studies—professors could never teach this stuff: you have to feel it. This is *real* education. Out here, it seared me like a branding iron. *Always protect and defend that blessed symbol and what it represents. Fight to the bitter end, and never desecrate the honor of those who gave everything to give me so much. The flame of freedom lives.* The image of that flag consumed me. *Whoa, I've accelerated, despite going uphill—fueled by its inspiration.*

I ended with a steep, five-mile downhill, cruising into the park at seven o'clock without pedaling a single stroke in that last stretch.

I rolled to a nice spot in the hikers and bikers area well ahead of the eight o'clock sunset, and several other campers immediately stopped to welcome me. One woman saw me eating the cardboard sandwiches from Lompoc and offered to make me something. I thanked her but declined, as I could see that her family had eaten and their campsite was already clean and shipshape. Once word of my journey spread, everyone stopped by and wanted stories. *I'm my own worst enemy! Once my lips start flappin', I get delayed in getting clean and warm.*

After the camp settled down for the night, I lay in my tent listened to the howling wind. *These gusts are ear-splitting! They'll test the outer envelope of my tent's design and sturdiness.* To avoid another beach-ball incident like the one in Oregon, I'd staked my tent to the ground tonight. *If it collapses on me, so be it. I'll just tuck in like a mummy and worry about it in the morning.*

Whoa! Another shredding gust! So cool! Leo Kottke has a song called "Hear the Wind Howl." I may just need to dial it up. If I can stay awake long enough.

Whoa again! I thought for sure that gust would split my seams! But I love sleeping in this stuff, so let 'er blow. As one of my good friends exclaims, "You can't break me!"

GAVIOTA STATE PARK, CA—
ABOUT 30 MILES NORTH OF SANTA BARBARA
Miles today: 100

PART 4

ALL GOOD THINGS MUST END

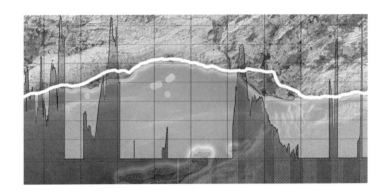

DAY 48
MONDAY, AUGUST 6, 2012—GAVIOTA STATE PARK
Miles to date: 3,337

For the first time in weeks, I awoke to beautiful sunshine and the air was warm from the get-go. Plus, today brought the flattest terrain I'd had on the entire trip.

In some areas, Highway 1 runs concurrent with 101 or turns into a freeway itself, and this morning I completely missed a sign posting that I was supposed to get off of Highway 1/101 and onto the Pacific Coast Route. When I missed my turn this time, however, it was dangerous. The freeway was packed with speeding Southern California traffic, so as I crossed highway on-ramps, off-ramps, and merges, I had to be hypervigilant. I was making great time and speeding along on the freeway when, once again, I was pulled over by the California Highway Patrol. This guy was a motorcycle cop with bloused pants, jackboots to the knees, and all. *I better suck the wind out of his sails right away and assume the blame.* When he walked up, I immediately said, "Where did I miss my turn?"

"About ten miles back," he replied. He was another decent man who simply directed me off the freeway, though he couldn't resist adding the approximately one hundred turns necessary to navigate through Santa Barbara while staying off the freeway. *Too much information!* I got the first three turns, then mentally checked out—my eyes crossed under the cover of my sunglasses.

Off the freeway, all the traffic lights and weaving through Santa Barbara slowed me down and got me turned around. Worse, I had a raging fight going on in my head regarding the readings on my GPS versus what I thought was true. I'd been heading south ever since Washington State. *Everyone knows the entire West Coast is north–south. And since I'm heading south, the ocean will always be on my right. What else do I need to know? Obviously, I know which direction I'm going.* Complicating the moment was the "guy gene," which doesn't allow me to stop for directions. *I'm the poster child for this affliction.* Even though I did my best to keep the coast in my sights, there were times when I lost it. When that happened, I checked my GPS to ensure I was heading predominantly south—which slammed me onto the immediate coast again. *Wait, when I'm heading south, I should be traveling along the coast, not be stopped by the coast. Going south, the ocean should always be on my right.* So I pedaled along, with the ocean on my right, but when I referred back to my GPS, it indicated that I was heading east. *I don't want to head east!* East was inland and off course! It didn't take me long to decide there had to be something wrong with my GPS—*because there can't be anything wrong with me!* Finally the ongoing problem got big enough for me to pull over. *Stupid me.* The minute I pulled out my physical map, I saw that my mental image of the West Coast had twisted me, and I'd forgotten about the east–west jog at Santa Barbara. Problem resolved. If it hadn't been for that guy gene, I would have checked my map earlier, avoided the entire dilemma, and made much better time. *From now on when I'm flying blind, I'll trust my instruments rather than relying too much on the guy gene.* Once resolved, I crunched out the miles, with the last three hours right on the water where the surfers and kite-boarders entertained me as I rode.

Huh, the biggest dangers and risks I've faced each day have changed markedly throughout the journey. In the remote far north they were illness, injury, or bear attack without nearby support. In Washington, Oregon, and Northern California, it was the logging and construction trucks, narrow bridges, and treacherous headlands rife with plunging drop-offs, often without shoulders or guardrails. Here in Southern California, the biggest danger is the traffic. Even parked, the cars are dangerous. The bike lane is just to the left of parallel-parked cars, and both cars and buses constantly pull in and out. *Be extremely vigilant and watchful! Too easy to get car-doored here! That would suck!*

As I rode along a surfing beach, a guy was walking to his car when his dog darted blindly between cars smack in front of me. It happened so fast there was no time for me to react. The dog was suddenly there, my spine blew a circuit as I reactively braced to smack it, and then *whooooooosh*, I winged his tail—a near miss! The dog avoided me more than I missed him. I was lucky—it would have taken me down. *My heart is still pounding. Don't go down!*

I eventually checked into a cheeseball motel in Malibu and was happy to see the motel's laundry only two doors down the alley from my room—*I'm woefully behind!* I had to wash everything, so, for the first time in semi-public, I wore just a towel to do my wash. It was pretty funny. Well, probably TMI. But funny to me.

Tomorrow will be wild, I'll spend the day finding my way through L.A. The California Highway Patrol obviously doesn't want me on the freeways, so I'll see if I can avoid them for a day.

MALIBU, CA
Miles today: 105

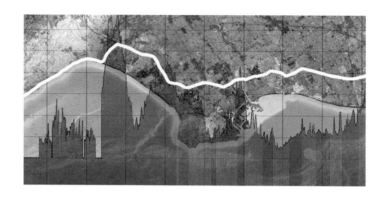

DAY 49
TUESDAY, AUGUST 7, 2012—MALIBU, CA
Miles to date: 3,442

As I turned in my room key this morning, the woman at the front desk started laughing. "I saw you traipsing down the alley last night with a mondo load of laundry in your arms—uh, wearing just a towel!"

"Yeah, I had to do *everything*."

"You could have split loads," she advised.

"Yeah, but *real* guys only do one load."

(Oh, and they also didn't have any laundry detergent, so when I'd checked in, I asked her to give me four room shampoos and did the load with those. *So, if I smell like a French massage parlor, that's my story.*)

It was another stunning morning as I rode along the Malibu strand. Although it was early, beach activities were already in full swing. Observing it all made the miles just blow by. I was hungry early but decided to get to Venice Beach, about twenty miles away, to have breakfast. I knew of a convenient sidewalk cafe with a clear vantage on the Venice Beach freak show. *I'm fascinated observing the underbelly of beach life, especially in bizarre areas like Venice Beach.*

I'd lost my bike lock, so when I arrived in Venice, I wasn't about to let my bike out of sight. I found a place to leave it in the grass right outside of the open-air cafe, but there was an unkempt guy loitering nearby with what looked like a folded card table and a beaten-up cardboard box. "Hey, man, how ya doin'?" I said as I laid the bike down. I was friendly, but at the same time I looked him in the eye— my body language and wordless communication said, "Focker, I've got my eyes on you." I even thought about doing the whole *Meet The Parents* two-fingers-to-the-eyes shtick.

The guy eyed my fully loaded bike. "Where you coming from?" he asked me.

"Anchorage."

"Gnarly, man!" he cried. *My new best friend, Gnarlyman.*

On the surface, Gnarlyman looked owlish, with his skin fried brown and leathery from way too much sun, but under the veneer, he was a great guy. When he asked where I was from and I told him Minnesota, he replied, "You betcha." I grinned at his humor and subtle knowledge of the Minnesota ancestral Scandinavian expression.

As we talked, an empty old man shuffled by, hardly lifting his feet or his eyes. "Doc, Doc," Gnarlyman called. "This guy just rode from Anchorage!" Gnarlyman turned toward me on the side and pointed as he explained, "Doc is an M.D., legally registered to prescribe medical marijuana in that shack right there across the boardwalk." *Everyone knows each other here within their little zone of influence.* But Doc merely glanced at me with the thousand-yard stare. *This dude has consumed way too much of his own inventory. Dead man walking— no, make that shuffling.*

As Gnarlyman finished setting up his folding table and chairs, he said, "Bring your bike right over next to me. Ain't nobody going to touch it with me here." *My instincts say trust this guy, he's got my back.* So, without ever saying a word about bike security, Gnarlyman became my bike guard, and someone I initially thought would be a problem had turned into my bike security solution. *I totally misjudged him—great core disguised by his outward appearance.*

Gnarlyman introduced me to a couple of his friends as they wandered by, so I met Buddha and Ocean, too. *Everyone has their beach name. I'm impressed that Ocean's parents had the foresight to name him Ocean at birth, as if they knew his ultimate destiny. I crack myself up!*

Gnarlyman was slightly cross-eyed and had no front teeth, so he struggled pronouncing his *F*s. *If he wants to shout a popular vulgar insult, it can't be the F-word—all he'd do is blow air! He has to pick a different expression! You just have to play to your strengths.*

Gnarlyman and I talked for a while. "Why isn't there anything on your table?" I eventually asked.

"When I'm ready you'll know what I'm selling. This whole table will be smoking—with incense." *Hmm, probably a front for a larger venture. Competition with Doc?*

Gnarlyman was kind enough to tell me that it would be tricky getting south past the marina area of Venice. "I don't want you to get boxed in by the harbor entrance to Marina del Rey and then have to backtrack." He went out of his way to direct me. *I never would have guessed that I'd like this guy. What a pleasant surprise!*

Once I settled in to eat at the boardwalk cafe, a teen rode past on his bicycle. He was scowling and rapping loudly, confusing the profane with profound, while simultaneously thrusting his hands skyward with splayed fingers. On a nearby rise, a fez-wearing Middle Eastern man was calmly chanting morning prayer under an umbrella with a star-struck sole admirer bearing an adoring Mona Lisa smile as his sidekick. Down the block, the Hare Krishnas were clanging their monkey-grinder mini-cymbals to the rhythm of a Hindu mantra. *My mantra? Just keep pedaling!* And next door, the guys at Muscle Beach were strutting like peacocks in heat, preening and ogling each other between sets—inflated as if they'd just sat on an air hose. It was their own form of religion. I could go on. *There's something for everyone.*

To me, beach life here was counterintuitive. You'd think it would contain the fountain of youth, but way too many of the young people looked old beyond their years. Obviously, Venice is a place where runaways, the counterculture, and those out of sync with the mainstream congregate and are accepted. *But beach life looks like it has taken its toll on way too many of these guys!*

From Malibu to well south of LAX International, there is a paved bike trail smack on the beach. Just past Venice, a retired man pulled alongside me on his bike and we rode side by side for about ten miles, just yapping away about my trip, our families, his occupation, and anything else that came to mind. The miles flew past. He led me all the way south to Redondo Beach and then pointed the way for me to avoid Palos Verdes and get back on the Pacific Coast Highway toward Long Beach.

Long Beach was an especially interesting city. It was dirty, noisy, and heavily industrial, with poor roads and stifling stop-and-go traffic. I got stopped at every single traffic light, so it took me forever to get through that section. The midday temperature was blistering—in excess of ninety degrees. I couldn't help but notice that every storefront had folding maximum-security barricades for nighttime protection of their businesses. And the McDonalds advertised "Spicy McDonalds," an ethnic variation from its standard fare. When I stopped in a convenience store to buy a sandwich and drink, the cashier stood behind floor-to-ceiling bulletproof glass. *Am I buying my chocolate milk from a Brinks truck?!* I hung out in the Long Beach 'hood and ate lunch while sitting on the curb in my highly stylish biking outfit. The locals eyed me, suggesting, *What the hell are you doing here, bro?* I never felt the least bit threatened, probably due more to my ignorance than strength. *But I probably need my bear spray here more than in the far north.*

Part of everyone's education should be navigating through the greater LA area on a bicycle. What a spectrum of cultures, with each city having its own unique character. The contrasts between Malibu, Venice, Manhattan Beach, Hermosa Beach, Redondo Beach, Long Beach, Huntington Beach, and finally, Newport Beach, were amazing: different microcultures in each respective area. From a broader perspective, the difference between Southern California and the Glenn, Alaska, Cassiar, and Yellowhead Highways of just a few weeks earlier brought home the immense contrast from one end of my journey to the other. *I've traveled from one of the last remaining true wilderness areas on the planet to the frenetic multicultural mass of humanity in greater L.A.— an exceptionally diverse geographic and demographic spectrum. Despite the vast differences of cultures, the goodness of people has been a common thread throughout the entire journey.*

About a week ago, when I was still north of San Francisco, my brother Steve, who lives in San Diego, had sent me an e-mail that said, "Hey, just by chance, I stay in Orange County every Tuesday night, so I have a hotel room just in case you make it this far by next week." At the time I'd ignored his e-mail. *There's no way in hell I'll be at that spot on that particular night.* But as I was riding through Huntington Beach, it was about 3:30 p.m. *Hmmm. Call him!*

Steve had a better sense of my time and distance than I did and said he had been expecting my call because he'd been tracking my daily progress. He'd even taken a room with two queen beds tonight, which he never does, because he was so sure I'd make it this far. I plugged his hotel's address into my GPS. *He's only eight miles away— and only about three miles off my route—perfect!*

Steve and I headed to Blackie's, a classic Newport Beach dive bar, for a couple of beers, and then had dinner on the Newport pier. Seals and dolphins screwed around just off the end of the pier, providing dining entertainment. We gabbed away as the sun plunged into the ocean and the large waves rattled the pier.

"How did you make the decision to go?" Steve asked. "Was it tough?"

"Nah, not really—I just didn't overthink it. My pea brain couldn't contemplate all the possible problems, so I basically ignored all the permutations and combinations of possible events—they just gave me an ice cream headache. I also didn't constrain myself with any set rules; rules are rigid and inflexible, and they start becoming obsolete the moment you make them. I operated by the laws of the jungle!"

"Jungle rules!" Steve exclaimed. "Like all our old volleyball games at the lake—anything goes! No rules, therefore no violations!"

"Yeah! It sure simplified the game and freed us up from all the lawyering and bitching at the net! I have been playing by jungle rules for sure—in total survival mode. I wasn't about to be constrained by the speed limit if I had a grizzly on my ass! So I wasn't rigid on anything. *Rigidity is not strength.* The way I look at it rules are merely guidelines, and hard rules are for soulless computers and robots, judgments are for people—judgment is my flex and give—constantly changing with rapidly changing conditions and thus making me readily adaptable. So my only real rule was to be honest with myself—to try my honest best and then take what each day gave me—but it had to be a real effort—no Cupcakeville! Some days gave me more, some less—it all works out. I trusted my judgment and it got me further ahead in the end. I knew I wouldn't make all good decisions—and I didn't. So I'm imperfect—so what? I can adapt and recover. I knew problems would occur and I'd be sidelined; with a bias toward action I'd just have to trust myself to adjust and flex when I confronted them. It's pretty liberating! So in that framework, I did minimal planning—got the obvious big things down, generally knew the direction I was headed—and I blew!"

"That simple?"

"Yeah, that simple. Did I ever tell you the story of when I bought my Harley? It's similar in a sense."

"Okay, but first, let's pay up and head out." As we walked back to the car, he said, "Now you can tell me your dumb-ass Harley story."

"Well, first, thanks for your sensitivity! Anyway, when I was forty-eight, I came home and told Sue, 'I think I'm going to buy a Harley.'

"She looked at me a little aghast and said, 'How long have I known you? In all our years together, you've never ever shown any interest in motorcycles, or even mentioned a Harley—who are you?' She went on, 'You know I'm afraid of motorcycles, but it's not that I

don't want you to have a Harley. We all set an example. I don't want
the kids to ever have one. What should I tell the kids?'

"'Tell them, when they're forty-eight, they can get one too!'

"She laughed and admitted, 'That's pretty good!'

"So, without ever having ridden a Harley, I went to the dealership
and inquired about a new model they had on the floor called a
V-Rod. The Hog salesman said, 'Yeah, it's a great bike; it's got its own
unique engine—different from all the other Harley models, the new
Revolution engine—a joint development between Harley-Davidson
and Porsche. It's Harley's most powerful engine, and it's faster than
hell! What are you coming from?'

"I looked at him and said, 'Uh, a ten-speed?'

"He was taken aback. 'Ten-speed bicycle?'

"'Yep.'

"He paused a moment and then asked me, 'Have you ever
ridden before?'

"'No, I've never had a bike—never ridden.'

"He cocked his head and said, 'And you want this? Don't you
think you should have a *starter bike* first?'

"'Naw, what's the big deal?'

"'Well, it's got so much power, it's pretty quick.'

"'What? You don't think I can ride it? It goes slow too, doesn't
it?' I said facetiously.

"'Yeah but it's just so much bike, especially for a novice.' The
dealership at the moment was full of customers, classic grizzled Hog
riders. I stated, 'Hey, look around this room—they all look highly
experienced. They all started riding at some point: if they can ride this
beast, then I'm pretty sure I can too.' And so I bought the V-Rod on
the spot without ever riding a motorcycle. The dealership delivered it
to my driveway a few days later. In the meantime, I took the written
motorcycle test, which enabled me to ride on a temporary limited-
time permit without any required behind-the-wheel time."

"How was the written permit test?" Steve asked.

"Shocking! It was about thirty questions, and all I needed to
pass was a pulse. So, when the bike was delivered to my driveway, the

dealership delivery person rolled it down the ramp of his trailer and placed it on its kickstand in the middle of my driveway. I looked at it and then burst into a little giggle.

"He said, 'What?'

"I said, 'Uh, um, how do you turn this thing on?'

"He cocked his head and replied, 'You don't know?' I shook my head slowly as a no. He went on, 'Have you ever had a bike before?'

"'No, never.'

"He exclaimed, 'And you bought this—the V-Rod? Man! Okay. Okay. Well—either get it in neutral or hold the clutch lever, turn the key to *On*, flip this switch to *Run*, and then depress the starter switch.' I giggled again, which gained his response, 'Now what?'

"'Uh, how do you shift this thing?'

"With a big grin he said, 'Okay, the lever on the right-hand grip is your front brake; this lever near the right foot peg is your back brake. The lever here at the left-hand grip is your clutch; the lever near the left foot peg is your shift.' By now, he was out and out laughing. 'As you depress the hand clutch, with your left foot on your shift lever, one down and four up takes you through the gears. And the reverse of it all gets you to your low gears again.'

"'Cool! What else do I need to know?'

"'Nothing,' he responded. 'Just get on and ride.'

"And so I did," I said to Steve. "To be honest, in hindsight I was a little dangerous for the first three thousand miles or so, but I naturally got better, as everyone would. Who's great at anything on their first shot? Have to start somewhere—but it was so much fun I got better pretty quickly. Now I've been all over North America—coast to coast. Some called it midlife crisis. Call it what you want: to me it was a new vehicle for feeling alive and growing. And that is essentially the same way I approached this cycling trip. I think these types of things absolutely gave me a looser and more cavalier approach."

"God! I thought that story would never end!"

"Well, I'm not done—I'm going to put you through more pain because there is a funny little twist at the end. After I'd bought the Harley, about a week later Sue said, 'Hey, I won't be around tonight.'

"'Yeah?' I said. 'Where are you going?'"

"'I'm going to play hockey with all the Minnetonka hockey moms. You know, chicks with sticks!'

"I looked at her and said, 'What, in your white figure skates and toe picks? In all the years I've known you, you've never played hockey, never even mentioned it—who are you?'"

"Well, who was she?" Steve laughed and slurped his beer loud enough for the whole bar to hear.

"I don't know who she was, but I can tell you who she wasn't—she wasn't no Wayne Gretzky! But at least she was out there—and that counts! All these new little experiences count—they shape you and who you are. Each in its own small way lowers the perceived barrier to trying new things."

We returned to the hotel and yapped for another hour, lying in the dark in our respective beds.

"Man, I doubt that I could do what you're doing. I mean, that's a hell of a distance," Steve plainly stated.

"What are you talking about? Before you got old and slow, you were a nationally competitive distance runner—and you don't think you could do this? Sheesh! How many miles do you think you've run in your life?"

"Well, I never kept a log, but roughing it out, I know pretty much how many miles I ran per week over a lot of years. I figure I've run about a hundred thousand miles, plus or minus a few thousand."

"Shit, bro! You're more equipped to do this pig than me—of course you could do it! How did you ever get through the big distances that you ran in your races, and the moments that you were eatin' it?"

"Well, I learned that races have different phases, phases that you feel relatively better or worse, and at times you even just want to quit. When I was eatin' chum, I also recognized that feeling that 'I've been here before—this will pass.' I broke the race down and focused on the intermediate distances, the splits, and tried to hit my split times. If I hit the splits, then I'd know I'd have a pretty good race, and it gave me something to focus on instead of my pain! Plus, you just know every runner was feeling it—they had no advantage in that department. So, it often boils down to who could mentally endure more. Someone's going to win—why not me? Of course, I didn't always win, but it gave me a mindset and framework to race with."

"Well," I smarted off, "when I'm not first, I just redefine winning. In the case of this journey, completing it will be winning, regardless of the time it takes. I'm on the homestretch—I think I have it licked from here. And what's carried me a long way is that I actually care about completing it. When I care, then my internal drive takes over—I try my best—and it's surprising how you often do better than you initially thought when you really care. I've also found that when I no longer care, I hit the ejection seat. I move on. And I'm doing that quicker than ever nowadays on things that don't matter to me—life's too short." It went quiet for a minute. "Hey, bro," I continued, "how about our splits in the Bay to Breakers in San Francisco—where we stopped for a beer at every pub along the route! I know the total race length wasn't a big deal for you, but I hated it—but funny how we broke the big distance into a bunch of achievable small distances—splits—because I knew I could achieve the next watering hole! Didn't do much for our time, but it sure turned that grueler into a ton of fun!"

"Always have to stay hydrated!" he joked.

"That we did! Well, the bike journey was a variation on that theme—but on a grand scale. Although I didn't know the total distance upfront, I knew it was big—and it felt daunting as hell. I'm just breaking it down to make some distance each day. Tomorrow will bring what it will—I'll worry about that tomorrow—I just had to survive today first! I don't know what the total distance will be, probably somewhere around thirty-seven hundred miles. But now when I break it down—Can I do a hundred miles thirty-seven times? Yeah! Can I do fifty miles seventy-four times?—yeah squared! Can I do twenty-five miles a hundred and forty-eight times? Piece of cake! So now, what seemed daunting upfront is not as daunting when it's all broken down. I honestly believe that anybody could do it."

"Did you have a bunch of doubters?" Steve asked.

"Yeah, quite a few actually."

"I'll bet you lowered the boom on them!"

"Naw, what's the use? That was the more fiery and combative me of the past. I just gave them a Mona Lisa smile and distanced myself as quickly as possible. It's a waste of time to argue or explain. Most doubters are trying to be helpful, but many are just energy suckers. I'd rather focus my energy on forward motion. But it's critical that you trust yourself because God knows you're always going to have those doubters and naysayers detracting you. Many will doubt you because what you try is outside of their zone of comfort or capability. So they transpose their own fears, uncertainties, and doubts onto you. You can't let their reference points dampen your enthusiasm for what you think is within your own realm of possibilities. If I'd listened to them, I'd never have gone! Everybody judges everyone else based upon their own unique frame of reference and experience level.

"Doubters can never know or duplicate your own reference points and capabilities. You are uniquely you—there never has been a duplicate before you and there never will be one again. So the world that opens before you is uniquely yours—run with it! Their fears of the unknown hold them back—you can't let them hold you back, too. So many people freeze in the safety and certainty of the knowns because their fears loom larger than they really are—so they're slow or never able to get off the dime. The corollary is that they also tend to be the over-planners—having a plan for every conceivable contingency—pushing paper in a great, wide, clockwise circle around their desks—so they're late to or never get into the game. I'm not saying you don't plan, but match the intensity of the plan with what you're really trying to do. I wasn't going to the moon—I was just going on a bike ride! So, unlike for a moon-shot, I didn't have to pack oxygen! In other words, just get on with it!"

"God, man! Take a breath—come up for air! What, are you a whale? Do you breathe from a hole in the top of your head?" Steve always leveled me on my long-winded answers!

"You can't flatten me."

"Hey, speaking of flattening!" Steve blurted. "Remember that night on a lark we went boogie boarding in Pacific Beach at one in the morning? And that big-ass rogue wave sent you over the falls?"

"Yeah, I didn't expect that bitch—in the pitch dark it took me by complete surprise! That mother sent me through the washing machine and floundering to the depths! And, you bastard, I heard your cackling laughter beyond the break-line when I eventually emerged choking and snorting saltwater!"

"What did you do when you realized you were scccrrrreeewwwweeeddd?" he exclaimed.

"I just instinctively grabbed my ass, tucked and rolled, and hoped for the best! I knew I wouldn't drown if I survived the initial pile-drive. Thank God I'm pretty strong in the water." I paused for a moment, then continued. "Funny, being out there in the black of night is a metaphor for my entire journey—casting our fate to the sea and not knowing what lurked above or below the waves, operating in the darkness of the vast unknown and instinctively reacting to what was thrown at us. We never really knew what to expect or what we'd run into out there. And yeah, I bit it for sure! Christ, I had sand coming out of every bodily crevice for a week! But what the hell, if you're never in the penalty box, you're not pressing the action— you'll miss the greatest plays and never be your best. Despite that rogue, we caught some unforgettable rides that night."

"Yeah, given some of the stuff we've done together, sometimes I'm surprised we're still alive," Steve replied, and he was not too far from the truth.

"I think we're regressing with age!" I quipped. "When I want to behave like a teenager, I get with you!" By now we were worn out and the conversation had become intermittent. "Do you realize that we've just entered the last trimester of our lives?" I pondered. "Let's make them count, bro! There's a lot lot lot more we're going to do. We're just starting."

"Let the games begin!" Steve exclaimed with all the depth of our brotherhood.

"Not to be morose, Steve, but when I'm on my deathbed, I want to look back and feel I've lived fully—no regrets from here forward. We have to . . ." *Zzzz.* I fell asleep mid-sentence.

COSTA MESA, CA
Miles today: 76

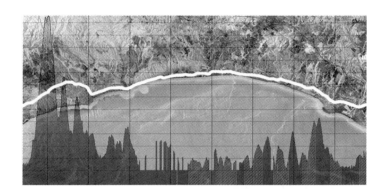

It was yet another sunny and warm start to the day. I hit rolling hills on the coast road into and through Laguna Beach, where I was expecting it to be flatter. *C'mon! I've done my time—please, no more hills!* Over the last two days, from Gaviota State Park south, the route had flattened out, and the flatter ride felt like vacation. *Funny how everything is relative to expectations. If I don't expect hills and then hit them, ugh! Whereas, if I expect the hills, I'm mentally prepared and more readily accept them. My mind is stronger or weaker relative to expectations.* After several thousand miles of *all* mountains and hills, these Laguna bumps were tiny—but I'd allowed my mind to reset to flat. *Ugh! I've become soft! Didn't take long.*

As always, people continually stopped and even went out of their way to strike up conversations with me and to help in any little way. They directed me through several tricky areas where I could have been dead-ended by the Orange County coast's inlets and harbors. I also received tons of honks, waves, well-wishes, and compliments. *In the future, I'll go out of my way to help or encourage others when I see them on their journeys. The kindness of strangers—even just a wave— offers a nice lift.*

About midday, I had to ride through Camp Pendleton, the large Marine base. They've accommodated cyclists by running a bike path through the base. A person in San Clemente had told me, "Go to the far side of the town and you'll hit the bike path into and through the base. You can't miss it." Well, I missed it and went the wrong way for about two miles, all the way to the wrong Pendleton entrance gate, where the young guard directed me back toward the proper gate.

Compounding my folly, this section back was hilly, and all of those hills could have been avoided. Then my front derailleur suddenly loosened from my bike frame, dropped on its support post, and jammed my chain in the sprockets as I ground to a halt. *Aargh! I hate working on bikes.* I spent about forty-five minutes by the side of the road ineptly trying to fix it in 95-degree heat. I could see what was wrong, but I couldn't seem to get it back into alignment. In the end, I jerry-rigged the front derailleur so it was inoperable and manually set the chain on the middle sprocket. *I've now lost my lowest and highest gears, but I'll make do.*

All that messing with my chain left my hands completely black with bike grease. *But there's a silver lining.* I wiped my hands on the asphalt to get the first grease layer off; the next wipe was on my black bike shorts. But what ultimately got them clean was when I washed my hair later—*and get darker hair in the bargain!*

While I was working on the bike, two older guys, also on bikes, stopped to ensure that I was okay and had the necessary tools. We struck up the usual conversation—where I'd been, what I'd done, my thinking and motivations, and so on. One of them then asked, "Did you have any trouble on the Big Sur?"

"Outside of some exhausting climbs—naw—can of corn!" I was obviously making fun, not expecting his next comment.

"Well, a few years back, I started biking the Big Sur, but it was so treacherous, I completely lost my nerve in the first couple of miles and immediately quit the ride. I turned back."

"Yeah, that's understandable—it's pretty treacherous," I replied in recovery mode, now not wanting to embarrass him. *I need to be empathetic here, I'm already behind the game—although quitting that segment never even remotely occurred to me. Y B Y A W C.*

Then the other man asked, "Have you ever been despondent on this trip? Many people on these types of journeys often hit periods of despondency."

That question surprised me. "Never," I told them. "Not even an inkling of despondency. As a matter of fact, quite the opposite—I've never felt more alive." But I did tell them about Catharina's big cry. I went on, "For me, it's been pretty easy to keep it all in perspective. I just feel that my worst days out here are better than many people's best days. Many people have debilitating diseases, injury, handicaps, or hardships—those people would give anything to change places. How can I complain?"

Along with my derailleur problem, going to the wrong gate in Camp Pendleton cost me about four unproductive miles and at least an hour of time. *I hate being set back.* As I made my way toward the proper Marine base gate, I spooked and chased a couple of coyotes—as mangy and free as this hillbilly. When I found the gate, I checked in with the young, ramrod-straight Marine manning it. "Hello, sir, can I see your ID?" he pleasantly said. I obliged. "Have a good ride, sir!" I looked him in the eye. *Such a fresh face, sunny disposition, and simple politeness. This is America's kid, all of our kids—he could be my kid—innocence juxtaposed with a forty-five on his hip.* As proud as I was of him, I thought of what he might be called on to do—*it tugs on my heartstrings.*

"Never—never let anyone tell you you're anything but exceptional. Thank you for serving," I simply but inadequately said.

I wasn't sure I would make San Diego today, but when I was about an hour out of La Jolla—*piece of cake!* I called Steve and said I'd arrive in a couple hours.

Everyone had warned me about the big hill that climbed up to Torrey Pines. And it was much tougher due to my jerry-rigged derailleur—*Quit your bitching and just get on with it.*

As I hit the top, I burst out laughing in an unexpected surprise. There was Steve with a big, shit-eating grin, waiting at the top of that grueling hill. "It's about time you got here," he said. "It's time to have a beer!" Who was I to argue? We detoured into the Torrey Pines Golf Course. The golfers laughed as I wheeled my loaded bike past the pro shop onto the outside courtyard. One golfer catcalled, "Are you confused as to what sport you play at a golf course?"

At hole 19, Steve and I fired down a couple cold ones on the outdoor patio of the clubhouse. We got into a fun and lively verbal exchange with two other tables of golfers next to us, each table lobbing hilarious insults at the other's apparel and the merits of their respective sports. In a normally quiet and reserved area, the patio became raucous and howling. *Whoa, I stood up too fast!* Dehydrated from the day, and replenished with beer, I wobbled slightly on my way out of Torrey Pines and continued on the last several miles on the back route to Steve and his wife Cathy's house. My GPS kept wanting to put me on the freeway, frantically beeping and flashing, electronically swearing at me every time I ignored its suggestions. *I swear this thing is pissed each time it has to recalculate a new route for me.*

Later, I sat on Steve's deck, perched on a hill, and watched the sun set behind the classic black silhouette of palm trees on the far ridge of the canyon. In the distance, to the southwest, we watched the shimmer off Mission Bay change color with the descending sun. The weather was perfect, and I had a cold beer in my right hand and two more longnecks in my left. *I am intoxicated with endorphins and an overwhelming feeling of well-being. Finality. I've survived. I'm here. It's over. I did it.*

I was mentally checking out and shutting down. *Tomorrow will be a simple twenty-five-mile ceremonial cruise to tag the Mexican border.*

Little did I know my dumbest decision of the entire journey lay before me.

SAN DIEGO, CA
Miles today: 91

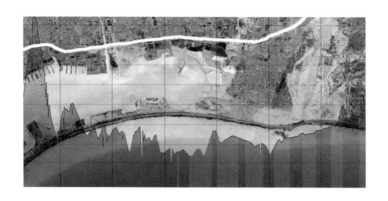

DAY 51
THURSDAY, AUGUST 9, 2012—SAN DIEGO, CA
Miles to date: 3,609

Alaska to Mexico in fifty-one days. Today's ceremonial cruise to the Mexican border will be a short, relaxed, and simple conclusion to this journey—my version of the winner's ceremonial ride on the last day of the Tour de France.

Cathy wanted to make this last day's ride with me in the worst way. My gut told me, *No, ride alone. She's like an unguided missile, and you'll never know where she'll blow you up. Just knock off the last twenty-five miles on my own.* But she was persistent. *Well, I'm staying at her house; I need to be a good guest, and it's a small thing to accommodate her. What's the harm? I've made it: what can possibly happen now?*

She saw my resolve to ride alone weakening and pounced. "I wanna go! I wanna go!" *Twice?* Then in for the kill. "I know the back roads to the border—I've ridden them before," she exclaimed.

"Why not?" I relented and reluctantly agreed. *Having her along will make it even easier. I won't have to think about the route—I'll just follow her. I won't even have to think . . .*

So I followed about a bike length behind her, running a mental commentary. *Cathy! What in hell was that move? I didn't like that decision.* But I was drunk in euphoria, the biker's version of the rapture of the deep. I gave her the benefit of the doubt and overlooked her decisions. *What's right for her may not be right for me. But, whatever, it will be over soon enough.*

There was a lot of road construction as we rode through the San Diego Harbor area, so I stayed behind Cathy, both of us cruising at a nice speed. As she approached a new patch of pavement, she cut inside some orange construction cones. I was adrift in my euphoric trance—just following her rear wheel, hardly paying attention. I'd quit making my own decisions.

And then, in a flash, Cathy hit something and was going down. I only had a millisecond to think, *Oh shit, that's going to hurt her*—and WHAM! I was down too! Like Cathy, unbraced, I creamed myself on the unforgiving concrete.

The concrete section we hit was so freshly poured it hadn't even begun to set. It was about three feet wide and twelve inches deep. Our front tires had dropped straight into the wet cement and slammed against the opposite wall, which dropped us both like a ton of bricks.

I lay there, curled in the wet concrete, forming my body imprint. My head and right shoulder were lying against the opposite wall. Slowly, I got up and did a self-assessment of just how badly I was hurt. My face and left hand were bleeding. *Did I tear my right ear off?* It was hard to tell at first because my face was so numb from impact. I'd also buried my right shoulder into the concrete, and it felt like a slight shoulder separation. *Is my head okay? Do I have a concussion?* But so far I was coherent and thinking clearly. Further fumbling confirmed that my right ear was still attached—but had the consistency of raw hamburger.

Cathy got up too, clearly dazed and talking nonstop—her shock mechanism—as she tried to make sense of what had just happened. She kept asking me if she was okay, wanting assurance. Outside of a pretty scraped-up face, she appeared to be in decent shape. I could tell that I was in worse shape than she was.

Meanwhile, the construction workers rushed over and offered to help and wanted to call an ambulance, but I waved them off. Then one of them re-troweled the fresh section so my twisted body print wouldn't be permanently fossilized in the concrete.

Our bikes were damaged, and we both blew our front tires, but I was determined to press on if possible. As far as I was concerned, it was time to fix the bikes and get to the border. After all, that's what I set out to do and that's what I was going to do, on my bike, today, come hell, high water, or wet cement. *Forget for the moment about the deep gash in my knuckle and the real possibility of infection. Forget about my bloody face. I'll deal with them later. I have a border to tag—today!*

Because it was my last day, I'd unloaded all of my bike gear and didn't carry my tools or spares. My front tube was blown and wouldn't hold air, and I thought I might have bent my front wheel because it wouldn't spin. After reassuring myself, and Cathy, that she would live, I said, "Cathy, if I can't fix my bike, I'm taking yours. I'm touching that son of a bitch today!"

Why is that so important? I don't know. I was that close, and nothing was going to stop me from finishing here and now. *I'm not unique; everyone would want that.*

I called Steve and told him which tools and supplies I needed out of my gear bag, and he came and found us. First I replaced Cathy's front tube, making her bike operable again. Then I replaced my front tire's tube; it would hold air, but the wheel still wouldn't spin—my front brake system was all messed up from the crash. I finally just loosened all the nuts and bolts and freed the front brake. *Shazam!* My tire spun with a slight wobble. But now I didn't have a front brake. No worries. Cathy assured me there weren't any hills between here and the Mexican border, only seven miles away. *Uh-huh. Sure.*

Wobbly and hurting, we limped to the border.

TAG—Elation! What started as a whim turned into an incredible expedition. Stealing a line from the Grateful Dead, "What a long strange trip it's been."

With my hand pressed flat against the border fence, my mind naturally rolled through the experience of this journey—now it *was* over. I'd been thinking about this moment from the very beginning, and it had seemed so far away. But now, more quickly than I could ever have imagined, I was finished. *I'm so happy: time to celebrate!* Except for one little thing: *I need a doctor.*

We loaded the bikes into Steve's car and dropped Cathy off at home. Then Steve took me to an urgent care center in Pacific Beach.

As I checked in, the nurse took my blood pressure. "Well, you're pretty calm despite what you've been through. Your blood pressure is one twelve over sixty-seven. That's pretty remarkable for [*a dinosaur*] your age." Now, I'd never had high blood pressure, but that was by far the lowest blood pressure reading I could remember getting. It distinctly showed the value of vigorous exercise and its positive effect on my systemic measures. I'd also dropped about twenty pounds of weight, even though I hadn't wanted to lose weight. But both measures were a strong reinforcement to forever keep moving—keep pedaling.

I knew I needed stitches, so when Patty, the doctor, came into the room, I asked, "Doc, do you know how to sew?"

"I'm a really good sewer," Patty said with a laugh. "Even outside of stitches, I can sew. But, I'm not a doc, I'm a nurse practitioner—a PhD nurse practitioner, and a professor at USC." *I'll take that!* She continued, "In the summer I come to Pacific Beach and work in the urgent care center to keep up my practical skills. I enjoy it, and I see so much."

Patty said she could see the raw knucklebone and tendons in the middle finger on my left hand, but I was lucky: no breaks or severed tendons. She gave me ten stitches (two internal and eight external) to close the large, thick flap of loose skin over my knuckle.

Adrienne, her assistant, was also amazing—she took her time to carefully and thoroughly clean the dirt from my face and ear.

She kept working and working, slowly and methodically, to get all the embedded dirt out of my skin. *So patient and thorough!* Despite a crowded lobby of others seeking medical assistance, those two women didn't rush me out the door. Instead they went above and beyond to fix my problems and to ensure proper healing. *This is no doubt the best urgent care center I've ever been to—and I've been to more than a few.*

As for my dumbest decision of the journey? I mentally checked out one day too early. *The final glide path is not a landed plane, and most mountain climbing accidents happen on the way down—I'm no different.* I entered this day thinking and behaving as if I was done when I clearly wasn't. *This crash was my fault.* Although I knew I should have ridden the last day alone, I didn't listen to my own instincts. And worse yet, during the ride, I hadn't liked her cycling decisions—but I didn't act on them! Thirty-six hundred and twenty-seven miles of making my own decisions—of straight success—the moment I followed, a scant seven miles to go, I ate it! *Worst of all—I knew better! Sheesh!*

Cathy and I lucked out: it could have been much worse. But, as if my getting battered wasn't enough, my new bike took it even worse. The crash bent the frame, changed its geometry, and destroyed its structural integrity. My sole companion for the past fifty-one days was now toast—a throwaway!

I, too, was toast. *But unlike my bike, I'll recover. And as sore and stiff as I am, the banged-up new is so much better than the automaton old.*

MEXICAN BORDER—TAG!
MILES TODAY: 25
Total miles: 3,634

POSTSCRIPT

Quicker than I ever thought possible, the trip was over. And so the bike ride ended, but not the journey. Oblivious, I had no idea how my actions were affecting others. In mid-August 2012, when I arrived home in Minnesota and saw my friends, many said they'd followed the journey through my nightly blog and went on to describe the ways it changed them—some small, some big.

Mark H. said, "My fishing buddies and I laughed every day— you provided great entertainment. But we were also inspired, so we've all gotten back on our bikes and are riding a bit together."

Nancy J. came up and, with a big bear hug and smile, said, "Dan and I thought, if you could do that, we should get on our bikes. So we're biking the city lakes a bunch—and we feel healthier!"

Dan interjected, "Now I'm also riding my bike to work every day, rain or shine, snow or sleet—and loving it! Every day is different."

Jack M. said, "It's made me think." He paused in contemplation, then said, "Think that I'm kind of boring—I can do so much more."

I saw where he was going and tried to redirect his thought. "I've been there, Jack: complacency kills—it was killing me. I was spending way too much time every day where nothing stood out. If nothing stands out, change your surroundings. And don't worry about mistakes—if you're afraid to make mistakes, you'll never press your best! Call it R&D, baby! Think about it: how can you ever get better if you don't change something? Strive for more—and I'm not talking about money, I'm talking about a more full and rich life. The fullest life possible is the endgame, isn't it? I don't have this well thought out, but I just have a gut feeling that if you're afraid to risk and potentially fail, then you're afraid to fully live. Never settle—it's such a waste of talent. And to me, the biggest waste of all is untapped talent—talent beyond ambition, talent suppressed by others, or raw talent frozen by fear."

"Funny you say that, Jerry," Jack said. "I've heard a related quote that 'Fear of failure is the enemy of ambition.'"

"I think fear paralyzes people into inaction. And it's counterintuitive, but in the hurricane of this rapidly changing world, inaction and complacency are more risky than movement. You'll get left behind. The world is rife with massive change and big problems, which also means it's ripe with new opportunity for great solutions. Regardless, there's *always* a new beginning in front of you, and with it comes tremendous excitement and the freshness of a new way."

Dan L. said, "I'd never do a journey like that on my own, but would you ever do a cycling trip with me? I want to see if I can do it, what it's like—and how I'd change."

"Of course, Dan, we'd have a blast!" I replied. "And you'll change for sure. These types of experiences always leave their DNA on your perspectives and outlook! Let's get one on the books." Dan and I cycled the Cape Breton Highlands of Nova Scotia in September 2015—yet another mind-blowing experience.

But perhaps the most inspiring conversation to me was the one I had with Anne M. while a small group of my friends met at a local establishment.

"I read your blog every day, Jerry," Anne said.

"You saw how a testosterone-fueled hillbilly floundered rogue in the wilderness, huh?" I grinned and brushed her off. "Bartender, I'll have a mongo Blue Moon!"

"No, Jer, you don't get it," she calmly stated in a soft whisper of introspection. "I've always wanted to do a humanitarian relief mission in Haiti, but I was too afraid—too worried about my personal safety there. After following your blog, I knew I *had* to go. That was it—it was the catalyst that pushed me over the top." She paused in further thought and then simply said, "So I just went. That was my stretch.

It's the boldest thing I've ever done—and, outside of my family, the most rewarding thing I've ever done. It was life-changing." She trailed off, her eyes looking past me and into nothing. "I would hate to have ever missed that experience."

Whoa, I didn't expect that. "I'm inspired by your courage, Anne. Thanks for letting me know." *She caught me off guard, and now I feel so shallow! Her journey was so much more meaningful and purposeful than mine.*

However, the funniest exchange with the best twist was with my youngest son, Justin. "Dad, you wanted a stretch, right?"

"Right."

"And you thought this might take you four or five months—or even more, right?"

"Right."

"And you actually did it in fifty-one days, a lot faster, right?"

"Right."

"So, Dad—it wasn't a big enough stretch!"

You're killing me, Justin! But he did have a point, because what had looked daunting up front now, in a funny way, didn't seem to be that big a deal. *Whoa, my boundaries have obviously expanded. I thought I was capable of this journey—but I was so much more capable than even I'd imagined.*

Finally, by happenstance, in November 2012, Justin's college hockey schedule with the Minnesota Gophers took him to Anchorage for a weekend series with the Anchorage Seawolves. So, three months after I came home to Minnesota, I returned to Anchorage and met up with Steve, who had flown up from San Diego, to watch Justin's games. Steve and I met at the Hotel Captain Cook in Anchorage— *Now there's a* real *explorer.* I'd last seen Steve back in August, when I left San Diego for home. I was so caught up in endorphins and celebration that I hadn't sat back and made broader sense of the journey. So, as Steve and I began a trek around Anchorage on the coastal trail toward Earthquake Park, we talked about the trip between bursts of a biting cold, steely gray wind.

"Would you do the trip again?" Steve asked.

"In a heartbeat! But I don't think I'd do it over again."

"What do you mean?"

"If I did it over, or a variation of it, it would feel like a reenactment, a replication with diminishing returns. For me, the firsts are the best—that's where the explosive growth takes place. *If you're not growing, you're dying.* Because my journey was so new and I was solo, I wasn't bound by daily norms or others' expectations, so there was a real freedom to forge and test my own new practices as I went—trying to thrive in the 'new normal.' But eventually the new becomes the normal, and if you let it, it eventually becomes the old. So I'd rather take on my next stretch doing something that I've never done before. That's when it's most fun and I feel most alive. I may not have been the best on the road, but it's when I felt I was at *my* best. Have you ever thought about when you're at your best, bro?"

"Not really. That stuff is too circumspect for me! I'm too busy just doing what I need to do to survive each day, so I've never really thought about it."

"Yeah, been there—sometimes you're so caught up in the daily swirl that you don't step back and think of that crap. But sometimes you have to step back in order to step forward. Pedaling all those miles, I had a lot of time to ponder—anything and everything came to mind on this trip. And that's when I asked myself, 'When am I at my best?' I realized it's when I smell an opportunity, I think I have all the stuff, but I'm a little uncertain—I think I have the pieces, but don't quite know if I can put it all together. But at the same time, my hair is on fire and I want to make *something* happen. And it's funny—my best is usually a self-inflicted activity that I could have easily avoided altogether, and often when I'm not the most comfortable. But all of it is when I feel most alive—I'm definitely going to spend more time there!"

"What do you think really carried you through it all?" Steve wondered.

"Well, a couple things. The first—and I know it's rare for me to compliment you, but I give you credit relative to a touchstone you gave me years ago—I've used it for years."

"Don't go soft on me!" Steve interrupted. "You've never given me credit for jack! Don't make me cry now!" We cracked up.

"Anyway," I continued, "I remember way back when you connived me into running the Mudball race at Theodore Wirth Park?" (It's one of the original Tough Mudder–type races.) "You knew I hated running—but you said, 'Remember, your body can always take more than your mind.' It stuck with me forever. You have no idea how many times I leaned on that during the journey. The second thing that helped carry me happened in the far north of the Yukon when I was standing at the crest of the Great Divide. I'd been climbing for a couple of days straight and eventually hit the crest—and I was exhausted. I stood in a stupor, looking into the vast wilderness as far as the eye could see, two different river systems flowing in completely different directions. I wondered which direction I'd flow. Then two brave US Army soldiers from Oklahoma appeared, and after a short conversation, they bestowed upon me the honorary decal sticker of their infantry unit—Y B Y A W C. I looked at them quizzically, and they proudly blurted 'You bet your ass we can!' I leaned on their battle cry from that moment forward. Both those touchstones are based on attitude. Attitude was more worthwhile to me than detailed plans. In the end, my journey was much more mental than physical."

"Do you think you'll write a book?"

"I don't know—I'm not quite sure. I certainly didn't go on the journey with the intention to write a book at all. I mean, c'mon, what the hell do I know about that? I do think I have the stories—but can I put it all together?"

"Well? Beyond the specific stories what would be your broader message? What would you tell anyone?"

"Beats the livin' hell out of me, Steve. Do I look like Obi-Wan friggin' Kenobi?"

"Uh, as a matter of fact . . ."

"Don't answer!" I cut him off. "Look, I'm just an ordinary dude. I'm not a writer. But in the last couple of months, I've had a chance to think about it all—what I learned and how I've changed. I initially rejected writing a book—too hard, where do you start? But as I've thought about it further, why not? It would be my new stretch! It's just another bike—another bear! Although it feels daunting, I'm pretty sure I'm capable. I didn't know where to start, so I just started pedaling—or in this case, writing—to get stuff on paper and see where it took me. So I created an initial draft manuscript while it was still fresh. But it's so funny, I gave the manuscript to a person—only one person—a woman who reads tons of books and who I trusted to give me straight feedback. I said, 'Scratch through this and tell me what you think.' So she took it and read my first rough cut."

"What did she say?"

"She said it sucked!" We both burst out laughing. "She was pretty blunt. But what do they say in sales? I think she likes me? I think it's a buying signal?"

Amused, Steve pressed, "Did she think you had the material?"

"Naw, not really. Or, more specifically, she thought I had the action, good stories for my buddies at the bar where I could carry the scene in the spoken word and expressively act out the antics. But for a book, I needed to dig deeper. The manuscript was lacking character development and introspection. But, I still think I have the stuff—now I just have to try to figure out how to rejigger it and put it all together. Each draft will get better. I'll never hit perfection. If I try for that lofty goal, I'll see my grave before I see a publisher. But what the hell, I'm redoing the manuscript and I'll see where it takes me."

"Yeah, why not? What's the risk?"

"Well, I'll have my critics for sure, it's inevitable. Look at You-Tube music videos as an example: there are thousands of clips of fabulous performances, and yet each of them inevitably has some people giving them the thumbs-down! There are *always* more critics than performers because it's so much easier to critique than it is to create and produce. Criticism just goes with the territory. Does that mean I shouldn't give it a shot? Hell, no! However, a book isn't without some risk: where the bike trip had the potential to cause physical harm, a book could expose to the world the extent of my illiteracy—and that, my friend, could be bad. Bruised pride, baby! Kills me!"

"Well your illiteracy won't shock me. I've had to live around your dumb-ass ideas my whole life!"

"Gee, thanks for your uplifting encouragement—I'll make sure to use you as my publicist! But the more I think about it, the more I want to see where it all goes, for one main reason: my blog, the one Julia *insightfully* made me write, the one I complained about updating, changed some people's lives. What if a book can inspire someone else to step forward—to step up and unlock their own true talent—who otherwise might not? Think of that possibility. I think the highest order is to inspire and unleash the full potential of other people. That potential would be worth enduring any criticism someone might fling at me. So, I think I'll go for it." I muttered slowly and somewhat distantly in afterthought, "I think it's my calling—I *have* to act on it."

"Hey, are you getting thirsty?" Steve yanked me out of my dream state. "We've both been to Earthquake Park before; should we use some of your professed flexibility, blow off the park, and head up to Simon & Seafort's? It's a great spot in town."

"Twist my arm! Uncle! Yeahhh—great idea! Take what the day gives us!"

When we got there, Steve blurted to the bartender, "Dos Alaskan Ambers!" Then he looked at me and said, "We're not drinking the bunny piss you like."

We each took a deep slug, and then Steve asked, "What happened along the way that you didn't expect?"

"Well, I didn't expect to be blown up on the streets of San Diego by your lovely wife!"

"Hey, welcome to my world!" Steve retorted.

"But she meant well—I guess that counts for something." I easily let her off the hook.

"But seriously, what surprised you? What did you discover?"

"Hmmm, I discovered a ton. I discovered that downhills and tailwinds mask talent and strength. They made me feel stronger and more accomplished than I really am. But then again, the downhills don't come free. I also discovered that I'm like my dog—I'm so much better when I'm off-leash and unrestricted. I've found I'm just better, and certainly happier, when I'm freewheeling and applying my own structure to a problem or opportunity, rather than behaving within the confines of someone else's judgment or policy. I loved having no oversight on this journey. I could adapt quickly to changing circumstances—moving faster. These journeys hone you to trust yourself in the gray zones where there are no clear answers. They point out when you need outside expertise, but even more so, they teach you to recognize when the best experts in the world can't make any better decisions than you do on your own—which I think is more often the case.

"I honestly think I've been blown up more by following others, including so-called experts, than by trusting my own feelings and instincts. Steve, what people need to realize is how unique they really are—there was never anyone like you before, and there will never ever be another you. You are the outcome of all your experiences. So take the unique things you bring—and *bring it!* Sure, experts can pull off some things I can't, but I can pull off many things that they can't, too—things they would insist are terrible ideas. You have to find your own zone of instincts and capabilities and then continually seek ways to expand that zone. These journeys do that, and stretch journeys push it further, on steroids. This trip vastly expanded the envelope of my capabilities. I discovered—and was even surprised by—how much more capable I was than I'd originally thought. And so I now define myself and accept projects by whether I think I can do something versus whether I've ever really done it. Now I want to give other people this confidence and trust in their own capabilities. That's what I learned on this journey—that's my surprise." We both drained the Alaskans.

"Two more!" Steve hollered to the bartender. *Tone it down, man— sheesh!* Then he looked at me. "I love to just wind you up," Steve said. "You're like the old toy doll with the cord on the back of its neck. I just pull the string and let you spew until it spools back in!"

"Well, I'm not done spewing. You know what's really funny? People are now calling and asking me about distance biking like I'm an expert! I had a great experience, but I don't consider myself an expert at all. Shit! I still can't fix a bike! But what I did learn was mental toughness and adaptability were far more critical than cycling expertise or mechanics."

"But I can see why they call—you have something to offer after doing that kind of distance solo and alone."

"Yeah, but the truth is, Steve, I didn't do this trip alone. Although I pedaled solo, I wouldn't have made it by myself. I relied on Sarah's patience and preparedness, Joel's knowledge, Claudia's humanity, Chen's creativity, Jerry and Bonnie's generosity, your hospitality, and countless other people's goodwill and encouragement. Otherwise, I'd still be staring forlornly into the wilderness on the Cassiar Highway, starving with a flat tire; or on the Alaska Highway with a greasy, broken bike chain draping from my hands like a dead snake. These people all covered my blind spots. I wouldn't have made it without everybody, so, yeah, I did this trip solo—but not alone. It's easy to forget or overlook those people around you that make things possible. Recognizing their contributions and genuine thank-yous matter!"

"What do you think you do differently now as a result of your journey?"

"Now I try harder to find the best in something, especially people—and let the little things go. People already know their faults; do I need to remind them? Instead, I try to find their greatness and play to their strengths—nurture their talent and let the deficiencies go. It means trading critique for imagination, which opens possibilities instead of closing them. There's something fascinating in everybody and everything: I try to find it. I now have a deeper curiosity about what's going on with every person or in every activity; what's the talent required, who are the players, how do you approach this, what forces are in play, how do changing variables affect the outcome, how or why does something work—or not? What are the opportunities and pitfalls? And then I boil it all down to the storyline: what is it, why does it matter, and how could I tell that story to make it come alive?"

"Do you think you've changed as a person?"

"Well, not wholesale. I pretty much am who I am, but on the margin I think I've changed in significant ways."

"Like what?"

"I'm much more willing to jump into new and unique activities that I never would have tried before. Whether you succeed or fail, you learn volumes. In many ways you can't lose—even failure is success!"

We both cracked up as Steve blurted, "Whoa! That's an inside-out thought. Have another cocktail!"

"But seriously, I don't go into things with the intent to fail, but now I don't worry as much about failure. And think about it, Steve: when I'm at a cocktail party, people don't want to hear about all my successes—I tend to bore the crap out of them. They want to hear about when I was in a pickle, got extremely embarrassed, or blew something: where I wallowed in the muck—but eventually slipped out, healed, or recovered. Christ, Steve, I'd just pedaled thirty-six hundred miles and change, but everybody wants to hear about how Cathy blew me up in the last seven miles! That's when they crack another beer, move in, and want to hear more. My decision to follow Cathy that last day was the biggest mistake of my entire journey. But I gained something from it. I've realized the struggles and crashes are where real empathy and human connections occur. Shared struggles are common ground for forming great friendships and deeper connections; they allow more meaningful conversations, which creates trust—and people want to do business with or just be around those they trust. That's all a hidden benefit of getting shredded."

"Shredsville—the price you paid to get schooled!" Steve cracked up as he wagged his finger in my face.

"That price was almost too high! But I'll give Cathy a pass: she wanted to be helpful but was simply overzealous, and I was mentally checked out—bad combination! But the thing was, the *overwhelming majority* of people wanted to be helpful. They placed themselves in my shoes and viscerally felt my struggles—some dumb-ass guy highly exposed to the whims of the wilderness or broken down in the middle of nowhere—and then they went out of their way to help me forward. Maybe they helped because they were lured in by the audacity of my self-inflicted journey, or perhaps just hoped someone else would bail them out in a similar position. But I think it's even deeper. There's an age-old raging controversy as to whether mankind is inherently good, or not. I'll leave that argument to philosophers, but all I can say is that I experienced firsthand that people were unbelievably good to me. In the most uncommon of circumstances, total strangers were commonly exemplary in how they treated me! They weren't looking for praise, credit, power, or heroics; they were simply looking out for my well-being and success. It was a core goodness toward me—and it was universal—it didn't matter if I was in the most remote wilderness of the Yukon or the toughest areas of Los Angeles. They have no idea how appreciative I was—and they taught me volumes. I now find myself going further out of my way to help others who are in a bind. That's new."

"I know a few people who have been inspired by your trip and now want to change their path or seek their own journey—but they don't know where to start. What should I tell them?"

"Uh—don't follow Cathy? Doh! Sorry, that was a cheap shot! Okay, seriously, I tell people you can't overthink it. Pick your general direction and just go. Start now! And, just say yes! Remember when I was with you in Palo Alto in 1978, and we went to see *The Last Waltz* when it premiered? Remember Bob Dylan and The Band's rendition of Dylan's 'Forever Young'? It's so inspiring. Now I'm trying to *live* that song. So, when people suggest I go somewhere or try something new, I just say yes! I may never get that moment back. New activities and experiences naturally keep me fresh and expand my frame of reference and perspectives, and my willingness to find and try the ever new. For me, I discovered it's the fountain of youth! And coincidently, it's also the antidote to my fragility! Look, it's a simple formula: the more you do and try, the more you *can* do across all disciplines—your performance explodes in all ways, both personally and professionally—it's a natural outcome. And when possible, I make it a stretch—a real stretch. When it makes sense, do your activities in the most adventurous way possible—sure, go to dinner by paddleboard! You may end up eating dinner drenched, but you also may get a forward surge surfing a rolling wave-front and see the most incredible sunset at water level—either way, it's so much more memorable. Like the signature note in your favorite song, it strikes a higher chord emotionally. Emotions engage—emotions sell—emotions connect—emotions move people!"

Committed to the point, I pounded it into him like a battering ram. "Look, you don't escape to your favorite music festival to think—you go there to feel! Get out and feel—and relate. Just say yes—you can't possibly conceive of how or when you may draw upon those new experiences in the future—but you will. I no longer spend money on things unless they are things that create great experiences—in general, I'm simplifying, unwinding, and getting rid of things—they're just clutter. Rather, I'm investing in experiences and memories because they make me happier and lead to a more full, fun, and worthy life—which is the real endgame, isn't it? When I'm taking my final breath, success to me is whether it was a full life for every breath before it. I've missed some opportunities in the past and had regrets. I'm actively trying to minimize my regrets in my remaining trimester. Those are the things this journey brought into clearer view for me."

Steve mimicked playing a sympathetic violin and then rubbing tears out of his eyes as I completed my last statement—but he couldn't hold back his grin.

"You are such a tool, bro!" I barked, laughing. By now he was deep into a huge slurp at the bottom of his Alaskan. *Did I actually just see that? He drinks like one of those dipping bird thingys!* "Hey, dude, tip the mug and let the beer come to you, you don't have to dive in after it!" I scolded in a lame attempt trying to get back at him.

"Hey, I'm just doing what you're preaching, gettin' after it—don't wait!"

"Fuck. Touché!" I dropped my head in resignation. "But you know what's pretty funny? Upfront, I thought that this trip would simply give me a set of kickin' stories—great campfire BS and a few laughs with my buddies as we'd fire the brews—which it has, by the way! But, in the end, I realized it was so much more than a bike ride. I wasn't out to 'find myself' or discover deeper meanings—you know I'm not that complicated. But, at the same time, I knew that I couldn't help but grow—I just didn't know in what ways."

Steve pantomimed taking ferocious notes, as though he was hanging on every word. *It's actually really funny—but don't encourage him.* Undeterred, I continued, "So my story is really a simple story of an ordinary person having an extraordinary experience by venturing into the unknown and seeing where it led. It's created an unforeseen renewal! Because of the scope of this stretch, new opportunities and a new future that I didn't even contemplate are coming my way—solely as a result of completing this journey. So as I thought about it, I realized that in the past, small stretches shaped my future, but now, this big stretch has made my future! So my story, in a way, is really a story of all of us—a story of what kind of person you will be—who you *choose* to be. You can't ever let anyone else define you—define yourself! And, don't define yourself by your accomplishments—that's the past. This is a story about defining yourself by your capabilities, big capabilities; it's looking forward at where you're going—it's your promise. I discovered that you *can* go make your future—and not just let it passively happen to you. If you wait for others to lead, or pave your way, you'll be waiting a long time. I discovered this all by accident. The bike was just a vehicle putting me in a position to discover it."

Steve looked at me and with a cold-weather yawn he said, "You hungry?"

"You didn't hear a goddamn word I said, did you?" I replied. "Yeah, I'm starving, but let's make our way to the F Street Station—best halibut sandwich in the world! And it holds sentimental value to me—it's where I ate the night before I pedaled out of Anchorage."

Steve and I entered the F Street Station—the same bar I went to on June 19th and jawed with a few locals on what I was about to attempt. Unbeknownst to me, the bartender, Tiffany, had overheard that conversation, but as an experienced bartender, she didn't interject. She was a master on human behavior and used to all the bar-talk bravado and BS that she'd observed over the years—yeah, she'd seen us all—and learned to doubt much of what she heard. She was bartending again tonight.

Steve and I bellied up to the bar and ordered two more Alaskans. Steve asked me, "Did you ever doubt whether you could do it?"

"Not really," I replied. "I just thought I could. I didn't overthink it. Of course I had uncertainties and knew I'd have setbacks—but I didn't have doubts. I was curious as to how I'd do. But I figured, I can pedal, I can camp, I know how to work out—this journey would just be a combination of those skills I already had, strung out over a bunch of days. That attitude turned out to be somewhat simplistic because so many other things happened outside of my control. But any new venture is probably bound to have some curveballs and discomfort—so what? Most discomfort ain't danger, and outside of a black swan event, I ain't dying. So find the humor in the discomfort and turn the negative to a positive—it's in there somewhere. But realistic or not, I just had faith that I could power through—and found that I had even more than I thought. I think everybody does, but many just don't know it, or are unwilling, maybe even afraid to test it. But I found that I always had fifty more miles when I needed it—we all do."

It went quiet for a moment. We both took a long draw from our beers before I continued. "These are almost as good as the beers we had that last night on your deck!"

"Yeah, and you don't even know good beer!" Steve shot back.

"You know, this is the exact same corner of the bar I sat in on the night before I left." I pointed with my frosty beer mug and added, "And she was bartending that night."

We noticed she was listening in, so Steve asked her, "Do you remember him?"

Tiffany looked directly at me and said, "Oh yeah, I remember you—I just didn't believe you."

Y B Y A W C.

DISCUSSION QUESTIONS

As I pedaled from one end of the continent to the other, I had hours upon hours to do nothing but think. Here are some questions that occurred to me mid-ride.

1. Who do you want to be? What is your purpose—rather than your mere daily activity? What's your battle cry? What will you fight for?

2. What do you personally bring to others? What are underused/unique personal capabilities that you can accentuate? Can you state these qualities succinctly (in under thirty seconds)?

3. What makes you feel alive? Which environment are you at your best in? Where and when do you do your most inspired thinking?

4. What have you always wanted, but held yourself back from trying? What's holding you back?

5. Where are you over-planning and under-acting? Trying to be too perfect and inhibiting larger productivity through inaction?

6. Do you think in terms of possibilities or problems, offense or defense? What's a recent example? Where was the problem? Where was the possibility?

7. Where do you project weakness when you really have authentic strength? Where do you confuse discomfort with danger?

8. What areas in your life are full of clutter that's not contributing? How can you simplify them?

9. Do you have policies and practices that you know are obsolete? Why do you continue to operate by them? How can you update yourself and offer the unexpected and exceptional?

10. Who around you matters? Why do they matter? Have you told them?

11. Do you consider what little moments stand out to you each day? Can you express why they stood out to you? How do you make the stories of those moments come alive?

12. Are there moments on your life where you've blown something? What did you learn? How did you change? What will you do differently next time?

13. Are there turning points in life where you wish you'd made different decisions? Why do you regret these decisions? What will you do going forward to live a life without regrets?

14. How will you make a new start for yourself beginning right now?

ACKNOWLEDGMENTS

What I learned riding solo from Alaska to Mexico is that while I performed every pedal stroke, I didn't really do the journey alone. I was stuck and in trouble multiple times along the way and numerous people helped me get out of trouble so I could proceed on the journey. That very same truth applied to writing this book. I couldn't have done it without great advice and counsel from the following people:

Sonia Marsh encouraged me to just simply get started and write the book. Dale Griffiths Stamos helped me structure the story. The late Lisa Lenard-Cook offered great expertise in critiquing earlier versions of the book. Thank you.

Amy Quale and her staff at Wise Ink Creative Publishing provided invaluable project management; Laura Zats did a great job keeping me on track, and editor Kellie Hultgren stretched me to improve my writing and had the wisdom and courage to tell me to delete some things that needed to be cut. Many thanks to Nupoor Gordon for the wonderful cover design, and to Neal Calvin Peterson, who cleverly combined satellite maps and elevation overlays to give a visual perspective of the grueling route.

I am grateful to you all for your keen eyes and expertise.